THE READER AND SHAKESPEARE'S YOUNG MAN SONNETS

Also by Gerald Hammond

The Metaphysical Poets: A Casebook (*editor*)

The Reader and Shakespeare's Young Man Sonnets

Gerald Hammond

To my mother

First published 1981 by
THE MACMILLAN PRESS LTD
London and Basingstoke
Companies and representatives
throughout the world

ISBN 0-333-28851-3

Printed in Hong Kong

Contents

Acknowledgements

The author and publishers wish to thank Stephen Booth and Yale University Press who have kindly given permission for the use of the text of the sonnets as given in *Shakespeare's Sonnets* (New Haven and London, 1977).

Textual note

The text of the sonnets is in a fairly respectable condition and I have preferred, wherever it makes sense, to retain the Quarto reading, even if proposed emendations sometimes make better sense. For the punctuation I have generally followed the example of Stephen Booth's edition. Any major deviation from the quarto or from Booth is signalled in the notes.

Introduction: 'The Well-Wishing Adventurer'

In 1946 L. C. Knights began a discussion of Shakespeare's Sonnets by questioning why there should have been 'so little genuine criticism.in the terrifying number of books and essays on the subject'. Part of the answer, he felt, lay in 'the superior attractiveness of gossip', but more important was the prevalence of two widespread unconscious assumptions, that the sonnets form a continuous and ordered collection and that they are, in the words of Benson, the publisher of the 1640 edition, 'serene, clear and elegantly plain'.[1]

Even before Knights' essay the second assumption needed to be qualified by reference to the analyses of sonnet complexities by William Empson and Arthur Mizener; and since 1946 that work has been continued by Winifred Nowottny, Rosalie Colie, and most importantly Stephen Booth.[2] Booth's book, *An Essay on Shakespeare's Sonnets*, and his recent edition of the sonnets, complete with analytical commentary, have made it impossible for any critic now to assume that a Shakespearean sonnet is anything but a highly complex structure of language and ideas, and my debt to his work is apparent on every page of this book. Most writing on the sonnets is still gossip, but genuine criticism is no longer the rare thing it was.

As for Knights' first assumption, I am not certain that it has ever been widely held. When Keats wrote to Reynolds that the sonnets 'seem to be full of fine things said unintentionally – in the intensity of working out conceits' he voiced what was, and despite modern criticism, remains, a common enough feeling, that the sonnets individually and as a collection lack coherence; and the critical consensus since the early nineteenth century has ascribed to the collection very different degrees of inspiration. That this is so is supported both by the venerable but still lively tradition, begun by Benson, of reordering the sonnets, and by the general state of appreciation of the collection which prizes sonnets like 18, 55, 94, 116, 129, and 146, and neglects the rest. Something of this common feeling is reflected in Knights' essay. Although he is disposed to write of the sonnets as if they present a developing thesis – at one point he says that 'in the Sonnets Shakespeare is working out a morality based on his own finest perceptions and deepest impulses' — he still finds it necessary to assert several times that they in no way constitute an ordered collection; for instance, 'they vary from the most trivial of occasional verses to poems in which a whole range of important emotions is involved'.[3] This book is written in opposition to that last statement, at least in so far as it applies to the first 126 sonnets. While the final 28 sonnets in the collection contain the unevenness which Knights describes, there is in the sonnets addressed to the young man an organised, coherent, and developing sequence of poems.[4]

Since it is one of my purposes to argue that the order of the sonnets in Thorpe's Quarto is substantially right, I think it appropriate to make use of the concluding words of Thorpe's dedication for the title of my introduction. 'The Well-Wishing Adventurer in Setting Forth' is most probably Thorpe's self-congratulation at having adventured the money for the volume and having had it published ('set forth'): but the sonnets encourage our most flexible responses to language and it is not unfitting to turn Thorpe's self-congratulation into congratulation of ourselves as readers, with the well-wishing adventurer becoming, to give an equivalent phrase, the good-natured reader, and his 'setting forth' the beginning of his journey through the sequence. The journey gives me my basic metaphor — better than the generic term 'narrative' because it involves progress and a goal without its having a story's watertight unity. That there is a narrative is not difficult to demonstrate: the sequence begins with friendship between a devoted poet and a self-centred young man, develops into a series of betrayals by the young man, with the poet's attempts to live with such treatment, and ends with the poet's own betrayal of the young man and consequent independence from him. But what makes the sequence truly sequential is not this narrative — after all, one betrayal by the young man is very like another — but the reader's developing experience of the nature of love poetry.

In tracing this developing experience I generally follow the numbered order of the sonnets. My first three chapters take most of their examples from the early sonnets and use them to explore some of Shakespeare's major poetic strategies: chapter 1 discusses the ways in which sonnets simultaneously require separate and often irreconcilable responses from the reader; chapter 2 treats obtrusive metaphoric structures in sonnets and groups of sonnets; and chapter 3 shows the rise of the sardonic tone in the sequence. In the remaining chapters I discuss what I take to be the sequence's major narrative concerns, with the aim of demonstrating its developing poetic complexity. The reader learns how to read sonnets, and what to read into them; and because the final stage of his journey, Sonnets 97—126, demands a significantly greater awareness from him of the subtleties of technique and meaning in Shakespeare's love poetry I devote my last six chapters to these final thirty sonnets.

Throughout the book I make three assumptions which need the reader's assent. Two of them I have already indicated, that the Quarto order is substantially right and that all the sonnets have the same young man as their subject. The first is made in the teeth of generations of attempted reorderings, but with the double security that no one of them has gained any kind of general acceptance, and that Thorpe's order contains enough defensible groupings to make a case for his having printed them as he found them. For the second, to assume that the subject is the same throughout is really only to agree that Shakespeare's sonnets share this characteristic with the majority of Elizabethan sonnet sequences.

My third assumption is implicit in the book's title, that it is possible to accept the existence of a character whom I can call 'the reader' and whose responses I can discuss and evaluate with some objectivity. In doing this my purpose is to argue for a critical approach to the sonnets in particular, and Renaissance poetry in general, which is not circumscribed by the ideas and ideologies of the sixteenth and seventeenth centuries. This is not to propose that the poetry ought to be approached as if we had an entirely innocent eye – as Gombrich has shown us, there can be no such thing anyway – but that we should take care not to have either our common sense or our moral responses subordinated to what we have been told are the Renaissance notions and values of such and such a thing. It is, after all, a peculiar literary belief of this century that we need to interpret a work of literature by way of the opinions of the age in which it was written, and it ignores our own feelings about the criticism of previous centuries, where the critical opinions we value most – Johnson on Shakespeare, or Blake and Shelley on Milton – are precisely those which insist on applying contemporary values and responses to the literature of the past.

Shakespeare's Sonnet 15 will help me illustrate what I mean:

> When I consider everything that grows
> Holds in perfection but a little moment,
> That this huge stage presenteth nought but shows
> 4 Whereon the stars in secret influence comment.
> When I perceive that men as plants increase,
> Cheered and checked ev'n by the selfsame sky,
> Vaunt in their youthful sap, at height decrease,
> 8 And wear their brave state out of memory.
> Then the conceit of this inconstant stay

> Sets you most rich in youth before my sight,
> Where wasteful time debateth with decay
> 12   To change your day of youth to sullied night.
> And all in war with time for love of you,
> As he takes from you, I engraft you new.

Within the sequence's opening group this sonnet marks an important change in the relationship between the poet and the young man: the first fourteen sonnets' insistence that procreation is the means by which the young man may gain immortality now gives way to a different suggestion – the major immortalising claim of the sequence – that the poet can give his subject eternal life through his poetry. By the end of this sonnet, though, the reader is still not aware that the change has happened – it needs the first quatrain of the next sonnet to make clear what was being proposed by the idea of engrafting in the couplet:

> But wherefore do not you a mightier way
> Make war upon this bloody tyrant time?
> And fortify yourself in your decay
> With means more blessed than my barren rhyme?

This kind of retrospective action of one sonnet upon another is one of the strongest arguments for the sequence's coherence; but what I want to emphasise here is that this major change of theme is entirely accessible to a modern reader who has very little experience of reading Renaissance poetry. This may seem an obvious thing to say, but it is important because a grasp of the basic intent of the sonnet is the reader's primary need – with it he is encouraged to make the discriminations and judgements which allow him to follow the twists of a sonnet's argument; without it he is lost. And my belief is that the modern, non-expert reader is seldom as precariously positioned to understand a Shakespearean sonnet as the commentators' comments might lead us to believe.

    To take a small example from this sonnet, consider the way Ingram and Redpath explain the word "holds" in line 2 in their edition: '"stays", as in "Hold still!" to a horse'.[5] The usefulness of this comment is that it makes the modern reader see that his instinct to take "holds in" as the verb (= 'contains') needs to be set against a more abstract alternative, where perfection is a state in which everything for one moment rests: but because they give only this gloss Ingram and Redpath actually diminish the reader's understanding of the sonnet, for by making him mistrust his own instinct to read the verb as "holds in" they have already begun to obscure the primary experience of the sonnet, which is for the reader to be caught between the abstract and the concrete, veering between the two throughout the fourteen lines.

Before I pursue this point let me attempt further to explore the modern reader's response to the details of Sonnet 15. One word which might give him trouble is "conceit" in line 9, although he will need very little exposure to Renaissance poetry to understand how restricted is the word's modern meaning.[6] Possibly more room for misinterpretation comes in the sonnet's theatre image: it is introduced in line 3, but how far it extends through the sonnet is difficult even for the expert reader to decide. That the world should be a "huge stage" is a persuasive metaphor for this poem because of its presentation of the poet in each quatrain as a looker on: "When I consider . . . When I perceive . . . Sets . . . before my sight." I would expect the non-expert reader to have the instinctive tact to appreciate that "stars" in line 4, despite its proximity to the theatre image, does not have its modern sense of 'stars of stage and screen'; but about "Cheered and checked ev'n by the selfsame sky" it is not easy to know how far the modern reader's instincts can be countered. Ingram and Redpath comment that 'Elizabethan audiences . . . "cheered and checked" as in line 6', but Stephen Booth adds the rider that "cheered" did not yet have 'its modern and special theatrical meaning "to shout applause"' (and neither did "sets", in line 10, have its modern theatrical meaning).[7] And, in the couplet, "engraft" will still have its primarily botanical sense, but again a modern reader will find it difficult to keep out of his mind the plastic surgery connotations of grafting skin; and to ask him to do so is artificially to stop the poem living for him – it becomes not so much a part of his actual experience, but instead an artefact with carefully defined historical parameters.[8]

There are also, it would seem from editorial glosses, a number of things which the non-expert reader will miss; in particular, the force of individual words. For example, it is not difficult to show that "influence" and "comment" in line 4, "brave" in line 8, and "wasteful" in line 11, have all stronger and more emphatic senses than they do today.[9] Editors spell these meanings out, but again I am not convinced that the modern reader is seriously handicapped. The very peculiarity of seeing the words used in what seem to be slightly off-centred ways requires him to make what are, in effect, only semantic adjustments of the kind he is used to making almost every day when new meanings are coined, or when he goes to see Shakespeare at the theatre. I can think of only one linguistic handicap for the non-expert reader of this sonnet, and that is so peripheral that the commentators seem largely to have missed it – namely, the ghost-pun on the word "weed". Sonnet 15 takes up two favourite images from the sequence, the world as a stage and men as plants: they come together in line 8, "And wear their brave state out of memory". As Ingram and Redpath note, this line not only completes the second quatrain's description of men growing and dying like plants, it also evokes the image of a faded theatrical costume: 'a decayed player continued to wear the finery (often originally handed over from noblemen's wardrobes) long after it had lost both gloss and fashion'. [10] Or, to put it in the words of Sonnet 2,

> When forty winters shall besiege thy brow
> And dig deep trenches in thy beauty's field,
> Thy youth's proud livery, so gazed on now,
> Will be a tottered weed of small worth held.

And for a man to be worn out means, in terms of the men as plants metaphor, that he will be overcome by weeds — as Sonnet 94 has it (and note the echo with Sonnet 15 in the verb "outbraves"):

> The summer's flower is to the summer sweet,
> Though to itself it only live and die;
> But if that flower with base infection meet,
> The basest weed outbraves his dignity.
>   For sweetest things turn sourest by their deeds;
>   Lilies that fester smell far worse than weeds.

Line 8 in Sonnet 15 provides something else worthy of comment in addition to the ghost-pun on "weed", and that is the word "memory". Few editors bother to gloss it; and why should they since its meaning in the sonnet is so obviously the same as in its modern usage? That, at least, would be the reaction of the non-expert reader, but the Renaissance specialist, brought up these days on the writings of Frances Yates, knows that although the word's meaning may not have changed, its connotations are very different. Almost the perfect specialist essay on a Renaissance poem takes this sonnet for its subject: Raymond B. Waddington's 'Shakespeare's Sonnet 15 and the Art of Memory' is a *tour de force* which sees the poem as very nearly a compendium of the accumulated culture of the previous eighteen hundred years. [11] Its declared purpose is to challenge the 'largely linguistic method' of reading a sonnet which Stephen Booth had developed in *An Essay on Shakespeare's Sonnets* and to illustrate 'the way in which certain kinds of reflective lyrics should be read'. [12]

Against my admiration for Waddington's essay as a piece of scholarly criticism I have to set my concern that the way in which he expects this

Shakespearean sonnet to be read will make it inaccessible to all but a handful of readers. Beginning with two Petrarchan sonnets for contrast and poems by Lord Vaux and Surrey for comparison he then goes on to consider the Renaissance's inherited tradition of Prudence, which means Cicero's *De inventione*, Titian's *The Allegory of Prudence* (via Panofsky), Albertus Magnus, Thomas Aquinas, Augustine's *Confessions* and *De doctrina christiana* (via Yates), Donne's *Sermons*, the *Rhetorica ad Herennium*, Quintilian's *Institutio oratoria*, Sidney's *Defence of Poesie*, Elizabethan 'Memory Theatres', Giordiano Bruno, Robert Fludd's *Ars Memoriae*, Pico della Mirandola, *The Faerie Queene*, Ficino's translation of the *Pimander*, and rhetorical training in the Elizabethan grammar schools. Not everything cited is an indispensable link in the chain, but the effect is to make Sonnet 15's 'meaning' dependent upon the reader's experience and knowledge of the breadth and the intricacies of Renaissance culture – much more, in fact, than any cultured Renaissance man could have been expected to bring to the poem. I shall do Waddington's essay harm if I attempt to summarise his interpretation of the sonnet – the argument needs to be followed stage by stage; but let me note that part of his summary is to say that this sonnet marks the poet's change from a passive state of mere observation to the activity of rational analysis, the latter state being signalled by the increasing abstractness of the sestet.

My belief – and it informs every chapter of this book – is that the great number of non-expert readers, so long as they are careful and engaged readers, may find a way of reading a reflective lyric which is as subtle and coherent as that of a scholar of Renaissance ideas, without their having to relate the poem to the entire culture within which it was written. In the case of Sonnet 15 the increasing abstractness which Waddington points out provides a useful example because, as so often in Shakespeare's sequence, the sonnet's initial hold upon the reader must inevitably be bound up with its perplexing juxtaposition of the abstract and the concrete. Set alongside words and phrases of clear imaginability are others of studied vagueness: the reader's mind grasps an image, but in the act of holding on to it meets immediately with an expression which loosens its hold. The opening lines present the movement in miniature:

> When I consider everything that grows
> Holds in perfection but a little moment

I have already touched on the concrete/abstract possibilities of "holds"/"holds in", but the reader's adjustments begin as early as "consider" in line 1. The experience of reading a sonnet is, from the first word to the last, a continuous process of forming expectations and anticipations which are either frustrated or satisfied. With "When I consider", as in the opening line of Milton's sonnet on his blindness, the reader begins to anticipate a sonnet of introspection, but "everything that grows" forces him to readjust those anticipations — the sonnet now seems to fit into a clearly imaginable context, that of the poet contemplating nature: at its most literal, gazing at a flower. But line 2 moves the reader back to the abstract by revealing that "everything that grows" had not been the direct and complete object of the poet's consideration but only the beginning of his description of the content of his introspection — i.e. 'when I consider *how* everything that grows holds in perfection . . .'

My claim is not that the reader makes such readjustments deliberately or even consciously, but that in any serious reading of Sonnet 15 he experiences at a basic level of his responses a process of anticipation – frustration – satisfaction, but with the satisfaction contaminated by the counter-image of the poet actually contemplating nature (rather than himself) which the first line had briefly established. And for the remainder of the sonnet these readjustments continue. In the first quatrain, for instance, in line 2 the image of the container in "holds in" surrounds the unimaginable abstraction of "perfection"; line 3's solid theatre finds itself governed by "stars" in line 4, and, moreover, stars which comment on the action. In the second quatrain the imaginable — the poet, men, plants, and players — is made vague by verbs which do not properly fit — "increase", "decrease" and "wear out". "Increase" in particular torments the reader, whose associations for the word have been formed by its being the opening rhyme word of the sequence:

> From fairest creatures we desire increase,
> That thereby beauty's rose might never die

There it stood as the definitive word to describe the procreation which the poet so strongly argues for. Procreate or die out is the message which Sonnet 1 has for the young man, and which the next thirteen sonnets repeat — a choice embodied in the rhyme word which the poet chose for "increase": not, as in Sonnet 15, "decrease", but "decease". Now, though, the reader's associations for the word — in particular its opposition to mortality — are frustrated; "increase" no longer signifies the eternity which procreation promises, nor any kind of eternity for that matter, but only the tiny spot of time when a thing stands at its highest point and when its "decrease" is about to begin. And it contrives to be, as I have said, not quite the right verb to fit either part of the simile: to have "men as plants increase" is a less satisfactory, because less imaginable, equation than having men as plants flourish or men as plants ripen (to take two characteristic words from the procreation group).

It seems fair to say that even to the entirely non-expert reader the increased abstractness which Waddington perceives in the sestet is not unprepared for: in essence it is the reasonable development of the readjustments he has to make at the sonnet's very beginning. There the abstractness was the poet's; in the sestet it comes to relate directly to the young man – "rich in youth", "your day of youth", "sullied night", these are all vague and hardly imaginable forms of description – while it clarifies the image of the poet as a dreamer who sees distinctly. The promise of the opening line, that the poet might actually be contemplating a natural object rather than an idea, comes to unexpected fruition when the object he contemplates turns out to be the young man, set carefully before his sight. At least, we have to take his word for the vision, for although we see the poet clearly, what he sees remains an abstraction to us.

No discussion of Sonnet 15 can be satisfactory without some consideration of its place in the sequence – I shall return to it in my treatment of the procreation group in chapter 1—but what I have described here should at the least act as an example of the kind of analysis I undertake in tracing the reader's experience of the sonnets.

1 'This Poet Lies':
Text and Subtext

I begin by wondering why Shakespeare's sonnets should be so unpopular. Despite their being the only collection of poems by our greatest poet, as a sequence they remain almost as unconsidered and unread as they were in his lifetime.[1] Individual sonnets are known and loved, but as exceptions to the general run of a collection of lifeless poems. Even literary critics have treated them with disdain. In the last forty years, apart from scattered forays by a handful of critics (most of them listed in my Introduction), they have been the happy hunting ground of biographical detectives, novelists, or the kind of literary moralist who constructs arguments by welding together lines and quatrains pulled painfully out of their context. And it is significant that, apart from the work of Stephen Booth, even the good critics have concentrated upon individual sonnets or sonnet groups, leaving the sequence as a whole in benign neglect.

Why should this neglect exist? It can hardly be the result of the intellectual complexity which generates so much silence about *The Phoenix and the Turtle*. The sonnets present few specifically intellectual problems, and if they did the vogue for Metaphysical wit has provided the techniques and the audience for that kind of explication. My suggested answer is that the sonnets cause reader and critic alike the more fundamental problem of determining the tone, both of individual poems and groups of poems, and of the sequence as a whole. This difficulty destroys the reader's basic allegiance to the sonnets, and only from such an allegiance does constant rereading of the work and eventually a good work of criticism emerge. It is, after all, quite possible to read a poem and have no clear understanding of its ideas, but be engaged with it all the same. In such a case we find ourselves responding intuitively to its level of seriousness and the poet's commitment to his subject. But the opposite is not easily done and even a fair degree of certainty about a poem's meaning may not overcome a reader's frustrating uncertainty at, to put it crudely, not knowing whether the poet means what he says or not.

My argument is that this kind of uncertainty is built into many individual sonnets and into the whole young man sequence with the aim of frustrating and alienating the reader—not forgetting that the chief reader, and in the terms of the sequence's fiction its only reader, is the young man himself. From very early in the sequence he encounters forms of wit, sarcasm, and innuendo which force him to reconsider his response to a sonnet or group of sonnets. Sometimes the reconsideration only begins in a sonnet's couplet, at others it begins as early as the first line, but, and this is a crucial difference between Shakespeare and his contemporaries, it is seldom complete. The poet's irony or sarcasm or bitterness do not replace the lover's pose: the two co-exist so disturbingly that the reader is often frustrated in his attempts to make a decision about the tone of the poem.

Let me begin to describe what I mean by means of a simple example, Sonnet 103, which develops a common idea in the sequence, that it is impossible to write to a perfect model:

> Alack what poverty my muse brings forth,
> That, having such a scope to show her pride,
> The argument all bare is of more worth
> 4   Than when it hath my added praise beside.
> O blame me not if I no more can write!
> Look in your glass, and there appears a face
> That overgoes my blunt invention quite,
> 8   Dulling my lines, and doing me disgrace.
> Were it not sinful then, striving to mend,
> To mar the subject that before was well?
> For to no other pass my verses tend,
> 12   Than of your graces and your gifts to tell;
> And more, much more than in my verse can sit,
> Your own glass shows you, when you look in it.

On the surface this sonnet is a piece of conventional self-abasement. In the first quatrain the poet admits that he falls short precisely where, as a poet, he should have most scope for his talents. The second and third quatrains then specify the reasons for the failure by concentrating on the face in the mirror. In one sense, in lines 7–8, the poet goes so far as to suggest that the young man could write the poem himself simply by concentrating on his own reflection, since that "overgoes" anything which the poet's blunt invention can produce. Then the couplet rounds off the whole argument by repeating the young man's action of looking in the mirror.

Looking in a mirror might originally have seemed an innocent action, but the couplet's repetition of the image alerts the reader to the possibility that the poet might not be entirely sincere in drawing our attention so forcefully to his subject's narcissism, and indeed it underscores a series of innuendoes which had begun in the second quatrain. The young man looking in the mirror and seeing "more, much more" than the poet could ever write implies that he sees more than anyone can ever write. "More, much more" may well recall to the reader the "no more" of line 5, and if it does then the innuendoes which he will earlier have avoided are now given retrospective force by the couplet: "O blame me not if I no more can write" carries the double implication that the poet is blamed because he does not describe the young man as better than he is, and because he does not write enough about him.[2]

The deliberate prosaicness of the couplet in its repetition of the image – in particular the harping on the second person pronoun in "Your own glass shows you, when you look in it" – also admits retrospectively all kinds of subversive possibilities into the body of the sonnet. The face which appears in the glass in line 6 is quite pointedly what the young man sees, and quite possibly not what the poet sees, depending upon the way in which "blunt" is understood as it applies to "invention".[3] Then the third quatrain plays tricks on the proverbial opposition of "mend" and "mar":

> Were it not sinful then, striving to mend,
> To mar the subject that before was well?
> For to no other pass my verses tend,
> Than of your graces and your gifts to tell.

Of course one may mar a subject with the best intentions, simply by being an inadequate poet – and something like that is the literal meaning of the quatrain – but now unavoidable is the innuendo that one may also mar a subject in his eyes, if no one else's, by trying to make him better. That innuendo is given life by the vagueness of "that before was well", a phrase which may carry all kinds of overtones, ranging from morally well to merely self-satisfied. Stephen Booth is right when he identifies 'the speaker's general tone of subservience' in lines 11–12, but they can also carry exactly the opposite tone.[4] "Graces" and "gifts", the "pass" to which the poet's verses tend, are in no way limited to the appearance of the face in a mirror, and the sense emerges of a subject who wants the poet to write about one thing only and stop writing about others, and of a poet who will not.

My purpose in treating the sonnet like this is not to substitute the innuendoes for the surface, but simply to recognise the existence of the innuendo throughout the last ten lines. A poem which, like so many of the sonnets, projects self-abasement to the point of humiliation, carries within itself rebellion and vindictiveness, a sub-text which says that the young man's vanity blinds him to his own faults and to the poet's talents. The sub-text never becomes the main text: the sonnet remains, substantially, the most moving kind of love poetry, wherein the lover-poet abnegates himself. The reader, though, ends the sonnet in self-distrust, having inadequate material to keep the surface uncontaminated by innuendo, but the innuendo is too vague for him to organise it into a counter-statement.

I can illustrate this point further by comparing two poems which treat the idea of the poet's death and its effect on the lover, Shakespeare's Sonnet 71 and Donne's 'The Apparition'. Shakespeare's sonnet is usually read as an exercise in sarcasm:[5]

> No longer mourn for me when I am dead
> Than you shall hear the surly sullen bell
> Give warning to the world that I am fled
> 4   From this vile world with vildest worms to dwell.
> Nay, if you read this line, remember not
> The hand that writ it, for I love you so,
> That I in your sweet thoughts would be forgot,
> 8   If thinking on me then should make you woe.
> O if, I say, you look upon this verse,
> When I, perhaps, compounded am with clay,
> Do not so much as my poor name rehearse,
> 12   But let your love ev'n with my life decay,
>   Lest the wise world should look into your moan,
>   And mock you with me after I am gone.

The sarcasm is evident from the opening lines – 'don't mourn for me any longer than it takes the bell to ring' – and bitterness carries through the sonnet, in the contrast of the poet's "vile world" with the young man's "wise world", the repeated ifs with their implication that he will not read the poetry or think of the poet, and the self-humiliation of the couplet. I describe the sarcasm as evident but a sensitive reader might well balk at that response, pointing out that the sonnet contains undeniable elements of self-sacrifice which my analysis ignores. In contrast with Sonnet 103 it is the self-sacrifice which is the sub-text here, but it nonetheless exists alongside the poet's bitterness. The central lines in particular are not easily resistible:

> for I love you so
> That I in your sweet thoughts would be forgot,
> If thinking on me then should make you woe.

The result is that where most critics detect sarcasm or self mockery, others like Philip Martin find that the sonnet 'breathes the most complete and noble selflessness'.[6]

Set that sonnet against Donne's 'The Apparition':

> When by thy scorn, O murderess, I am dead
> And that thou think'st thee free
> From all solicitation from me,
> 4 Then shall my ghost come to thy bed,
> And thee, feigned vestal, in worse arms shall see;
> Then thy sick taper will begin to wink,
> And he, whose thou art then, being tired before,
> 8 Will, if thou stir, or pinch to wake him, think
> Thou call'st for more,
> And in false sleep will from thee shrink,
> And then poor aspen wretch, neglected thou
> 12 Bathed in a cold quicksilver sweat wilt lie
> A verier ghost than I;
> What I will say, I will not tell thee now,
> Lest that preserve thee; and since my love is spent,
> 16 I'd rather thou shouldst painfully repent,
> Than by my threatenings rest still innocent.

Here the opening lines plunge the reader straight into the convention of coy mistresses murdering their unrequited lovers. In true Petrarchan fashion the poet seems to take his figurative death to the literal extreme and looks forward to the time when his ghost will return to torture the disdainful lady. The poem can easily be read in that way, and usually is; Joan Bennett's comment that it shows the poet's 'contempt for the woman who has refused him' being typical of what critical discussion there has been of the poem.[7]

But 'The Apparition' is much more a poem of disgust than the conventional reading will allow. "Feigned vestal" in line 5 gives the first indication of the lady's character and by the centre of the poem she has emerged as distinctly nymphomanic, in the poet's eyes at least, for whatever man she has next will be "tired before", hence her doomed efforts to pinch him awake at the ghost's appearance. The poem's location, it turns out, is in bed, and its content an address from one experienced lover to another, rather than the originally anticipated conventional suing for a look or a favour. Murder and death have literally occurred, but only as slang expressions for orgasm, and behind the bluster of the last lines – not even "I'll do such things", but "I'll say such things" — is the humiliation of a lover upon whom too great demands have been made ("and since my love is spent"). The joke played on the reader is typical of Donne. The poem opens in a traditional way and then turns the stock phrases on their head so that the reader is forced to see a different kind of "scorn", "dead", and "solicitation" from those he will have expected. But once he perceives the joke then the effect is complete; the poem will not permit co-existent opposites in the way the Shakespeare sonnet does. The reader's experience of 'The Apparition' is first one of chastity, unrequited love, and righteous anger, and then one of sexual humiliation and impotent rage, but there is no point at which the two can sustain each other. In Shakespeare's sonnet no such reversal is made. Self-sacrifice and sarcasm are kept side by side and the reader's doubts that they can possibly co-exist make him the more perceptive of the nature of those contraries.

The difficulty of responding to such co-existent contraries in the majority of sonnets in the sequence probably explains why the sonnets have, in Winifred Nowottny's words, 'proved to be remarkably resistant to generalisations'. Every reader is likely to find areas in the sequence where he senses the possibility of innuendo but doubts its probability, or its reasonableness, or even its probity. And these difficulties begin early in the sonnets, as early indeed as the procreation group which opens it. Few critics have questioned the superficial claims of these sonnets to be plain encouragements to the young man to marry and breed, and the theme has proved so uninteresting that they are often dismissed as a poetic exercise, Shakespeare learning the art of sonnet-craft. I do not believe that the experience of reading the group seriously leads to such uncritical acceptance of its claims; instead it is within this group that the reader feels his first uncertainties about the relationship between the poet and the young man and, if only subconsciously, begins to detect the existence of a subversive sub-text. Consider Sonnet 4:

> Unthrifty loveliness, why dost thou spend
> Upon thyself thy beauty's legacy?
> Nature's bequest gives nothing but doth lend,
> 4   And being frank she lends to those are free.
> Then beauteous niggard why dost thou abuse
> The bounteous largess given thee to give?
> Profitless usurer, why dost thou use
> 8   So great a sum of sums yet canst not live?
> For having traffic with thyself alone,
> Thou of thyself thy sweet self dost deceive.

Then how when nature calls thee to be gone,
12   What acceptable audit canst thou leave?
Thy unused beauty must be tombed with thee,
Which used lives th' executor to be.

For a start, any response to this sonnet must clearly take in the financial metaphor which runs through it, presenting the young man as spendthrift and usurer, bequeather and legatee. The apparent purpose of the metaphor is to convey the beauty and worth of the young man, a design supported by the form of gentle persuasion which the sonnet provides, with stern vocatives softening into questions whose implied answers can only reinforce the young man's image of himself. But the metaphor also carries the undermining innuendo that the young man masturbates, spending upon himself and trafficking with himself alone both being phrases which unavoidably signify this extreme of sexual miserliness.

It is worth exploring in a little detail the way these phrases work upon the reader. After the stylised opening vocative "Unthrifty loveliness" he meets the question "why dost thou spend/Upon thyself thy beauty's legacy?" Intact the question is typical sonnet wit, beginning the development of the financial metaphor with the paradox of a spendthrift miser; but the reader only maintains the intactness of the question by suppressing the masturbatory innuendo of "spend/Upon theyself". He does this willingly in the knowledge that the innuendo could not have been intended – it must be the product of his own mind and the poet's clumsiness in working out the conceit, for it is not probable that so conventional and formalised a poem as this sonnet, asking a young man to breed, could raise so graphic an image as that of the young man masturbating. It is, of course, a most reasonable image to use in an argument for procreation – why masturbate when you could easily copulate? – but not in a poetic argument where basic human actions are avoided or euphemised. But in line 9 "having traffic with thyself alone" forces the reader to reconsider: one masturbatory phrase may be an accident, two can not be and the sexual innuendo of other words in the sonnet – "frank", "free", "abuse", "use" – is also absorbed into the spending and trafficking metaphor.

By the sestet the reader has contradictory responses to the sonnet. He follows the controlled wit of the argument, especially its paradoxical metaphor aimed at describing the priceless beauty of the young man, but against that he can no longer ignore the elements of the metaphor which work to debase that beauty. Simultaneously with that response the sestet begins to move the argument into the prospect of the young man's death, its direction seeming to come from the apparently neutral rhetoric of line 8, "yet canst not live". Originally the phrase is interpreted as meaning 'yet does not know how to live properly'; now, unexpectedly, its meaning is limited to a shadowy way of saying that the young man is bound to die, no matter how much he lives for himself. That prospective death raises a matter basic to the whole procreation group.

From Thomas Thorpe onwards commentators have found it most natural to discuss the sonnets as immortalising agents – 'that eternity promised by our ever-living poet'. It is quite possible that Thorpe never looked beyond the first sonnet in the sequence, but that would have been enough for him to characterise it in the way he did. Indeed, the very first quatrain promises immortality:

> From fairest creatures we desire increase,
> That thereby beauty's rose might never die,
> But as the riper should by time decease
> His tender heir might bear his memory.

It is perhaps fanciful to see this as a miniature Fall narrative – starting with Adam and Eve ("fairest creatures"), their procreation ("increase"), and their prospective immortality, but then declining into ripening, decease, and the memory of the dead – but even without that Miltonic analogy there is sufficient tragic generalisation here to have warned Thorpe that the immortality is a highly qualified and not necessarily desirable one. In fact the quatrain, whilst promising eternity, does so in the alienating terms of demand and stipulation. "We desire increase" makes the fairest creatures the suppliers of a commodity to the rest of the world, and valuable more for the commodity than for themselves; and in "should . . . decease" there is a general acceptance of the rightness that those creatures will inevitably die. Initially the coldness of expression here may be put down to the understandable formality of opening a sonnet sequence, but actually it sets the tone for the poet's sustained argument from this point, that procreation is the only way to cheat death.

Shakespeare never uses the *carpe diem* convention in his sonnets, but his asking the young man to procreate contains the same internal contradiction as do most good *carpe diem* poems. Use decay and death as a threat and its very graphicness may overwhelm the persuasion: what is the point of making love, or breeding, if one must inevitably age and die? And who can make love with thoughts of death uppermost in the mind?

In the procreation group the prospect of death's annihilation works on both the young man and the reader. In this opening sonnet, for instance, there is something almost attractive, and certainly sympathetic, in the young man's self-sufficiency, particularly in its dramatic ending with a picture of him sitting by a grave, eating "the world's due".[8] Sonnets 2 and 3 oppose our normal human desires, the fair child and the eared womb, to the obduracy of the young man's self-containment which will lead to deep-sunken eyes and a tomb. But the opposition is only apparent, not real. Deep-sunken eyes and the tomb will still come whatever action he takes, and the poetry can not deny the inevitability of cold blood and wrinkles. The prospective child functions as memory, an excuse for age, and a vision in age of a past golden time.[9] This may be some consolation but to see it as a positive vision is to suppress the forcefulness of the image of decay and death which these sonnets present. One pertinent example comes from the sonnet we have been looking at, number 4, where the couplet does more than merely round off the poem with a final conceit about inheritance; it opens up wider images of the horror of life leading to death:

> Thy unused beauty must be tombed with thee,
> Which used lives th' executor to be.

The irresistibility of the process by which children bury their parents comes not only in the completion of the financial metaphor – the whole thing is a deal with nature which the son winds up – but also in the final pun which suggests that the son's primary purpose is to live to execute the father.[10] Like the other sonnets in the opening group Sonnet 4 imposes a double allegiance upon the reader, primarily to the poet's exhortation to recognise higher values than mere existence, but, increasingly inseparable from that, to the young man's sense of the purposelessness of action. Masturbation may not be a heroic gesture but it makes one kind of sense in a world where procreation symbolises death.

One further parallel which makes the procreation sonnets reminiscent of *carpe diem* poetry, despite their obvious differences, lies in the initial detachment of the poet. A *carpe diem* poet often begins disinterestedly, giving good objective advice to make hay while the sun shines, but he eventually comes round to self-interested exhortation. Similarly, the procreation group displays no self-interest to begin with; so much so that the first nine sonnets leave out the poet almost entirely, except perhaps for his inclusion in "we" in the opening line. Then, from this detached preparation, the second half of the group introduces the poet so that he may begin a seduction whose end is poetic immortality.

One effect of the poet's initial detachment is to emphasise the young man's isolation, as in Sonnet 4, and in the sun image which is used to describe the young man in Sonnet 7:

> Lo, in the orient when the gracious light
> Lifts up his burning head, each under eye
> Doth homage to his new-appearing sight,
> 4   Serving with looks his sacred majesty;
> And having climbed the steep-up heav'nly hill,
> Resembling strong youth in his middle age,
> Yet mortal looks adore his beauty still,
> 8   Attending on his golden pilgrimage.
> But when from highmost pitch, with weary car,
> Like feeble age he reeleth from the day,
> The eyes ('fore duteous) now converted are
> 12 From his low tract and look another way.
> So thou, thyself outgoing in thy noon,
> Unlooked on diest unless thou get a son.

Suns, we know, rise, set, and rise again, and it is impossible for the reader not to bring to the sonnet the Ovidian and Christian overtones which that image normally carries. As Stephen Booth writes, 'the Christian references never solidify, never add up to the sacrilegiously complimentary analogy they point toward; they do, however, give an air of solemnity and miraculousness to the equation the poem implies between the sun's cyclical birth, death, and rebirth and human victory over mortality by procreation'.[11] But alongside this symbolic content, and perhaps what stops it solidifying, is the image of one quite individual life. We see, behind the symbol of the sun, a body moving, in the lifting of the head, the climb to the top of the hill, and the weary decline; all forming the image of a man whose isolation is emphasised by his being the object of all eyes. The couplet's "so" is slightly misleading: unlike, say, Sonnet 55 ("so, till the judgement that yourself arise . . .") this does not introduce a summing up of the whole extended simile of the sonnet. It actually only expands on the last quatrain and presents a stark choice between two kinds of decline and death; one entirely alone and unlooked on, the other with someone looking on. However much the sonnet builds up the symbolic vision of rebirth and transcendence of death, its final image is of a man dying with his son looking on.

In effect Sonnet 7 manages to be two things at once. It uses one traditional form of symbolic language to elucidate great truths — we die in order to live again, all men are part of an eternal natural process, no man is an island — but it fixes in the reader's mind a counter-statement — we are isolated in life, we are neglected in age, and we die alone. To die "looked on" is better than, but not profoundly better than, to die "unlooked on", given the way "looks" works earlier in the sonnet to emphasise the subject's isolation.

This couplet's presentation to the young man of such bleak alternatives emphasises both his isolation and the poet's power over him. Despite the poet's first appearance not coming until Sonnet 10, from the opening of the sequence we have begun to be aware that his manipulation of metaphor and simile is bent towards making his values dominate the young man's. The opposition is implicit in the first sonnet's "beauty's rose" which isolates the one element of the young man, his appearance, which the poet thinks most valuable to others, while it ignores all other possible interpretations of "fairest creatures" (i.e. pure, righteous, just, pleasing, truthful, gentle). The potential cruelty of this process, which the reader is asked to condone as a member of the external world who will benefit from the young man's procreation, appears nakedly in Sonnet 5. Here the subject's preservation is given in the metaphor of a flower's distilled perfume:

> Those hours that with gentle work did frame
> The lovely gaze where every eye doth dwell
> Will play the tyrants to the very same
> 4   And that unfair which fairly doth excel:
> For never-resting time leads summer on
> To hideous winter and confounds him there,
> Sap checked with frost and lusty leaves quite gone,
> 8   Beauty o'ersnowed and bareness everywhere.
> Then were not summer's distillation left
> A liquid pris'ner pent in walls of glass,
> Beauty's effect with beauty were bereft,
> 12   Nor it nor no remembrance what it was.
> But flowers distilled, though they with winter meet,
> Leese but their show, their substance still lives sweet.

"Though they with winter meet" is a trick. Flowers distilled, even in mid-summer (which, of course, will always come round again) leese their show. Those who meet winter are those still alive, like the poet, and for them the distilled flower still has substance. For the young man, whose pleasure lies entirely in his show, it is hardly a consolation, even if the only way for him to be remembered is to be a liquid prisoner pent in walls of glass. Again our allegiance is contradictory. We presumably accept the poet's values in the way that Winifred Nowottny does: 'This triumphant transfer to Beauty of the movement formerly associated with Time, is of a piece with the imagery of the next line . . . where Beauty's distillation is at once arrested ("prisoner", "pent") yet free ("liquid") and visible ("glass"); this image of course reverses the implications of the earlier images of winter, where the sap was checked with frost and beauty was o'ersnowed.'[12] This is a moving vision, but the vision of an observer, not the subject. His future is to be a shadow. "Pent in walls of glass" glances at the idea of a reflection trapped in a mirror, and in the third quatrain not beauty but only "beauty's effect" (probably the perfume of the flower) governs the syntax of line 12,

> Nor it nor no remembrance what it was;

in other words neither perfume nor the remembrance of perfume would remain. As for the flower, its loss is inevitable, and the poet's detached acceptance of that fact prevents the reader from finding any way of mediating between the two sets of values, the poet's belief in "substance" and the young man's life of "show".

Compare this sonnet by Samuel Daniel which is similar in imagery to the procreation sonnets, is also built upon an exhortation not to make too much of present beauty, but whose effect is quite different because of the poet's concern for his subject:

> Beauty, sweet love, is like the morning dew
> Whose short refresh upon the tender green
> Cheers for a time but till the sun doth show,
> 4   And straight 'tis gone as it had never been.
> Soon doth it fade that makes the fairest flourish;
> Short is the glory of the blushing rose,
> The hew which thou so carefully dost nourish,
> 8   Yet which at length thou must be forced to lose.
> When thou surcharged with burthen of thy years
> Shalt bend thy wrinkles homeward to the earth;
> When time hath made a passport for thy fears,
> 12   Dated in age, the Kalends of our death—
> But ah, no more, this hath been often told,
> And women grieve to think they must be old.[13]

Daniel's sonnet is planned, from the opening vocative to the knowing couplet, to set against the implied exhortation (be it to make love or to have children) the poet's knowledge of and sympathy with the acts which a human being vainly does to defy time. As in Shakespeare's procreation sonnets the poet's superiority is always evident, but unlike them it does not use its subject's decay and death to make a well-rounded artefact. Actually it does the opposite. After an octave made up of two complementary statements about the certainty of beauty's loss it moves into apparent preparation for its ultimate purpose in the third quatrain: but the anticipatory syntax of the two whens is choked off in a couplet which scorns the poet's perpetual preaching.

The development of Shakespeare's procreation sequence from the time the poet allows himself explicit entrance is not towards the synthesis of double allegiances which Daniel's sonnet reaches. For one thing the repeated argument to procreate becomes so dulled that the sonnets seem to exist more for their imagery of the horror of death than for the proposed consolation. In the couplet of Sonnet 11 the young man is seen as nature's seal made to print copies, but the verb is "carved", not "made", and it introduces the sense of lined and trenched faces. In Sonnets 12–14 the phrases of consolation seem flat and insipid when set against the poet's descriptions of death: in Sonnet 12 "breed to brave him" opposes "the wastes of time"; in Sonnet 13 "your sweet issue your sweet form should bear" opposes "barren rage of death's eternal cold"; and in Sonnet 14 "if from thyself to store thou wouldst convert" opposes "thy end is truth's and beauty's doom and date". In the couplet of Sonnet 15 the idea is one of rebirth but the image one of cutting:

> And all in war with time for love of you,
> As he takes from you, I engraft you new.

This is the first mention in the sequence of the poet as eterniser but the word "engraft", as Stephen Booth points out, is nowhere recorded in the Renaissance 'where its direct object is the receiving stock and not the grafted scion'.[14] In other words the image is not, as a modern reader might understand it, of grafts being added to the young man but of he himself being the graft. What the poet does in Sonnet 15 is to take seriously his perceived analogy between men and plants. The sonnet opens with the world as a stage under the eyes of a cosmic audience:

> When I consider everything that grows
> Holds in perfection but a little moment,
> That this huge stage presenteth nought but shows
> Whereon the stars in secret influence comment.

The second quatrain lowers the analogy several pegs — the men become plants and the cosmic audience the poet:

> When I perceive that men as plants increase,
> Cheered and checked ev'n by the selfsame sky,
> Vaunt in their youthful sap, at height decrease,
> And wear their brave state out of memory.

The third quatrain takes images from the first two:

> Then the conceit of this inconstant stay
> Sets you most rich in youth before my sight,
> Where wasteful time debateth with decay
> To change your day of youth to sullied night.

The image is still the stage with the poet as spectator. The play he is watching has one hero, the young man, and two villains plotting his downfall, time and decay. The couplet grants the poet the same kind of superiority as the secret influential stars of the first quatrain, one which allows him to use the knife of his own plant metaphor in the couplet.

This sonnet's effect on the reader is to make him perceive a great distance between the two men. The young man presented as the isolated figure on the stage is particularly vulnerable to the master plotters – "rich in youth" and in his "day of youth" – as if the very period of his inconstant stay were determined merely by the length of their debate. To have his little moment of perfection fixed in so arbitrary a way would make the play a tragedy but for the detachment of the poet, for whom the play is only one more "show", part of the pattern which controls men as completely as it does plants. As a spectator the poet is already superior to the actors in the drama, a point made more forceful in the couplet where his image of himself as an engrafter excludes him entirely from the common metaphor of all men as plants, turning him instead into their preserver and renewer.

To the reader this claim is an unexpected piece of self-characterisation. The idea of immortalising poetry has not yet emerged so that the image of engrafting will still be connected to his role as marriage broker. But the claim is more personal than ever before and the opening quatrain of the next sonnet, number 16, immediately recontextualises it as the claim of a poet for poetry, if now more humbly put:

> But wherefore do not you a mightier way
> Make war upon this bloody tyrant time?
> And fortify yourself in your decay
> With means more blessed than my barren rhyme?

"But" joins the quatrain so closely to the previous sonnet that the reader is jarred by the sudden subordination of the newly found immortalising agent at the very moment that it is defined: "my barren rhyme" hardly fits the claim the poet has just made for himself to be an engrafter. Still, the reader suspends judgment awaiting the "mightier way" which the poet will propose for the young man to make war upon and fortify himself against time. That way, as it emerges in the second quatrain, is in all respects bathetic:

> Now stand you on the top of happy hours,
> And many maiden gardens yet unset,
> With virtuous wish would bear your living flowers,
> Much liker than your painted counterfeit.

Unexpectedly the poet ignores the military nature of the first quatrain's promises and creates a series of images in apparent opposition to one word in the first quatrain, "barren". The argument is, of course, the old argument for procreation, but now it has been reduced to the level of coy sexuality built around the paradox of deflowering maidens in order to plant flowers. The sestet unites procreation and poetry as immortalisers by way of of the much discussed ambiguities of "lines of life":[15]

> So should the lines of life that life repair
> Which this time's pencil or my pupil pen
> Neither in inward worth nor outward fair
> Can make you live yourself in eyes of men.
>   To give away yourself keeps yourself still,
>   And you must live, drawn by your own sweet skill.

In the act of denying poetry any power and insisting upon its inferiority to procreation the poet contrives to give it a complexity and mystery which the ideal of procreation has lost. The couplet, as many times before, exhorts the young man to have children, but gives the palm to poetry by arguing that to do so will make the young man become his own artist.

By now poetry has become the dominant subject of the sequence and the next sonnet, number 17, takes up the whole of its three quatrains in describing how barren poetry must inevitably decay and be disbelieved. But the couplet, in resurrecting procreation a final time, causes an unexpected sub-text to emerge:

> Who will believe my verse in time to come
> If it were filled with your most high deserts?
> Though yet heav'n knows it is but as a tomb
> 4 Which hides your life, and shows not half your parts.
> If I could write the beauty of your eyes,
> And in fresh numbers number all your graces,

The age to come would say, 'This poet lies —
8 Such heav'nly touches ne'er touched earthly faces.'
   So should my papers, yellowed with their age,
   Be scorned, like old men of less truth than tongue,
   And your true rights be termed a poet's rage
12 And stretched metre of an antique song:
      But were some child of yours alive that time,
      You should live twice in it and in my rhyme.

In his comment on the final line of this sonnet Stephen Booth notes that the reader has a choice of two possible interpretations depending upon the chosen punctuation (i.e. a comma after "twice" as in the Quarto, or after "it" as above). They are: '(1) "You would live twice in it [i.e. have a second life, live again, in your child] and [have a third life] in my verse." (2) "You would have two chances at immortality, in your child and in my verse." ' [16] The problem with these alternatives is that although they seem reasonable readings of the line in isolation, they both contradict the argument of the preceding thirteen lines so far as poetry is concerned. In these lines the sonnet has developed an almost cynical conceit: so beautiful is the young man that the greater success poetry has in describing him, the more certain it is to be disbelieved in time to come and the less likely is the young man's immortalisation in verse. One implication of this which is never quite brought to the surface in this sonnet, although it appears later in the rival poet sonnets, is that only poor poetry will work for future ages, or for a subject whose eye is on the opinion of future ages. The other implication, which the poet takes up here, is the paradox that only if the young man is *not* unique will his uniqueness be appreciated in the future. To make sense of the final line as a completion of the sonnet's argument we have to add to Booth's alternatives the more extreme assertion that only if the young man breeds can he be immortalised in verse, because only in his beauty as it appears in his child — "much liker than your painted counterfeit" — will future readers find a metaphorical equivalent for the picture the poet paints in his own verse and therefore believe that it could describe a real person. Otherwise, "this poet lies".

Sonnet 17 is even more an observation about the nature of poetry than it is about the young man's beauty: readers will not believe what the poet writes unless they have a metaphorical equivalent before them, and the art of the poet is to find the right equivalent. The effect of the last line on the sonnet is to put all of its claims for the inadequacy of poetry into a fresh context. The poet had speculated on the possibility of being able to "write the beauty of your eyes,/And in fresh numbers number all your graces". These formulations lean towards an ideal of pure description not obscured by any use of metaphor, almost a listing of the young man's points of beauty and grace. But lists will no longer work when the subject is dead, and the sonnet's couplet points towards the need to find the right metaphor. This is a procreation sonnet still — the last of them, in fact — but now procreation has taken on the subservient role of giving support for the poet's metaphors.

That very point, the search for the best metaphor, is the subject of Sonnet 18, perhaps the best known sonnet in the sequence and probably one of the least discussed. In place of analysis one normally, and understandably, finds only praise:

> Shall I compare thee to a summer's day?
> Thou art more lovely and more temperate:
> Rough winds do shake the darling buds of May,
> 4 And summer's lease hath all too short a date;
> Sometime too hot the eye of heaven shines,
> And often is his gold complexion dimmed;
> And every fair from fair sometimes declines,
> 8 By chance or nature's changing course untrimmed:
> But thy eternal summer shall not fade,
> Nor lose possession of that fair thou ow'st,
> Nor shall death brag thou wand'rest in his shade,
> 12 When in eternal lines to time thou grow'st.
> So long as men can breathe or eyes can see,
> So long lives this, and this gives life to thee.

A full response to this sonnet ought to take in all the implications of the opening line. "Compare" carries the substance of all love poetry, the finding of the right image to convey the subject's beauty. The proposal is for a metaphor to be built around the image of a summer's day but it is no sooner made than it is rejected on the grounds that the young man is more lovely and more temperate than any single summer's day could be. Then the sonnet gives two separate, consecutive descriptions, the first in listing the reasons for rejecting the image actually describes various summer's days, the second describes the young man. The strange thing is that the first description is more human and attractive than the second. The clue is given in line 2: to be more lovely than a summer's day may be desirable, but to be more temperate is not.[17] To be a darling bud of May shaken by rough winds, to be too hot and then to be dimmed is almost a summary of beauty, which depends upon chance and change; and lines 7–8 read as if they were a definition of beauty, especially when one thinks that among the possible meanings of "untrimmed" are 'free of ornaments' and 'with hair hanging loose':[18]

> And every fair from fair sometimes declines,
> By chance or nature's changing course untrimmed.

In essence, part of the nature of beauty is some time to decline from beauty. But then the poet switches in the sestet to an ideal who is incapable of change — eternal summer, perpetual beauty, immortality, a never-ending poem (one sense of "eternal lines"). To be stuck in time in such a way, to be always 'the same we were today or yesterday' is a peculiarly poetic fate, and to have the power to do that to his subject gives the poet absolute rule.[19]

Thus the two opposed tones inhere in this sonnet too. The reader needs to set against the grandeur of the poet's claim to immortalise the threat which such a claim carries for its subject. The more the poet's creation gains eternal life the more the actual subject is destroyed, its extremes reduced to an unchanging permanence, so that it is fitting for Sonnet 18 to be followed by a sonnet which raises the poet to the rank of time's controller, permitting and then forbidding him to act. This is Sonnet 19:

> Devouring time, blunt thou the lion's paws,
> And make the earth devour her own sweet brood;
> Pluck the keen teeth from the fierce tiger's jaws,
> 4 And burn the long-lived phoenix in her blood;
> Make glad and sorry seasons as thou fleet'st
> And do whate'er thou wilt, swift-footed time,
> To the wide world and all her fading sweets;
> 8 But I forbid thee one most heinous crime,
> O carve not with thy hours my love's fair brow,
> Nor draw no lines there with thine antique pen.
> Him in thy course untainted do allow,
> 12 For beauty's pattern to succeeding men.
>   Yet do thy worst, old time; despite thy wrong,
>   My love shall in my verse ever live young.

The imagery of the sestet transforms time into a poet. Instead of the poet's "antique song", as Sonnet 17 had described it, time now has the "antique pen"; and in a similar reversal, just as quill pens are normally carved so time's pen now does the carving, making lines on the love's brow analogous to lines of verse. The whole sonnet enacts the reversal of roles: time's actions in the octave are, we perceive intellectually, those which span lifetimes and centuries, but we also perceive the actions poetically and they transform the lifetimes and centuries into frenetic action – the images are of a sudden blunting, plucking, and burning. The "antique/antic" pun carried over from Sonnet 17 develops the picture of time's frenzied scoring of lines across the young man's brow, all in contrast with a poet in obvious and imperious control, from the orders addressed to time in the first quatrain to the final permission in the couplet.[20]

The great unifying concept of Sonnets 1 – 19 is the image of the young man as "beauty's pattern to succeeding men". In every one of the nineteen sonnets it is the poet's ideal: it opposes both the young man's wishes and time's rule, and it is ultimately achieved by turning the young man into a kind of mummy preserved in poetry. The reader's experience of the group is disturbing. He begins with remonstrations against the independence and individuality of the young man and eventually sees both of those human qualities sacrificed to poetic immortality. The text immortalises but the subtext embalms.

2 'Some Good Conceit of Thine': The Obtrusive Metaphor

The extent of the reader's doubt about the tone of a sonnet is often bound up with the use and presentation of metaphor; and in this chapter I shall describe some of the ways in which specific metaphors are used to trouble and perplex the reader — what I shall call the obtrusive or frustrating metaphor. I ought to begin, though, by emphasising that by no means all of the sonnets in the sequence use this kind of metaphor; indeed a number, if not a great number, use metaphor to free the reader from doubt. Sonnet 29 will stand as a good example of this liberating use of metaphor and provides a useful initial contrast to set against the remainder of the sonnets which I shall be discussing in this chapter.

In Sonnet 29 the liberating metaphor is the lark ascending:

> When in disgrace with fortune and men's eyes
> I all alone beweep my outcast state,
> And trouble deaf heav'n with my bootless cries,
> 4   And look upon myself and curse my fate,
> Wishing me like to one more rich in hope,
> Featured like him, like him with friends possessed,
> Desiring this man's art, and that man's scope,
> 8   With what I most enjoy contented least;
> Yet in these thoughts myself almost despising,
> Haply I think on thee, and then my state,
> Like to the lark at break of day arising
> 12   From sullen earth, sings hymns at heaven's gate;
>   For thy sweet love remembered such wealth brings,
>   That then I scorn to change my state with kings.

The liberation comes partly from the metaphor's action upon the syntax of the sonnet and partly from the aptness and clarity of its image of the lark.

First the syntax: the "when" which opens the sonnet leaves the reader anticipating a "then" clause which never comes; and the check at line 9, after eight lines of syntactic expectation, seems, for that line at least, to emphasise all of of the negative elements of the octave. Then lines 10–12 use the image of the lark to transform all of these elements into intense celebration. Syntactically there is a release both in the fulfilment of the apparently frustrated promise of the initial "when" and in the sweep right through line 11 and into line 12 in contrast with the end-stopping of lines 1–9. In its image the metaphor provides a release from the oppressive man-centredness of the octave: a world peopled by the rich, famous, and neglected suddenly finds a new, bird's-eye perspective, and the sheer pleasure of singing for the sake of it raises the bird to the heaven's level where the man in line 3 had called fruitlessly up to it. The idea of the outcast is the same – a lark in the sky is an excellent figure of isolation – but his "state" has been transformed, so that when the couplet comes to recapitulate the change of state in the worldly terms of the octave the reader now perceives ecstatic undertones in the mundane words "wealth", "scorn", "change", "state", and "kings".[1] The effect of the one image of the lark is total, preventing us from reading the couplet in any other way but as a triumphant vindication of the outcast poet. It would, for instance, be wrong-headed to say that it shows the poet imprisoned in the attitudes of envy ("brings such wealth"/"scorn to change my state") which had created the melodramatic self-pity of the octave. There are many such ironic ambiguities in the sonnets but here one metaphor wipes them out.

In the metaphor's clarity of purpose Sonnet 29 is unusual and for the rest of this chapter I intend to consider some of the more frustrating metaphoric structures in the sonnets. Sonnets 25 and 26 provide a useful place to start. In substance Sonnet 25 is very close to Sonnet 29, especially in its couplet:

> Let those who are in favour with their stars
> Of public honour and proud titles boast,
> Whilst I whom fortune of such triumph bars,
> 4 Unlooked for joy in that I honour most.
> Great princes' favourites their fair leaves spread,
> But as the marigold at the sun's eye,
> And in themselves their pride lies buried,
> 8 For at a frown they in their glory die.
> The painful warrior famoused for fight,
> After a thousand victories once foiled,
> Is from the book of honour razed quite,
> 12 And all the rest forgot for which he toiled.

> Then happy I that love and am beloved
> Where I may not remove, nor be removed.

The text of the sonnet here is an emended one. In the Quarto "worth" is printed as the rhyme word of line 9 and a suggested, and equally possible, emendation to the sonnet would be to leave "worth" where it is and alter "quite" in line 11 to "forth". It would be equally possible and equally acceptable since the image carries no kind of conviction whatsoever; rather like the whole poem in fact, which seems to be a deliberate exercise in sonnet making. On every level – rhythm, syntax, image, and metaphor – it does its best to repel interest, a feeling expressed as early as 1780 when Steevens remarked of the third quatrain, but with the whole sonnet no doubt in mind, that it 'is not worth the labour that has been bestowed on it'.[2] But since I assume the sequence to have been carefully planned in its effects, instead of treating the sonnet entirely negatively as an example of Homer nodding I am inclined to see it as a conscious demonstration of the workings of a naïve mentality; so naïve that his summary of his state in the couplet strains the reader's credibility to the limit.

How far does the banality of the couplet lead us to reconsider what has been said in the three quatrains? Little, I suspect, because neither of the sonnet's dominant metaphors, the princes' favourites or the marigolds, allows us any room for manoeuvre. Each is introduced in text-book manner, as if learned by rote, and together they have no more effect than to reveal the self-satisfaction of the speaker, content in his own obscurity. But the reader who carries the naïvete of these images into Sonnet 26 will be pulled up short:

> Lord of my love, to whom in vassalage
> Thy merit hath my duty strongly knit,
> To thee I send this written ambassage
> 4 To witness duty, not to show my wit.
> Duty so great, which wit as poor as mine
> May make seem bare, in wanting words to show it,
> But that I hope some good conceit of thine
> 8 In thy soul's thought, all naked, will bestow it;
> Till whatsoever star that guides my moving
> Points on me graciously with fair aspect,
> And puts apparel on my tottered loving,
> 12 To show me worthy of thy sweet respect.
>   Then may I dare to boast how I do love thee;
>   Till then, not show my head where thou mayst prove me.[3]

This sonnet seems often to have been read in isolation, and usually for the purposes of demonstrating the claims of Southampton to be the addressee of the Sonnets. But its taking up of the theme of Sonnet 25 – duty paid to a lord of love – is sufficiently marked for me to treat the two as a pair. After having seen the text-book fate of great princes' favourites in Sonnet 25, "Lord of my love" is a dangerously ironic opening to Sonnet 26; and even if we treat it as a logical following-up of Sonnet 25 – i.e. 'I am not a great prince's favourite, but I am your favourite, so you are my lord' – the irony still holds, for lords of whatever kind, we have been told, have only to look askance to shrivel up marigolds. Verbal echoes join this sonnet to its predecessor too: "star" (line 9 with 25:1), "moving" (line 9 with 25:14), "fair" (line 10 with 25:5), and "boast" (line 13 with 25:2).

Where Sonnet 25 had revealed invincible naïveté Sonnet 26 reveals extreme vulnerability. It is an "ambassage" dedicated to the poet's lord, but the poet must function primarily as a diplomat, not a poet (hence the parallels with the dedication of *The Rape of Lucrece*). Ambassages, unlike poems, do not show their wit. They show duty; and the language of duty runs a double risk. Duty demands metaphor, as in the opening line of the sonnet; but duty also demands self-effacement, and self-effacement of this kind ought to be witless, for too witty a metaphor shows too much of the poet's personality. The result is a sonnet whose argument is genuinely difficult to unravel. In contrast with Sonnet 25 metaphor is kept circumspect: bare, all naked, tattered, not worthy to be shown, describe the poet's expression, and the metaphorising of this expression will, for the moment, be the young man's – "some good conceit of thine" – while perhaps eventually some astrological help will put the poet in a position to find his own metaphorical apparel. Until then obscurity allows him to keep free of the challenge from the young man which he expects to come some day.

Sonnet 26 provides a strange reversal of Sonnet 25. In place of the desire for, and celebration of, obscurity comes the description of the humiliations and limitations of that state. Where Sonnet 25 had precise, clear, and ultimately banal metaphors, Sonnet 26 presents fragments of metaphor and innuendo.[4] In neither case can the reader respond to metaphor and image in the way that he is encouraged to do in Sonnet 29; and in this respect the interaction of Sonnets 25 and 26 increases the confusion. The two polarise. Sonnet 25 becomes even more naïve, almost the kind of flat use of metaphor which would appeal to the addressee of Sonnet 26, and Sonnet 26 becomes more ironic in emphasising the dependence of the only just proclaimed free man.

Sonnet 52 uses metaphor even more self-consciously than Sonnet 25:

So am I as the rich whose blessed key
Can bring him to his sweet up-locked treasure,
The which he will not every hour survey,
4   For blunting the fine point of seldom pleasure.
Therefore are feasts so solemn and so rare,
Since seldom coming in the long year set,
Like stones of worth they thinly placed are,
8   Or captain jewels in the carcanet.
So is the time that keeps you as my chest,
Or as the wardrobe which the robe doth hide
To make some special instant special blest,
12   By new unfolding his imprisoned pride.
　　Blessed are you whose worthiness gives scope,
　　Being had to triumph, being lacked to hope.

The experience of reading this sonnet is to move by way of metaphor from
the security of wealth and possession to insecurity and poverty. The
metaphors, or better, similes, are all connected with the possession of wealth,
but they deal with it in significantly different ways. The image of the miser in
the first quatrain leaves all the power over sight and deprivation of sight in
the poet's hand, the power in the verb "will not" and the reason for
depriving himself in line 4. The second quatrain switches the metaphor from
treasure to festivals and then to jewels in a necklace. In both the passage of
time and the setting of jewels the poet's power over his sight is more limited
than in the first quatrain. Then the third quatrain gathers the earlier images
together. The locked-up treasure reappears in the chest and wardrobe of
lines 9 – 10, and the robe itself contains both the festive and jewel associations
of the second quatrain; but the young man as a robe available only on special
occasions is a more fragile vision, from the poet's view at least, than coins
locked away to be surveyed at any time – the adjectives mark the contrast
between "sweet up-locked treasure" and "imprisoned pride". Through the
metaphors the sense of time contracts too, from "not every hour" to
"seldom" to "rare" to "thinly placed" to "some special instant". Finally the
couplet is ironically loaded, for "blessed" is carried over from the key which
unlocks the treasure in line 1 and which defines the special instant of line 11.
Those have both gained their blessedness from their proximity to the young
man, and in the couplet his blessedness is set directly parallel to his
"worthiness", itself a pun on the accumulated wealth of the three quatrains.
Being both holy and wealthy the young man is seen as the granter of scope,
the poet as dependent upon his gifts.
　　A similar metaphoric structure governs the well-known example of

Sonnet 73, where the contraction from season to day to dying fire is rounded off in an ironic couplet which matches the young man's strength of love to his sense of the poet's decay.[5] But Sonnet 52 has none of the force of Sonnet 73. The obvious sequence of metaphorising may be similar in the two poems, but from its initial "so" Sonnet 52 makes it clear that the metaphorising is a deliberate search for similitudes. It maintains a syntax of explanation – "So am I as . . . Therefore are . . . Since . . . So is the time . . . as my chest, Or as the wardrobe . . ." – thereby insisting upon a distance between subject and metaphor, where Sonnet 73 fuses the subject into its metaphor so fully that, for example, the exact degree of reference of "bare ruined choirs" to the poet's age can never be fully described by the reader. The deliberate metaphorising in Sonnet 52 only reinforces the progression from possession to deprivation which I summarised earlier. The reader's experience of the sonnet, as he meets a succession of metaphors which maintain their detachment from the point of reference, is to reduce their force from the poetic to the explanatory, and finally, perhaps, to the status of mere excuses. In other words, 'I put up with this constant deprivation because I can deceive myself that I am the possessor of great riches'.

This type of conscious, too deliberate metaphorising occurs repeatedly in the first half of the sequence. Sonnet 37, for instance, develops the idea of the poet being given life and strength by the young man. It seems to follow the argument of Sonnet 36 where the poet accepts that "we two must be twain", and in the couplet employs the conceit that he loves the young man so much that any revelation of their relationship would harm him as much as it would the young man:

> I love thee in such sort,
> As, thou being mine, mine is thy good report.

Then Sonnet 37 opens with a simile which, in the light of the procreation sonnets, has no small irony:

> As a decrepit father takes delight
> To see his active child do deeds of youth,
> So I, made lame by fortune's dearest spite,
> 4   Take all my comfort of thy worth and truth.
> For whether beauty, birth, or wealth, or wit,
> Or any of these all, or all, or more,
> Entitled in thy parts do crowned sit,
> 8   I make my love engrafted to this store.

> So then I am not lame, poor, nor despised,
> Whilst that this shadow doth such substance give,
> That I in thy abundance am sufficed,
> 12   And by a part of all thy glory live.
>   Look what is best, that best I wish in thee.
>   This wish I have, then ten times happy me.[6]

The bizarre, if picturesque, nature of Sonnet 37's opening simile is something which the reader can hardly forget through the rest of the sonnet — its solidity is incidentally testified to by the number of eccentric attempts at proving Shakespeare's lameness from it. But the metaphoric structure of the sonnet is one of increasing vagueness, as if trying to dissipate the self-pity of the poet's picturing himself as a decrepit voyeur of his lover's deeds of youth.[7] The second and third quatrains, in contrast to the first, give only shadows of metaphor: after the abstract qualities and considerations of lines 5 – 6 — beauty, birth, wealth, wit, or all, or more — lines 7 – 8 glance at images of kingship, grafting, and hoarding. Line 9 recalls "lame", but demetaphorises it by insisting upon its abstract sense, making it the first in a sequence of three disabilities, lame, poor, and despised; and the rest of the quatrain, with "shadow" and "substance", "abundance" and "glory", concentrates the reader's imagination on abstractions. In this way the reader's experience of the sonnet may be puzzling in contrast to, for example, a sonnet like 143, where a similarly explicit opening image — "Lo, as a careful housewife runs to catch/One of her feathered creatures broke away . . ." — is maintained throughout the sonnet. Here, though, the unusually direct and obvious opening image contaminates the rest of the sonnet. Where the poet seems to be arguing for his transformation from decrepitude to vigour by way of the young man's worth and truth, the reader is given no opportunity to abandon or replace the image of dependence at the beginning; hence the flippant couplet whose tone would make it a strange summation of lines 5 – 12 were it not for our memory of the humiliations of the opening image.

So far I have been content with fairly obvious examples where the reader's over-consciousness of the metaphor makes a sonnet's immediate argument difficult to accept. Other sonnets cause similar frustrations, but in a way less easily described. Sonnet 75 is a case where two metaphors vie with each other:

> So are you to my thoughts as food to life,
> Or as sweet seasoned show'rs are to the ground;
> And for the peace of you I hold such strife,

 4 As 'twixt a miser and his wealth is found;
   Now proud as an enjoyer, and anon
   Doubting the filching age will steal his treasure;
   Now counting best to be with you alone,
 8 Then bettered that the world may see my pleasure;
   Sometime all full with feasting on your sight,
   And by and by clean starved for a look;
   Possessing or pursuing no delight
12 Save what is had or must from you be took.
      Thus do I pine and surfeit day by day,
      Or gluttoning on all, or all away.

"Peace of you" in line 3 presents insuperable difficulties for the reader or commentator. It might be possible to find some paraphrase which sums up all of its connotations, but in the process of reading the sonnet the reader mainly perceives the contrast between "peace" and "strife" together with the pun on 'piece' which anticipates the money image of line 4, and secondarily, perhaps, a general sense of "peace" summing up the opening images of providential succour. Certainly the contrast in the quatrain between the first two lines and the fourth is immense. Sublime is hardly too strong a word to describe the complete dependence of the poet upon the young man in the images of food and rain, but the sublimity evaporates after "peace" and "strife" with the image of the miser and his wealth. The degradation of that metaphor spreads through the second quatrain: "proud", "enjoyer", "treasure", "counting best", "bettered", and "see my pleasure" all take on the taint of the miser, where they might otherwise have been used to sustain the grandeur of food to life and showers to the ground. When the sestet returns to the initial image, through "full", "feasting", and "clean starved", it does so only to revise it radically downwards by carrying into it the values of the miser. The body's dependence upon food has become the neurotic's obsession with whatever fuels his neurosis, and the final vision of the poet caught between times of gluttony and times of starvation does more than merely describe his self-humiliation, it also completes the reader's frustration. A sonnet which opens in the high metaphorical fashion enacts the degradation of its subject by allowing one metaphor to contaminate another.

The dangers of this kind of analysis are obvious. One man's obtrusive metaphor may well be another's poetic gem, and all readers are susceptible to the shifts of time and taste which will flatten some metaphors and bring others to prominence. But in a sequence of poems so intensely concerned with image and metaphor the reader is constantly forced to make decisions about them. Consider Sonnet 53, where Adonis and Helen are brought in to exemplify the young man's beauty. The sonnet does not merely use the mythological characters as models, but draws the reader's attention to the fact that these are models being used by an artist. "Describe", "imitate" "set", and "paint" are the operative verbs, and they leave the reader floundering:

> What is your substance, whereof are you made,
> That millions of strange shadows on you tend?
> Since everyone hath, every one, one shade,
> 4   And you, but one, can every shadow lend.
> Describe Adonis, and the counterfeit
> Is poorly imitated after you;
> On Helen's cheek all art of beauty set,
> 8   And you in Grecian tires are painted new.
> Speak of the spring and foison of the year;
> The one doth shadow of your beauty show,
> The other as your bounty doth appear,
> 12   And you in every blessed shape we know.
>   In all external grace you have some part,
>   But you like none, none you, for constant heart.

The first quatrain may not be easy to follow in detail, with its play on Platonic forms, but its gist is clear: the young man is the central substance which controls all other individuals, and those individuals serve him. The whole quatrain is a question: what are you that you can have such power? The second quatrain begins the answer in artistic terms, but with a vagueness calculated to confuse the reader by forcing him simultaneously to consider the nature of art generally, the nature of this kind of art, the nature of the young man, and the nature of the poet. That might be thought an ambitious summary of a few seconds' reading, but the mind is capable of it and the quatrain will permit nothing less.

The nature of art is to describe, usually by comparison. If the artist wants to describe Adonis or Helen he must counterfeit, since the originals have long departed, and base his attempt upon his imagination of what Adonis's and Helen's beauty were like. That process will gain its power from observation of the most beautiful thing in the present world, in other words the young man. "Poorly imitated" becomes, therefore, a comment on all poetry – on all things in fact. We are only shadows of the past and our best models fall far short of the mythical archetypes; hence the unnervingly discordant vision of the young man as a painted Greek lady in full costume. However, this response to the nature of art in general runs counter to the demands of this kind of art: the love sonnet celebrates one being who transcends everything which has gone before. In this respect Adonis and Helen are themselves only shadows foretelling the substance of the young man, as the spring foretells the harvest. The lines shift in this focus. All past descriptions of Adonis have become poor imitations of the young man because those poets whose subject was fabulous beauty never had the real model to work from. Give Helen's cheek as much cosmetic help as possible: that artificial beauty may eventually lead to a vision comparable to the natural beauty of the young man.

But the syntax of the quatrain gives the reader another focus, into the nature of the young man. "Describe" and "set" are imperatives, and we are best advised to consider them in the way that I have been doing so far, as rhetorical imperatives addressed to the world in general – let anyone try to describe Adonis or Helen. However, the first quatrain of the sonnet has a firm object of address in the young man – not "what is his substance . . .?" but "what is your substance . . .?" – and one part of the reader's mind will see the logical syntactic continuation in the imperatives: 'you describe Adonis and Helen'. And when the young man describes Adonis and Helen the result is self-centredness, a poor copy of Adonis based upon his view of his own charms and a Helen rouged in the same way that he is ("I never saw that you did painting need"). Opposed to that response, though, is the realisation that "describe", "imitate", "set", and "paint" are the actions of an artist, most relevant to the poet himself. Applied to him, as the metaphoric logic would require, they shift the reader's focus back to an experience which runs through the sonnets, namely the effect of the young man upon the poet's art. Describe Adonis, as of course Shakespeare did in *Venus and Adonis*, and the poem fails because the young man gets in the way; paint Helen and the image of female beauty invariably reads like a picture of the poet's young man.[8]

The way in which this quatrain deals with the metaphorical process of art should prevent any reader coming to any kind of definite conclusion about it. The sonnet insists upon multiplicity of focus and eventual frustration; and after so packed a quatrain the sestet's apparent simplicity completes the reader's torture:

> Speak of the spring and foison of the year;
> The one doth shadow of your beauty show,
> The other as your bounty doth appear,
> And you in every blessed shape we know.
>> In all external grace you have some part,
>> But you like none, none you, for constant heart.

Summarised, this comes down to the assertion that the young man plays a part in all visions of external beauty; it is natural to use him as a metaphor for spring and foison or to use spring and foison as a metaphor for him. But "show" and "appear" are literally superficial words, the more so when contrasted so heavily with the final rhyme word of the three quatrains, "know". Stephen Booth glosses "know" in two ways, we recognise you in every shape, and you appear in every shape known to us.[9] I would suggest a third, more sinister possibility, of knowing the young man for what he is, whatever shape he takes.[10] With that possibility added to the other meanings the sonnet goes a little way towards answering its opening question—"What is your substance, whereof are you made"—or at least putting various answers forward. The couplet, with its obvious irony, only summarises the variety. No reader can really choose, as one commentator does, to read the sonnet as simply 'a piece of direct irony', or as another does, as 'a peace offering of abundant flattery', without having closed his mind to part of the metaphorising process which the sonnet parodies in such a deadly fashion.

The argument of this chapter is that the reader's experience of the sonnets is intimately bound up with his response to individual metaphors. A metaphor which is obtrusive or vague may well undermine, or at least obscure, a sonnet's literal statement. That literal statement will not usually be abandoned but it will have to co-exist with a potentially frustrating metaphoric competition. In some sonnets, though, the competition between metaphor and statement is a sustaining, not frustrating, element. An example is Sonnet 30 which has one of the most exhaustive metaphors in the sonnets:

> When to the sessions of sweet silent thought
> I summon up remembrance of things past,
> I sigh the lack of many a thing I sought,
> 4   And with old woes new wail my dear time's waste.
> Then can I drown an eye, unused to flow,
> For precious friends hid in death's dateless night,
> And weep afresh love's long since cancelled woe,
> 8   And moan th' expense of many a vanished sight.
> Then can I grieve at grievances foregone,
> And heavily from woe to woe tell o'er
> The sad account of fore-bemoaned moan,
> 12   Which I new pay as if not paid before.
>   But if the while I think on thee, dear friend,
>   All losses are restored, and sorrows end.

Coldly abstracted Sonnet 30 says the following: 'When I mediate I remember dead friends whom I have long since ceased mourning over. I feel their loss anew until I think of you; with that thought I cease grieving at their loss.' That statement pays a great tribute to the power of the young man but it also has strong negative, reductive undertones which are only held in check by the distance between the sonnet's statement and the metaphor it uses. The metaphor is, of course, a legal/financial one, beginning at "sessions" and continuing through "summon up", "precious", "cancelled", "expense", "tell o'er", "account", "pay" and "paid", to "losses are restored". Added to those obvious images there is a strain of words which carry secondary legal/financial senses: "lack", "dear", "waste", "unused", "dateless", "foregone", and "dear" again in the couplet. Nonetheless I can sympathise, if not agree, with Martin Seymour-Smith's judgement that the legal metaphor is 'unobtrusive', largely because it has to compete with another line of imagery, the poet's sorrow: "sigh", "old woes", "new wail", "drown an eye", "unused to flow", "weep afresh", "moan", "grieve at grievances", "heavily", "from woe to woe", "sad", "fore-bemoaned moan", and "sorrows". I call this a line of imagery because it does not quite have the standing of a metaphor; elements of it are metaphorical, but the reader's vision is on sighs and tears—a literal sadness opposed to a figurative financial court. And what prevents the literal and the figurative from overcoming each other is the surprising degree to which they fail to interact. Put simply, the part of the mind which sees Thought presiding over his court and summoning witnesses, the cancelling of debts and the spending of money, will not directly, or even indirectly, relate these images to sighs and tears.

There must, of course, be some kind of fusion at work, otherwise the sonnet would be merely ludicrous, the kind of thing which Sir John Davies mocked in his gulling sonnets – one of them begins "Into the Middle Temple of my heart/The wanton Cupid did himself admit." I believe that the fusion comes in the second quatrain, where the death of friends which causes the poet's literal sorrow is related to the figurative cancelling of debts and spending of money. But it is important to emphasise that this is a shadowy fusion. "Dateless" has its double reference – death has no end, like a lease which has no fixed term – but neither it nor the rest of the metaphor can be absorbed into the sonnet's statement. This might seem an odd thing to say, especially if we remember Sonnet 4, where a similar metaphor is absorbed into the poet's statement that the young man should marry. But the contrast with Sonnet 4 is worth pursuing, for there we were aware that we were probing such essentially poetic themes as the good life, the way to immortality, and the eventual decay of beauty. Here the death of friends can not be so conveniently labelled. It exists, of course, as a poetic subject, but not normally as a subject, let alone a vehicle, for love poetry, one of whose conventional metaphors is the legal/financial. In essence Sonnet 30 preserves the balance between subject and metaphor, permitting the reader neither to turn it into the reductive statement 'you are all my dead friends', nor to read it as the involved love conceit which so much of its language points toward.[11]

Finally in this discussion of obtrusive metaphors I mean to consider the group of three sonnets, 33–35, which first raises the matter of poetic metaphor implicitly and then, in Sonnet 35, considers its function explicitly. Sonnet 33 introduces into the sequence the idealising metaphor of the young man as the sun:

> Full many a glorious morning have I seen
> Flatter the mountain tops with sovereign eye,
> Kissing with golden face the meadows green,
> 4 Gilding pale streams with heav'nly alchemy,
> Anon permit the basest clouds to ride
> With ugly rack on his celestial face,
> And from the forlorn world his visage hide,
> 8 Stealing unseen to west with this disgrace.
> Ev'n so my sun one early morn did shine
> With all triumphant splendour on my brow;
> But out alack, he was but one hour mine,
> 12 The region cloud hath masked him from me now.
> Yet him for this my love no whit disdaineth;
> Suns of the world may stain where heav'n's sun staineth.

This is a sonnet which treats the reader courteously and expects courteous treatment in return. The experience of reading it is almost to fall into collusion with the poet, for everything about it, from its poetic and syntactic structures to its use of metaphor and pun, invites acceptance. The single sentence octave broadcasts its heightened poetic nature by its regular use of adjective +noun structures; not merely their abundance but their ordering makes the reader conscious of the rhetoric. In the eight lines only the fifth and the eighth do not have their second major stress on an adjective; and what these patterned adjectives do is to help construct not an elaborate but an elegant metaphor of the sun as a noble countenance, normally given to blessing by his blaze and kiss but often obscured by base elements. The third quatrain then brings the metaphor home -- or at least it should, but it refuses to make the necessary identification. "My sun" is still one stage removed from 'my friend' or 'my love', and it requires a response from the reader along the lines of, 'you still wish to describe what has happened by the use of this metaphor; do so, and I shall not inquire too closely into the nature of the region cloud or its masking'. Indeed any reader who did wish to enquire would be frustrated for he gets more information from the signalled metaphor in the octave — "basest", "ugly", "disgrace" — than from the part of the sonnet where he might have expected ultimate clarification. All that the sestet does is to restate the octave in exactly the same metaphoric terms: the puns on "sun" and "stain" in the couplet stay on the level of superficial wit and the final line reads like the poet's prepared excuse for his friend's crime, a lame excuse were it not for its metaphorical dress.

Sonnet 34 follows directly and seems to gain a more personal tone immediately because of its direct address to the young man:

> Why didst thou promise such a beauteous day
> And make me travel forth without my cloak,
> To let base clouds o'ertake me in my way,
> 4 Hiding thy bravery in their rotten smoke?
> 'Tis not enough that through the cloud thou break,
> To dry the rain on my storm-beaten face,
> For no man well of such a salve can speak,
> 8 That heals the wound, and cures not the disgrace.
> Nor can thy shame give physic to my grief;
> Though thou repent, yet I have still the loss.
> Th' offender's sorrow lends but weak relief
> 12 To him that bears the strong offence's loss.
>   Ah, but those tears are pearl which thy love sheeds,
>   And they are rich, and ransom all ill deeds.

Here the first quatrain, even with its direct address, has much of the detached quality of Sonnet 33, reinforced by its use of the same sun metaphor. In the second quatrain, though, the metaphor shifts dramatically. Line 5 gives no warning of what will shortly happen: we are still on the level of the sun breaking through the clouds. But line 6 carries a remarkable double weight. In no way does it let down the metaphor — the sun reappears and dries the rained-on face — but it creats a potent second image, that of one man wiping away tears from another man's face. The effect is retrospective too, giving to the verb "break" in line 5 the sense of reaching through the clouds. Lines 7–8 complete the metaphoric change. Drying tears leads to "salve" (i.e. comfort) which leads to healing wounds but leaving scars (at least that is what I assume the metaphoric sense of "and cures not the disgrace" to be). By the end of the second quatrain, then, the reader has begun to readjust himself to the rapid movement of images which governs most sonnets, in contrast to the near stasis of Sonnet 33. The third quatrain continues the disintegration of metaphor, giving the reader little to grasp hold of in the way of imagery: abstract terms dominate but with almost none of their normal figurative load – "shame", "repent", "loss", "sorrow", "relief", "bears", "loss" – the emphatic non-rhyme of "loss"/"loss" emphasises the lack of poetic substance. [12]

With the fading out of metaphor the sonnet begins to come to terms with the nature of the young man's offence and the poet's sorrow; but as emotional battle begins to be joined the couplet quite disarmingly retreats to the safety of metaphor:

> Ah, but those tears are pearl which thy love sheeds,
> And they are rich, and ransom all ill deeds.

The "ah" is an exclamation of sarcasm rather than, as it purports to be, of revelation – and the metaphor of the redeeming pearl is retrograde. By such a metaphor crime and suffering no longer appear what they really are and become, respectively, permissible and bearable. This is a matter which the next sonnet, number 35, directly considers:

> No more be grieved at that which thou hast done:
> Roses have thorns, and silver fountains mud,
> Clouds and eclipses stain both moon and sun,
> 4   And loathsome canker lives in sweetest bud.
> All men make faults, and even I in this,
> Authorizing thy trespass with compare,
> Myself corrupting salving thy amiss,
> 8   Excusing thy sins more than thy sins are;
> For to thy sensual fault I bring in sense –
> Thy adverse party is thy advocate –
> And 'gainst myself a lawful plea commence.
> 12   Such civil war is in my love and hate,
>   That I an accessory needs must be
>   To that sweet thief which sourly robs from me. [13]

As the beginning of the third and final part of the poetic analysis of the young man's fault, and further analysis of what poetic metaphor involves, the first quatrain of this sonnet is calculated to baffle the reader further. The quatrain says that the young man should not feel any further remorse for his actions since it is in the nature of beautiful things that they have their darker side. But being a poem the sonnet does not simply say that, it uses images to make the point: roses have thorns, silver fountains have mud, etc. The implications of the small catalogue of images, following Sonnets 33 and 34, build into the quatrain a series of possible qualifications, none of which the reader feels confident in making, but none of which he can ignore. For example, it is normal for roses to have thorns, but not for poetic roses to have them. Poetic roses, as in Sonnet 1, tend to be idealised images of beauty with no negative thorns. The same thing applies to poetic silver fountains as opposed to real ones. In this respect the sonnet has already declared itself to be distinctive — "mud" is an emphatically unpoetic rhyme word. Lines 3−4 amplify the matter. This sonnet sequence is different; it has just shown a metaphoric sun stained by cloud as, earlier, it had explored the potential of the canker-worm for destroying roses. But qualifications to this immediately occur to the reader because, for all of their challenging of poetic decorum, lines 2−4 contrast heavily with the opening line. "No more be grieved at that which thou hast done" is direct, intimate, and unavoidable; the next three lines are oblique and have the resistible detachment of proverbs. The reader senses in the opening line the potential for a real description of what has happened but finds in the rest of the quatrain only a retreat into metaphoric generalisations. But that, too, is capable of qualification. The shift from the personal to the general is, after all, a more serious view of the crime. For it to have become the meat of proverbs is bad enough, but worse still is for them to be the kind of proverbs whose general implication is that the young man's behaviour is so intimately bound up with his character that it is inescapable. In other words the opening line's meaning is revised from 'do not repent any further over what you have done, you have repented enough' to 'do not repent any further . . . it will make no difference, it is in your nature'. But no man's nature is that easily described: the very proverbial nature of the images makes us retreat again and consider that thorns, mud, clouds, eclipse, and cankers only gain their metaphoric force by simplifying human actions — the idea that the sweetest bud is chosen by the canker-worm may be a pretty fiction, but it is nonetheless a fiction for all that; just as our interpretation of the meaning of an eclipse is fictional, or any of our glossing over of natural phenomena with moral qualities.[14]

From out of this frustrating playing around with metaphor comes, in the second and third quatrains, open discussion of what the poet actually does. The sarcastic drift of the second quatrain is clear:

> All men make faults, and even I in this,
> Authorizing thy trespass with compare,
> Myself corrupting salving thy amiss,
> Excusing thy sins more than thy sins are;

'You are bad, but I am worse because I make excuses for you.' The excuses made are now directly related to the roles of poet and subject: "even I in this" takes up the frequent meaning of "this" in the sonnets to mean 'poem', and "compare" is the sequence's basic word for making metaphors (note the pun on "authorizing" too). The effect of poetry like the sonnets is threefold. It corrupts the poet, glosses over the crimes of the subject, and still contrives to make these crimes worse than they actually are – or seem worse, depending upon one's interpretation of line 8, which could equally mean offering more excuses than necessary.

At this point in the sonnet metaphor seems to have been extinguished: through lines 5–8 there are only shadows of metaphors. "Authorizing thy trespass" carries the promise of a legal metaphor but it is not continued; "corrupting salving" hints at disease and cure, but that too fades out; and line 8 – "Excusing thy sins more than thy sins are" – provides one of the typical sonnet repetitions which through their very abstractness force the reader to bend his mind to their decoding. But the sestet revises the order:

> For to thy sensual fault I bring in sense –
> Thy adverse party is thy advocate –
> And 'gainst myself a lawful plea commence.
> Such civil war is in my love and hate,
>   That I an accessory needs must be
>   To that sweet thief which sourly robs from me.

Word repetition moves back into punning, and punning into restoration of metaphor: "sensual . . . sense . . . adverse . . . advocate". By line 12 the legal metaphor promised in line 6 has been fulfilled, and it governs the rest of the sonnet. The most effective part of this movement is the verb "bring in" in line 9; it carries simultaneously and inseparably the senses of introducing as a witness and including in a poem. The sestet of Sonnet 35 is a marvellous example of a poem acting out its meaning. The small group of sonnets, 33–35, repeatedly raises the potentiality of metaphor for dealing with human conflict; here, eventually, the poet emerges as witness against himself and accessory to every crime against himself – and the whole is achieved through paradox and punning.

The true paradox of the sestet of Sonnet 35 is that such a "civil war" can only be fought in terms of metaphor: the kind of psychological state where a man will happily degrade himself for his lover's sake can only be described in fictional terms, fiction requires metaphor, and metaphor's effect is a civilising one, so that any war it describes is a civil one. The act of writing poetry and addressing it to a lover who exploits the poet is, in sonnet terms, all that is implied in the paradoxes of Sonnet 35. But something else is implied too, and that is the nature of the poet's betrayal of his subject. In the logic of paradox "thy adverse party is thy advocate" means that the odds are so much on the young man's side that even his opponent argues for him, but it takes very little alteration of perspective to see another paradox in the line, that even his advocate is his opponent. In that respect bringing in "sense" to the sensual fault in the preceding line is not so much to argue away the young man's sensual faults by finding good reasons for them, but to compound the crime by adding sense to sense (both in the sensual sense of sense). The plea in line 11 is "lawful", but that has as many overtones of 'full of law' as it has of 'just', and the civil war in line 12 may be between love and hate, or it may describe separate wars, one within the poet's love, the other within his hate. And, finally, to have an accessory like the poet in one's robbery might well mean that one is not going to get away with the crime, real or metaphorical.

3 'So True a Fool': The Sardonic Tone

In the group of sonnets numbered 33 – 35 the reader encounters for the first time the kind of unmistakable criticism of the young man which will dominate the rest of the sequence: negative in direction and ranging from amused cynicism to bitter disgust. That the sonnets should criticise their subject is not strange. It is normal for sonneteers to find fault with their mistresses for non-compliance, rather in the way that the opening procreation group had criticised the young man for not giving the world a facsimile of his matchless self. That is all in the cause of poetic hyperbole – positive criticism leading to greater praise – but as early in the sequence as Sonnet 35 the hyperbole begins to be turned away from the young man's praise and towards consideration of his vices, and central to this change is the introduction and growth of a sardonic tone which undermines any attempt at praise. Significantly, Sonnets 33 – 35 make use of the imagery of the procreation group, but in a purely negative way so far as the character and deeds of the young man are concerned, thereby forcing the reader not just to look forward to more of the same but to reconsider what has gone before. In this chapter I shall examine the sardonic tone of individual sonnets and the way in which it contaminates neutral or even apparently positive declarations about love and immortality.

I begin with the way the contamination works retrospectively. A number of sonnets which have seemingly treated conventional topics in conventional ways may have already lodged possible discordancies in the reader's mind. Consider Sonnet 24, a poem which usually makes commentators throw up their figurative arms in horror. Murray Krieger, for example, confesses 'to being totally baffled by the couplet . . . which, in its derogation of the eyes and its distinction between eye and heart, runs counter to all that precedes'.[1] Stephen Booth, as usual, has the wisest comment: 'The sonnet is carefully designed to boggle its reader's mind (make his eyes glaze), but some sanity may be retained if he holds on to the idea of two people looking into one another's eyes.'[2] The sonnet takes up two conventional ideas, one the contest

48

between eyes and heart, the other the image of one lover in the eyes of another:

> Mine eye hath played the painter and hath steeled
> Thy beauty's form in table of my heart.
> My body is the frame wherein 'tis held,
> 4   And perspective it is best painter's art,
> For through the painter must you see his skill
> To find where your true image pictured lies,
> Which in my bosom's shop is hanging still,
> 8   That hath his windows glazed with thine eyes.
> Now see what good turns eyes for eyes have done.
> Mine eyes have drawn thy shape, and thine for me
> Are windows to my breast, wherethrough the sun
> 12   Delights to peep, to gaze therein on thee.
>   Yet eyes this cunning want to grace their art;
>   They draw but what they see, know not the heart.[3]

Vital to an understanding of the sonnet is the view, literally, that the reader takes of line 4. "Perspective" is the popular form of Renaissance painting whereby everything in the picture appears distorted until it is looked at from one particular angle. The line presents its own problem of perspective, namely how we are expected to look at the juxtaposition of "perspective" and "it". Do we read "perspective it" as if "perspective" were used adverbially, or as if "it" were in apposition to "perspective"? In his edition Stephen Booth admits both possibilities, but in theirs Ingram and Redpath are firm in insisting on "perspective" as an adverb, damning the other reading with that terrible word 'ingenuity'.[4]

An innocent reader might well be content with the Ingram and Redpath stricture but I doubt whether a reader of the sonnets stays innocent for long. Here the reader is encouraged to go back into the sonnet and apply his ingenuity, partly by the very complexity of the artefact – no one could possibly take it in at first reading – and partly by the couplet's unexpected suggestions of the young man's hypocrisy. The result of such a review, especially if it admits the appositive reading of "perspective it", is for the reader to find in the second quartrain implications pertinent to the roles of artist and subject which Sonnets 33–35 will later bring into the open. The quatrain says that constructing such a perspective portrait is the best way for the artist to work, because only "through" the artist – i.e. by giving him proper attention, literally and figuratively – can one find the proper angle from which to view the picture. The third quatrain expands on this view of an artist in ideal harmony with his subject, the subject giving him not only a good shape to draw but the gift of sunlight too. But viewed from the couplet the effect is ironic. "Now see what good turns eyes for eyes have done" is, of course, an action of the eye, and eyes, the couplet warns us, lack cunning. All actions of the eyes in this sonnet are thrown into confusion by, in Krieger's words, 'the derogation of the eyes' in the couplet. The artist believes that he has captured his subject's beauty and true image; the subject believes that the artist's reproduction is genuinely of what he has seen. Either or both may be mistaken since neither knows the heart. Looking into each other's eyes, as they do throughout the sonnet, is, as the sonnet implies, the only perspective which will make them both happy; but already in the final line the artist's perspective has begun to shift from his subject's shape and image to his subject's heart – and from such a shifted perspective the love between the two will inevitably appear distorted. [5]

Other suspicions which will have occurred to the reader I have described in discussing the naïveté of Sonnet 25 and the vulnerability of Sonnet 26. [6] Phrases and statements whose undertones have been suppressed earlier now begin to take on a retrospective double-edgedness; in particular a sonnet like 32 may well become more barbed than it had originally appeared because of its proximity to Sonnet 35. This is Sonnet 32, a poem it seems of nearly total self-effacement:

> If thou survive my well-contented day,
> When that churl death my bones with dust shall cover,
> And shalt by fortune once more re-survey
> 4 These poor rude lines of thy deceased lover,
> Compare them with the bett'ring of the time,
> And though they be outstripped by every pen
> Reserve them for my love, not for their rhyme,
> 8 Exceeded by the height of happier men.
> O then vouchsafe me but this loving thought:
> Had my friend's muse grown with this growing age,
> A dearer birth than this his love had brought
> 12 To march in ranks of better equipage.
>   But since he died, and poets better prove,
>   Theirs for their style I'll read, his for his love.

This sonnet will probably be initially read as it declares itself to be, that is a self-deprecating wish, by a poet who senses that his poetry will soon be dated, that his lover will still read it if only for what it says. But either the sonnet is so poorly written that it is self-enacting – an example of how dated the poet's work already is — or its ironies are carefully planted to lie dormant in the reader's brain and take full effect later. Thus, the opening quatrain is a strange departure from convention: 'when thou survive . . .' would have been a much better opening, since love poets normally promise to die before the subjects they address (at least in sonnet sequences they do); "by fortune" in line 3 implies that the poet is going to be lucky indeed to be read by the young man; and the description of the poet's work may well be the poet's own, but equally well may be the poet repeating the young man's opinions — "these poor rude lines . . . the bettering of the time . . . outstripped by every pen". The young man is an expert judge of poetry, quite probably familiarly addressed by many more poets — "happier men" — and confident in his prospective analysis of the poet's work as reported in the last five lines of the sonnet. Line 12 seems to be his idea of what makes good style: one gets the sense of columns of iambic pentameters like a well drilled army. Finally, "since" in the couplet may be only a time marker to follow the desire expressed in line 10 that the poet had lived on, but it also retains its other sense of 'because', embodying a statement something like: 'as long as my poets live I'll read them for their style, when they are dead it is safe to take their love seriously'.

Much of this will seem over-ingenious, a way of reading into the sonnet implications which pervert its obvious meaning; but I would suggest that the ironies I describe are really only the product of cynical common-sense. If we were to approach the sonnet with an entirely innocent eye — innocent, that is, of poetic convention — we would be immediately suspicious of such a self-deprecating, self-abasing statement. What prevents our suspicion is our knowledge of convention: sonneteers regularly write sonnets which contrast their own unworthiness to their lovers' greatness. But this sonnet sequence is unique in its probing into the effect of writing such poetry upon the poet and the effect of reading it upon the reader.

As in Sonnet 32 some of the strongest effects in the sequence come from the reader's readiness to suppress his common-sense as part of the suspension of disbelief which convention requires, and then finding that those unliterary responses can be suppressed no longer. For different readers this will occur at different places in the sequence, but it is a strange reader who can exclude them throughout. What happens is that the more the reader suppresses his cynicism, the more he has to place his trust in the conventions of love poetry. That trust is betrayed in a number of ways. One is the frustration of metaphor which I described in chapter 2. Another, the subject of this chapter, is the perception first of a sardonic undertone, and then the feeling that the undertone is taking over the whole sonnet. Sonnet 57, for example, might affect readers in different ways. Superficially it is servile; but how much of the servility is ironic contempt for the way in which the young man treats the poet?

> Being your slave, what should I do but tend
> Upon the hours and times of your desire?
> I have no precious time at all to spend,
> 4 Nor services to do till you require.
> Nor dare I chide the world without end hour
> Whilst I, my sovereign, watch the clock for you,
> Nor think the bitterness of absence sour,
> 8 When you have bid your servant once adieu.
> Nor dare I question with my jealous thought
> Where you may be, or your affairs suppose,
> But like a sad slave stay and think of nought
> 12 Save where you are how happy you make those.
>   So true a fool is love, that in your will,
>   Though you do anything, he thinks no ill.

Martin Seymour-Smith reads this sonnet as emphatically sardonic: 'a more direct tone of heavily sarcastic bitterness is introduced for the first time into the Quarto sequence' is his general comment on it, and with regard to lines 3–4 he writes 'forthright and even savage irony, reflected in the rhythm, rescues Shakespeare's state of subservience from utter pusillanimity'.[7] Philip Martin notes that this is a sonnet whose irony is often missed by readers, but feels that even if we detect it 'we need not go to excess like Seymour-Smith'; instead he argues for the sonnet as a kind of double-take – the young man first reads it as a compliment, then sees the possibility of sarcasm.[8] I do not intend to legislate between these two, but what interests me is their attitude to the sonnet which immediately follows, number 58:

> That god forbid, that made me first your slave,
> I should in thought control your times of pleasure,
> Or at your hand th' account of hours to crave,
> 4 Being your vassal bound to stay your leisure.
> O let me suffer, being at your beck,
> Th' imprisoned absence of your liberty –
> And patience tame to suff'rance bide each check,
> 8 Without accusing you of injury.
> Be where you list, your charter is so strong,
> That you yourself may privilege your time
> To what you will; to you it doth belong

12   Yourself to pardon of self-doing crime.
I am to wait, though waiting so be hell,
Not blame your pleasure, be it ill or well.[9]

In his book Martin makes no mention of this sonnet at all, while Seymour-Smith, in his poem by poem commentary, describes it as 'a less emotional version of 57 in which Shakespeare acknowledges to himself, so to speak, his state of dependence, and determines to act the part of an unselfish lover'.[10] The link between Sonnets 57 and 58 is so obvious that no reader is likely to miss it and this makes both critics' responses difficult to understand. Martin's argument for the balance in Sonnet 57 between sarcasm and devotion ought to be tested against what is said in Sonnet 58, while Seymour-Smith takes for granted that the reader will happily move from heavy sarcastic bitterness in the one sonnet to unselfish love in the next.[11] Martin's case must be hurt at least a little by a sonnet which follows and labours the same point in almost the same words: the "being your slave" which opens Sonnet 57 becomes an ironic refrain in Sonnet 58 – "that made me first your slave . . . being your vassal . . . being at your beck . . . I am to wait", even a spaniel can fawn too much. Seymour-Smith, though, does not allow the sardonic tone of 57 to influence 58. For example, he glosses line 3, "Or at your hand th' account of hours to crave", as 'demand from you an account of how you have been spending your time', apparently ignoring the strong sense the line gives of the poet as an animal begging food from his master's hand – an image reinforced later by "bound", "tame", and "bide each check".

In other words, read after 57 Sonnet 58 may lack the bitterness Seymour-Smith finds in 57, but it carries so much contamination from that sonnet that its gestures of unselfishness reveal an even greater self-pity. Where Sonnet 57 describes an apparently volitional state—'I love you so much that I'll be your slave' – Sonnet 58 turns the screw by bringing destiny into the argument: 'I love you so much because I was fated to do so ("That God . . . that made me first your slave") and my servility is inescapable and undesired.' The couplet completes the tremendous pressure which the sonnet has laid upon the verb 'to be': "I am to wait" is not merely a definition of the poet's task, it defines his whole nature; and that definition of inescapable servility is more horrifying than the mere sarcasm of Sonnet 57 where one lover ticks off another in the guise of showing him how much he loves him.

However far back the reader may go before he detects the same type of ironic response which governs Sonnets 57 – 58, he is likely, as I began this chapter by saying, to see Sonnet 35 as the watershed. It is a sonnet which takes up the probing into the poet's role and potentialities which earlier sonnets had begun to explore (Sonnet 18 for example), and which delineates the emotional responses – self-sacrifice, accusation, betrayal, revenge – which supply the rest of the sequence:

> No more be grieved at that which thou hast done:
> Roses have thorns, and silver fountains mud,
> Clouds and eclipses stain both moon and sun,
> 4   And loathsome canker lives in sweetest bud.
> All men make faults, and even I in this,
> Authorizing thy trespass with compare,
> Myself corrupting salving thy amiss,
> 8   Excusing thy sins more than thy sins are;
> For to thy sensual fault I bring in sense –
> Thy adverse party is thy advocate –
> And 'gainst myself a lawful plea commence.
> 12   Such civil war is in my love and hate,
> > That I an accessory needs must be
> > To that sweet thief which sourly robs from me.

Not only future emotions but future language and imagery are delineated too. The "sweet"/"sour" contrast of the couplet will occur several times over; indeed "sour" becomes the key descriptive word for the young man's actions.[12] The canker in the bud will be constantly held up as an emblem of the young man's actions, and not as before, as an emblem of his failure to act.[13] And the most important element in the sonnet, the one which unites emotion and language, is the strategy of making excuses – hardly apparent before Sonnet 35, from now on it becomes the major function of the poet and his poetry.

Sonnets 40 – 42 form an early group which take up the pattern of offering excuses begun in 35.[14] Sonnet 40, in fact, never quite gets round to finding an excuse although it always seems on the point of offering one:

> Take all my loves, my love, yea take them all:
> What hast thou then more than thou hadst before?
> No love, my love, that thou mayst true love call;
> 4   All mine was thine, before thou hadst this more.
> Then if for my love thou my love receivest,
> I cannot blame thee for my love thou usest;
> But yet be blamed, if thou thyself deceivest
> 8   By wilful taste of what thyself refusest.
> I do forgive thy robb'ry, gentle thief,
> Although thou steal thee all my poverty;

And yet love knows it is a greater grief
12   To bear love's wrong than hate's known injury.
      Lascivous grace, in whom all ill well shows,
      Kill me with spites, yet we must not be foes.[15]

The first quatrain of this sonnet comes closer to song than any other in the
sequence, an effect which is carried into the second quatrain by way of the
feminine rhymes; but this lyricism is a camouflage which allows the poet to
slide from "love" to "love" with the reader never quite sure whether the
abstract sense of the emotion or the specific person of 'lover' is intended.
Both quatrains play with the idea of the faithless young man stealing the
poet's lovers and, making the appropriate qualifications, the possibility of his
deserving blame for it. The sonnet turns, though, on line 9, where rhythm,
rhyme, and image take the lyric into the mainstream of sardonic sonnetry.
The image of the thief stealing the poet's poverty is an unmistakeable
harking back to Sonnet 35 — that sweet thief which sourly robs from me" —
and lines 11 – 12 complete a dramatic transformation of the sonnet: "and yet
love knows" echoes its opening lyricism, but the echo fades away into the
accusatory sententiousness of "it is a greater grief/To bear love's wrong than
hate's known injury". The end to it all is one of the most loaded couplets in
the sequence where the sardonic and the lyrical are inseparable. Lyrically we
are given the glide through liquid consonants and variform vowel sounds in
"in whom all ill well shows", as well as the stock language of courtly love
framing line 14, "kill" and "foes"; but the sardonic tone also appears in both
lines, in the oxymoron "lascivious grace", and in "spite" which carries
especially vicious connotations from two recent sonnets, "a separable spite"
in Sonnet 36 and "fortune's dearest spite" in 37.[16]

The sonnet's failure to find an excuse for the young man's actions is bound
up first with the poet's determination to play the matter down — witness the
lyrical form of the octave — and then his failure to keep playing the role of
poetic forgiver — witness the third quatrain. The couplet restores some
balance, but with "lascivious" and "spite" it comes close to rejecting the
half-suggested excuses of the young man's being motivated by his affection
for the poet — "if for my love thou my love receivest" — and his being
justified by his nobility — "gentle thief". Sonnet 41 not only tells us more
about the nature of the theft, it also gets down to the business of finding
excuses for it:

      Those pretty wrongs that liberty commits,
      When I am sometime absent from thy heart,
      Thy beauty and thy years full well befits,

4   For still temptation follows where thou art.
   Gentle thou art, and therefore to be won,
   Beauteous thou art, therefore to be assailed;
   And when a woman woos, what woman's son
8   Will sourly leave her till he have prevailed?
   Ay me, but yet thou might'st my seat forbear,
   And chide thy beauty and thy straying youth,
   Who lead thee in their riot even there
12 Where thou art forced to break a twofold truth:
   Hers, by thy beauty tempting her to thee,
   Thine, by thy beauty being false to me.

The sardonic undertones of the octave show the art the poet brings to finding the bitterest irony in everyday locutions and turns of thought. "Pretty" and "liberty" in the opening line make sure that we appreciate the continuation from the couplet of Sonnet 40. They suggest the first excuses, that the wrongs are trivial and, anyway, necessary for a free individual. Line 3, "Thy beauty and thy years full well befits", carries a remarkable amount of irony; behind it, especially behind its verb, lurk all of our commonly accepted excuses for the thoughtless behaviour of the young and the beautiful.[17] Given that the young man is young and handsome line 4 binds guilt and excuse indissolubly together: "for still temptation follows where thou art" means, of course, that he is always being tempted wherever he goes, but it means more, that wherever he is there temptation follows him – not that he is tempted, but that he tempts others. The second quatrain continues making excuses by offering the reasoning of the world, first by way of its two therefores – therefore to be won and therefore to be assailed, the causes being, respectively, gentleness and beauty – and then by its vocabulary redolent of nudge and a wink reasoning – "woman's son" as a synonym for 'man' which explains his susceptibility to the fair sex, and "sourly" which makes his leaving her before she seduces him an impossibly puritanical act.[18]

From this display of ironic excuses the change of tone in the sestet is as dramatic as in Sonnet 40. Where the octave had paraded the poet's apparent detachment the sestet now moves the search for an excuse onto a personal level:

   Ay me, but yet thou might'st my seat forbear,
   And chide thy beauty and thy straying youth,
   Who lead thee in their riot even there
   Where thou art forced to break a twofold truth:
   Hers, by thy beauty tempting her to thee,
   Thine, by thy beauty being false to me.

The word which marks the change is "yet" and its effect is unexpected, since it conveys a strong sense of wistfulness whilst contriving to keep its logical, cold connective sense with a meaning close to 'therefore'. I say that its effect is unexpected, but that is to ignore the importance of the word in the preceding sonnet, where it occurs three times in the last eight lines; and where it has both its simple connective sense ("But yet be blamed"), its wistful sense ("And yet love knows"), and in the final line the same combining of the two ("yet we must not be foes"). Here, in the sestet of Sonnet 41 the double nature of "yet" preserves an important balance, for while these lines make slightly more clear the pathos which underlay the brave worldliness of lines 1–8 they also preserve much of the detachment of those lines. Here the poet finally faces the horrifying fact that the young man's infidelity is not simply a matter of wanton youth, but that it includes a special kind of vindictiveness which takes pleasure in stealing the poet's mistress. But simultaneously with the facing of the fact comes the excuse for it – one that only the poet could make – that the real culprits are the young man's beauty and youth, two independent forces which actually lead the young man on. Poetic abstractions are useful things if they can help avoid fixing the responsibility for his actions upon the young man: as line 12 puts it, he is forced to break his word (as well as the mistress's). In the couplet it is the beauty which tempts and is false; a separation of the young man from his sinning elements which had begun in the opening line of the sonnet, where "liberty", rather than the young man, had committed the pretty wrongs.

Such personifications and abstractions are part of poetry's strategy to absolve the guilty of their guilt. Sonnets 40 and 41 educate the reader in poetry's capacity to make excuses for even the vindictive infidelity which the young man has shown. Sonnet 42 completes his education:

> That thou hast her, it is not all my grief,
> And yet it may be said I loved her dearly;
> That she hath thee is of my wailing chief,
> 4   A loss in love that touches me more nearly.
> Loving offenders, thus I will excuse ye:
> Thou dost love her, because thou know'st I love her,
> And for my sake ev'n so doth she abuse me,
> 8   Suff'ring my friend for my sake to approve her.
> If I lose thee, my loss is my love's gain,
> And losing her, my friend hath found that loss;
> Both find each other, and I lose both twain,
> 12   And both for my sake lay on me this cross.

>   But here's the joy, my friend and I are one;
>   Sweet flatt'ry then she loves but me alone.

This is lyrical poetry in the same way that Sonnet 40 was, with the rhythm of the second line, the feminine rhymes scattered through the octave, the saturation of the sonnet with verbal repetition, especially "love" in its various senses but also "loss"/"lose", "find"/"found", "my friend"/"my sake", and the obvious parallelism of statement both within the quatrain (e.g. lines 1 and 3) and within the line (e.g. line 6, line 11). All make the reader very aware that he is in the artificial, heightened world of the lyric poem. Almost too aware, in fact, because it becomes increasingly difficult for him to resist the sonnet's logic which announces itself in line 5; give yourself up to the pattern and organisation and it is not easy to refuse the message.

The message, of course, is ludicrous; a fact which the poet recognises in the couplet where he pushes the sonnet's logic to its extreme − 'my friend and I are one, so if he sleeps with my mistress she is not being unfaithful to me'.[19] Hamlet used similar chop-logic to taunt his uncle. Still, the lyric patterning is very useful to the poet for it allows him to insinuate two contexts for our understanding of what has happened. One, which comes to a head in the third quatrain, is the desire for self-sacrifice on the poet's part. He projects himself as a martyr, ultimately a Christ-like figure bearing his cross. That projection begins at line 5, where "loving offenders" may be read equally as a vocative or as a piece of self-description − 'it is in my nature to love those who offend against me'. The second context recalls the implications of Sonnets 40 and 41, namely that the whole impetus for the double betrayal has come from the young man. The insinuation of this charge is twice as effective because of the way the sonnet opens, for taken out of context the first quatrain would seem to suggest the opposite, that the blame is the woman's. But the second quatrain uses its parallels and antitheses to uncover the young man's motives and actions. He seduced her because he knew of the poet's feelings for her, and I can use the word 'seduce' because, as lines 7−8 imply, her response is to suffer the young man to approve her. Underlying the second quatrain of Sonnet 42 is a murky combination of the poet's capacity for martyrdom and the young man's readiness to hurt the poet: the repeated "for my sake" in lines 8−9 gives more than a hint that the poet helped in the seduction.[20]

Perhaps the sonnet which deals most frustratingly with the young man's deeds and the excuses the poet is prepared to offer for them is Sonnet 49:

Against that time, if ever that time come,
When I shall see thee frown on my defects,
Whenas thy love hath cast his utmost sum,
4   Called to that audit by advised respects;
Against that time when thou shalt strangely pass,
And scarcely greet me with that sun thine eye,
When love converted from the thing it was
8   Shall reasons find of settled gravity;
Against that time do I ensconce me here
Within the knowledge of mine own desert,
And this my hand against myself uprear
12   To guard the lawful reasons on thy part.
 To leave poor me thou hast the strength of laws,
 Since why to love I can allege no cause.[21]

The key word in the sonnet is "against". Introducing each of the three
quatrains it carries the solemnity of an oath, a promise made in anticipation
of his future abandonment by the young man. The development of the
octave – "When I shall see . . . When as thy love hath cast . . . when thou
shalt strangely pass . . . When love . . . shall reasons find" – makes that
day inevitable, and the parenthetical qualification in the opening line – "if
ever that time come" – seems more and more to be merely a polite gesture.
Sardonically the octave suggests reasons for the abandonment. The young
man's love is subordinate to more worldly things: the poet's "defects"
outweigh his value (lines 3 – 4) and policy requires the suppression of love in
the name of reason and gravity (lines 7 – 8).

 Despite its suggestion of looking forward to one time in the future when
he will have been abandoned – "that time" – the octave actually traces the
process of abandonment. The first quatrain envisages the beginning of the
end as calculation leads the young man to frown at the poet; in the second
quatrain even such recognition as a frown might indicate has gone, leaving
only the pathos of distanced contact in "that sun thine eye". With such a
clear perception of what will happen and the reasons for it we might expect
the third quatrain to complete the sentence which has been held in suspense
from the opening line. From "against" which begins the sonnet and "when"
which opens line 2 the reader is prepared for some kind of declaration. When
it comes in the third quatrain it does so with a surprising degree of literalness.
Now "against that time" sums up the whole of lines 1 – 8, and it brings the
poet into his own poem – "ensconce me here" – to make his oath: but lines
11 – 12 are entirely unexpected, especially following "the knowledge of

mine own desert" which can only carry the octave's implications of a shallow young man and sincere poet. In line 11 "and this my hand" has all the solemnity of an oath-taking; "against" retains the solemnity of the openings to the three quatrains, but now its connotations have to be completely revised. It is not, as we will have anticipated, one more "against that time", but "against" in its normal opposing sense, "against myself". To uprear one's hand against oneself, either as an oath or as an offensive gesture, is a return to the self-abasing paradoxes of Sonnet 35, and line 12 completes the parallel, its "lawful reasons" recalling that sonnet's "lawful plea". The sestet mimics a painful deflation of the poet, from the nobility which can foresee and prepare for betrayal, to "poor me" who is forced to accept the logic of a betrayer who demands reasons for everything. Such a deflation leaves the reader stranded. After sharing the assumptions of nobility opposed to infidelity which the octave contains he is required to participate in the abandonment of all nobility in the sestet; and the irony is that the abandonment occurs at the very moment the poet moves into literal action by raising his hand.

That gesture at the end of Sonnet 49 signifies future defencelessness, but perversely it hints at one very certain line of defence, for the phrase has a further possible range of reference to the poet's verse, i.e. 'this my writing'.[22] It may even be that so unexpected is the move from self-defence to self-attack in line 11 that the reader ghost-reads the line as ". . against *thy*self uprear", but whether or not that happens the sestet does quietly convey the idea that poetry is a weapon. Here the weapon is going to be used for the young man: 'in the future, when I feel bound to blame you for your abandoning me, these poems will defend your actions by showing that I was never able to give sufficient cause for you to love me'. But that argument works both ways and it is only a short step to seeing poetry as the poet's weapon on his own side in the predicted battle of estrangement.

4 'The Living Record of Your Memory': Promises of Immortality

The retaliatory possibilities of poetry appear early in the sequence, before the raising of the prospect of the young man's infidelity and abandonment of the poet. In chapter 1 we saw how Sonnet 18's opening question "Shall I compare thee to a summer's day?" makes full use of its poetic status: as a rhetorical question it implies the answer 'yes' and gives the opportunity for a celebration of the variety of summer, but as a question addressed by the poet to the young man, the answer, even though it is the poet's answer, is 'no', with the reasons for saying so withheld until the third quatrain. The reasons are initially reassuring: 'I shall not make that comparison because it does not do you justice since you are eternal where summer's days are subject to time.' Only the couplet reveals the disturbing fact that the young man is eternal because the poet's verse is eternal,

> So long as men can breathe or eyes can see,
> So long lives this, and this gives life to thee

not, as the sonnet's logic might have seemed to dictate, 'and this gains life from thee'.

After the poet's joust with time in Sonnet 19 and his full-bodied portraiture of the young man in Sonnet 20, Sonnet 21 returns to considering the poet and his subject:

> So is it not with me as with that muse,
> Stirred by a painted beauty to his verse,
> Who heaven itself for ornament doth use,
> 4 And every fair with his fair doth rehearse –
> Making a couplement of proud compare
> With sun and moon, with earth and sea's rich gems,
> With April's first-born flowers, and all things rare

8   That heaven's air in this huge rondure hems.
    O let me true in love but truly write,
    And then believe me, my love is as fair
    As any mother's child, though not so bright
12 As those gold candles fixed in heaven's air.
        Let them say more that like of hearsay well;
        I will not praise that purpose not to sell.

Rather than speculating about the identity of the other poet I prefer to consider this sonnet with regard to its effect upon the young man. For one thing, it makes the praise of Sonnet 18 seem even more qualified. In both sonnets "fair" is the word which characterises the young man: in 18 he is promised that he will not lose possession of the "fair" he owns, and the poet says that he will not compare him to any other fair thing, since "every fair from fair sometime declines". This sonnet copies that refusal to make such a comparison but gives a very different reason for it. Because it is the shoddy poet who "every fair with his fair doth rehearse" this poet will maintain some kind of realistic connection between his subject and the similitudes he chooses for him – "my love is as fair/As any mother's child". Whether Sonnet 21 is attacking Daniel, Watson, Sidney, or Chapman, it would seem to be attacking the poet of these sonnets as well, at least the poet of Sonnet 18 for whom even the examples of "proud compare" given here are inadequate for his subject. [1] So even this early in the sequence two kinds of poetry have been described: one idealises and immortalises its subject, the other tells the truth.

The conflict between these kinds recurs in the complementary sonnets, 38 and 39. Sonnet 38 takes as its theme the conventional idea that the young man is the sole and unparalleled source of poetic inspiration:

    How can my muse want subject to invent,
    While thou dost breathe, that pour'st into my verse
    Thine own sweet argument, too excellent
4   For every vulgar paper to rehearse?
    O give thyself the thanks, if aught in me
    Worthy perusal stand against thy sight;
    For who's so dumb that cannot write to thee,
8   When thou thyself dost give invention light?
    Be thou the tenth muse, ten times more in worth
    Than those old nine which rhymers invocate;
    And he that calls on thee, let him bring forth
12 Eternal numbers to outlive long date.

If my slight muse do please these curious days,
The pain be mine, but thine shall be the praise.[2]

Literally this sonnet contradicts the claim that the poet can immortalise. It seems instead to suggest that the young man's inspiration will enable the poet to find the right style – "eternal numbers" – so that future ages may recognise his worth. The reader can not be entirely sure of the power the poet has over his own style, however, because of the syntactic blurring in the third quatrain. In line 9 the poet puts the young man in his rightful, inspirational place – "Be thou the tenth muse" – but it is not possible to know whether the order given to the would-be poet in line 11 – "let him bring forth" – is syntactically complementary to "be thou", in other words still the poet giving orders, or whether it is the young man's action, having become himself the tenth muse. This might seem to be accidental imprecision were it not for a similar, if less obvious, blurring of the issue in the first two quatrains. The sonnet's opening rhetorical question suffers from the same kind of susceptibility to innuendo as the question which opens Sonnet 18. The reader is likely to interpret its primary intention as one of hyperbolic praise, but he may also carry through the quatrain two other shadowy meanings which subvert the hyperbole. The main one comes from the possibility of the question marker "how" operating also as an exclamation marker. The first line, "How can my muse want subject to invent", must, if only briefly, lodge itself in the reader's mind as equivalent to 'I still lack subject matter'. The second and third lines may relegate that possibility to innuendo and assure the reader that hyperbole is intended by introducing the idea of the young man pouring his own sweet argument into the verse, but not before they themselves raise a second shadowy meaning: "while thou dost breathe" extends the first innuendo to 'I shall always lack subject matter while you are still alive'. The second quatrain, too, teases the reader by encouraging him to see something which should not be there by way of a rhetorical question. In line 7 the poet simply asks "For who's so dumb that cannot write to thee", a question which raises all kinds of possibilities about the young man's inability to tell good poetry from bad, and his suitability for either kind.[3] The next line, "When thou thyself dost give invention light", goes some way towards removing the innuendo, but not entirely, given the possibilities which cluster around "subject to invent" in the opening line.

Several other things in the sonnet also encourage the reader to suspect its surface meaning. The playing with the young man's value of "ten" in line 9 – "Be thou the tenth muse, ten times more in worth" – echoes the obvious hollowness of the couplet of the preceding sonnet, number 37:

Look what is best, that best I wish in thee.
This wish I have, then ten times happy me.

Then through the whole sonnet runs an undertone of the young man's self-praise. In lines 2–4 his inspirational action, and his choice of this poet to inspire rather than more vulgar ones, has this self-centred aim: "thou . . . pour'st into my verse/Thine own sweet argument". So, too, "give thyself the thanks" and "thou thyself dost give invention light" in the second quatrain recall the self-centredness of the procreation sonnets. And all of this prepares us for a couplet which contrasts the poet's "pain" and the young man's "praise":

> If my slight muse do please these curious days,
> The pain be mine, but thine shall be the praise.

As Stephen Booth points out with regard to "pain", 'the plural was more usual and would have more efficiently prevented a reader from momentarily hearing a reference to the speaker's suffering. By choosing to use the singular, Shakespeare gives the line a bitter undertaste.'[4] The conflict between pain and pleasure is the theme of many love poets; what makes it so bitter here is that it clarifies the conflict which the sonnet has so far kept under the surface, between the poet's estimation of his subject's worth and that subject's requirement for the poet to immortalise him.

One further element which plays its part in the conflict is the seemingly slippery way in which the word "muse" is used. The near dead metaphor of the poet's muse is given only a little life in the opening line, with responsibility for the poetry being assigned to it rather than the poet. In the third quatrain, though, it is brought completely to life, with the young man taking on himself the role of the tenth muse. In this role he not only ensures himself eternal fame, but he makes all past poetry — written of course to other subjects — seem antiquarian. Therefore the reversal to "slight muse" in the couplet seems inconsistent, but the inconsistency is well planned because it indicates the young man's failure as an inspirational force. Either the poet's muse is still slight because the young man has not yet assumed the role, in which case the innuendo of the opening quatrain gains a greater weight in retrospect, or the poet's muse remains one of the old nine, in which case the poet is not to be readily associated with "he that calls on thee".

Sonnet 39 continues the poet's internal debate over his incapacity to describe the young man's worth:

O how thy worth with manners may I sing,
When thou art all the better part of me?
What can mine own praise to mine own self bring,
4   And what is't but mine own when I praise thee?
Even for this let us divided live,
And our dear love lose name of single one,
That by this separation I may give
8   That due to thee which thou deserv'st alone.
O absence, what a torment wouldst thou prove,
Were it not thy sour leisure gave sweet leave
To entertain the time with thoughts of love,
12   Which time and thoughts so sweetly dost deceive,
And that thou teachest how to make one twain,
By praising him here who doth hence remain.[5]

As much as this sonnet is a continuation of 38, it also returns to the theme of
Sonnet 36 in its concern with the young man's absence – "twain", in the
couplet, recalls the opening line of 36, "Let me confess that we two must be
twain", and there are other verbal echoes, such as "remain" as the rhyme to
"twain", the rhyme "one"/"alone", and one sonnet has "divided" the other
"undivided" – but the important difference between the two is that in
Sonnet 36 the poet had proposed his own "bewailed guilt" as the reason for
the separation, while now in Sonnet 39 the cause seems to be bound up with
the nature of poetry itself. That is a vague phrase, but then Sonnet 39 seems
deliberately vague. When the poet introduces the prospect of separation in
line 5 – "Even for this let us divided live" – whatever "this" is he makes its
consequences seem as drastic as separating the phoenix and the turtle, "our
dear love" losing the name of single one. What is "this"?

Within the logic of the sonnet "this" is the reasoning of the first quatrain,
i.e. that the poet can not write about the young man with "manners"
because his writing only redounds to his own credit. But any such attempt to
encapsulate the quatrain's meaning is bound to miss much. For example, the
second line – "When thou art all the better part of me" – glances at a
number of possible ways of describing the relationship between the poet and
his subject. Stephen Booth points out three ramifications of "better part":
Ovid's 'parte . . . meliore mei', meaning 'my soul' and used explicitly in that
sense in Sonnet 74; husband or wife, as in the modern 'better half'; and, from
Plato's *Symposium*, a pair of lovers as a single individual.[6] These variously
allow the poet in line 3 to play on "mine own self" as the young man (a
conceit which takes up the whole of Sonnet 62) and to follow in line 4 with
the paradox that to praise a lover is to praise oneself (the same paradox which

is used grimly in the final line of Sonnet 42). All of these elements in lines 2 – 4 make the opening line's "with manners" distinctly incongruous. The various glosses proposed by editors – decently, politely, with proper modesty, not unbecomingly – bring out the distinction between a poet and a lover. Where a lover may be described by the paradoxes of two in one and thine is mine, a poet is required to keep his distance and merely do the describing – like "the bird of loudest lay" in *The Phoenix and the Turtle*. This is the reason why the poet must part from his lover, and it carries the implication, following Sonnet 38, that the request for the separation is the young man's. Again innuendo has been planted by a rhetorical question at the beginning of the sonnet: before lines 3 – 4 make it clear that the poet is arguing himself into the separation, lines 1 – 2 may well seem an exasperated answer, in question form, to the charge that his poetry does not show sufficient decency/politeness/modesty. Therefore at least part of the meaning of "even for this" in line 5 can be summarised as something like 'precisely because of this failure of mine to subordinate myself to your praise'.

The sestet is taken up with the consequences of the separation:

> O absence, what a torment wouldst thou prove,
> Were it not thy sour leisure gave sweet leave
> To entertain the time with thoughts of love,
> Which time and thoughts so sweetly dost deceive,
> And that thou teachest how to make one twain,
> By praising him here who doth hence remain.

The poet has turned from addressing the young man to addressing absence, but his use of the same pronoun encourages us to see behind the "thou" of absence not only the figure of the young man but also the behaviour of such a patron to his poet: he has the capacity to torment, but in his leisure gives the poet leave to entertain with thoughts of love – "entertain the time" is a beautiful summary of patronising boredom. Then the couplet gives a painfully witty contrast between poet and lover. Its first line repeats the thesis of the octave, the idea of two lovers as one unit and the splitting of that unit back into separate parts. The final line, though, forces the reader to reconsider: the "one" that is made twain is the absent lover, whom poetry can split into two, one still absent, the other with the poet. But poetry can do no such thing, and the line, whilst raising that literary ideal, squashes it flat by the words it uses. "By praising him here", with a shadowy pun on 'upraising', gives "praise" a sense it cannot properly bear of transporting through space; and "remain" as the final rhyme word emphasises the impossibility of "praise" achieving that aim.

"Remain" does one other important thing by clarifying the reader's perplexity about the actual situation of the sonnet. From the first quatrain it had appeared to be an argument for future separation – imminent, perhaps, but still to come – but now "who doth hence remain" describes an already existent state of separation. Possibly the sonnet imitates the movement through time in the poet's mind from foreseeing separation in the first quatrain to experiencing it in the couplet; but equally possibly the whole sonnet is situated after the break, so that "let us divided live" in line 5 means 'let us keep living apart as we are', "this separation" in line 7 has a present not a prospective reference, and "what a torment wouldst thou prove" in line 9 also defines a present hypothesis rather than a future one. Located after the separation rather than before it, the poet's position becomes even more futile and his poetry even more wishful thinking.

In its position in the sequence Sonnet 39 presents a further irony. In essence it argues for more than merely the separation of poet and young man which I have concentrated upon for it uses as grounds for that separation the idea that the young man needs isolation from everyone to reveal his transcendent worth. This idea is cunningly conveyed in the second quatrain which comes to rest on the word "alone":

> Even for this let us divided live,
> And our dear love lose name of single one,
> That by this separation I may give
> That due to thee which thou deserv'st alone.

The primary sense, of course, is that the young man alone deserves such praise, but the rhyming emphasis on "alone" carries the second sense of the need for such praise to find him in isolation, as if any society he kept, and not just the poet's, would detract from him. The particular irony is that this sonnet comes immediately before the triangular three, 40–42, where the poet, the young man, and the mistress are inextricably interlinked. However, the poet's recognition of the young man's need to be isolated remains, despite the intervening ironies, and re-emerges in Sonnet 55 where he is seen, in the third quatrain, triumphing over time like an Antony bestriding the world:

> 'Gainst death and all oblivious enmity
> Shall you pace forth; your praise shall still find room,
> Ev'n in the eyes of all posterity
> That wear this world out to the ending doom.

Most critics, John Crowe Ransom excepted, agree that Sonnet 55 immortalises its subject; in it the poet's self-appointed task is to build a monument to the eternal praise of the young man. However, Sonnet 54 which precedes it is much more speculative, finally raising a question which has as much to do with the poet's sense of his own worth as with the worth of his subject — and which might strongly affect our response to the following promises of immortality. This is Sonnet 54:

> O how much more doth beauty beauteous seem,
> By that sweet ornament which truth doth give.
> The rose looks fair, but fairer we it deem
> 4 For that sweet odour which doth in it live.
> The canker blooms have full as deep a dye
> As the perfumed tincture of the roses,
> Hang on such thorns, and play as wantonly,
> 8 When summer's breath their masked buds discloses;
> But for their virtue only is their show,
> They live unwooed, and unrespected fade,
> Die to themselves. Sweet roses do not so;
> 12 Of their sweet deaths are sweetest odours made.
> And so of you, beauteous and lovely youth,
> When that shall vade, by verse distils your truth.

This sonnet would fit well into the discussion of obtrusive metaphors in chapter two. From the taking up of the rose in line 3 it becomes a poem built up around the single metaphor of men as plants — but at the end of the first quatrain that had not been a predictable development, because lines 3−4 seem merely to be a metaphoric extension of the more abstract statement of the first two lines. Quite unexpected is the rest of the sonnet's continuation of the metaphor by contrasting canker blooms to real roses.

The sonnet presents little difficulty in interpretation. Within the metaphor of men as plants the young man is the rose which has a genuine and lasting substance, in contrast to other, deceptive people who are all fair outside but rotting within. But the very easiness of that interpretation masks a number of oddities in the sonnet's presentation of its argument. For a start, why exactly are the canker blooms in the sonnet? If simply to act as a contrast to the young man, then they surely do their job too well. In fact most of the metaphoric substance of the sonnet is taken up with them: although the deep dye, hanging on thorns, wanton playing, and disclosing of their buds are elements and actions which they have in common with roses, the reader is always aware that the poet is describing the canker blooms rather than the roses. And, of course, the reader is familiar with the way canker blooms have been used earlier in the sequence as a warning to the young man not so much of what he will become as of what he may already be.[7] Here, in contrast with the variety of description given to the canker blooms is the monotony of the rose. It is essentially "fair" and "sweet"; indeed "sweet" acts as a frame to the body of the sonnet, used twice in the first quatrain – to describe the ornament of truth and the odour of the living rose – and three times in the third quatrain – to describe the rose, the rose's death, and the odour derived from the dead rose. The only difference is that while the living rose gives a sweet odour, the dead rose gives the sweetest.

The similarity between this sonnet's imagery and that of the procreation group is not an accident. Like that group it contains two threats, both related to the nature of poetry. One is that the poet, as he does in the second quatrain, can turn roses into canker blooms, and *vice versa* – it is all a matter of metaphor. If the young man is the rose, then he finds himself being graphically reminded of how little difference there is in appearance between him and the rest (remember this sonnet follows directly the cosmetic imagery of Sonnet 53, Adonis and Helen). The only way to tell the difference is to distil his essence, a task which the poet reserves for himself in the couplet. On the other hand, if the young man is really a canker bloom then of course the poet can find images which make him indistinguishable from the rose.

The second threat comes in the difference between "sweet" and "sweetest". The poet works best when he works with a dead subject, an idea developed in the sonnet's complex game with "live" and "die". Life occurs first in line 4, but it is the odour's life not the rose's – "For that sweet odour which doth in it live". As if to show up the distinction between odour and rose the next line uses "die" as its rhyme word, even if it is "die" in a different sense – "The canker blooms have full as deep a dye" (spelt "die" in the Quarto). In the sestet we see the life story of the canker bloom in a line and a half – "They live unwooed, and unrespected fade,/Die to themselves" – but remembering "dye" in line 5 the canker's story may not actually be what it seems, life, fading away, death, but instead a perpetual cosmetic job, life, fading, repainting (i.e. dying). The possibility of such an ambiguity comes from the peculiar syntax which makes "die to themselves" stand alone, unrelated to what has gone before unless one interpolates an "and". In contrast are the sweet roses. They do not so (die to themselves, or dye to themselves?); instead, "of their sweet deaths are sweetest odours made". At this point the metaphor has run itself into an odd conclusion for no rose which dies naturally can be distilled into perfume. To obtain the perfume the distiller has first to kill it; it may be a sweet death but the metaphor is a drastic one to convey the process of poetry, and the couplet seems to reflect this by using a deliberately imprecise syntactic structure:

> And so of you, beauteous and lovely youth,
> When that shall vade, by verse distils your truth.

"And so of you" appears to relate the young man to the rose by a parallel with the preceding line – "Of their sweet deaths" – but such a parallel would require "my verse" in the final line, not "by verse" (as, of course, many editors have suggested). If we keep "by", and we ought on principle keep any Quarto reading which makes sense, then "and so of you" will have to be taken to mean 'with regard to you', which is not to say that the reader will also abandon the parallel with the reference to the rose in line 12. Finally "that" in line 14 – "When that shall vade" – could mean almost anything. The reader might, in desperation, defy syntactic incongruity and relate it to one or other (or both) of the qualities of the preceding line, beauty and loveliness, but "vade" should make him reconsider. "Vade" is carefully chosen to echo "fade" but has the stronger meaning of 'decay'; and the "that" which decays may again be the dead subject which the poet requires for his distillation.[8]

As well as its syntactic imprecision the couplet of Sonnet 54 has one other point of significance: its introduction of the work of poetry is quite unexpected. Nothing earlier in the sonnet prepares the way for the intrusion of "verse", and its suddenness makes the poet's claim to power the more emphatic. In this it recalls the couplet of Sonnet 19, where poetic immortality is promised for the first time, and it anticipates Sonnets 60, 63, and 65, all of which add to their analyses of the workings of time couplets which promise the eternity only poetry can give. More directly, though, Sonnet 54's couplet acts as a springboard for Sonnet 55's promises of immortality:

> Not marble nor the gilded monuments
> Of princes shall outlive this powerful rhyme,
> But you shall shine more bright in these contents
> 4 Than unswept stone, besmeared with sluttish time.
> When wasteful war shall statues overturn,
> And broils root out the work of masonry,
> Nor Mars his sword nor war's quick fire shall burn
> 8 The living record of your memory.
> 'Gainst death and all oblivious enmity
> Shall you pace forth; your praise shall still find room,

Ev'n in the eyes of all posterity
12 That wear this world out to the ending doom.
So, till the judgement that yourself arise,
You live in this, and dwell in lovers' eyes.[9]

The parallels between this claim to poetic immortality, and the last lines of Ovid's *Metamorphoses* and Horace's 'Exegi monumentum' ode, are noted by every editor, and many critics have drawn usefully upon the fact that where Ovid and Horace are referring to themselves, Shakespeare's is a claim for the immortality of his subject. One recent example is Philip Martin, who concludes his study of the Sonnets by comparing this sonnet with Spenser's Sonnet 75 from *Amoretti*, and makes this distinction between the classical sources, Spenser, and Shakespeare:

> Where the Roman poets are celebrating their own immortality, Shakespeare lays his stress elsewhere and characteristically transforms his sources completely. The Romans say: Because of my poem *I* will never die. Shakespeare says: Because of my poem *you* will never die. Of course, plenty of his contemporaries made that amendment too; but here again, in the couplet, Shakespeare rings an all-important change on the received idea. Most poets are content to say: You are immortal in my poem. Spenser goes a step further: You are immortal in my poem, from which our love will reach out to enhance later lives. Shakespeare goes further again: You are immortal in my poem, and in yourself, and you will live in the poem, in yourself and in the eyes of later lovers. What distinguishes Shakespeare is that he values the identity of the beloved; he recognizes that the beloved has his own personal immortality, in no way dependent on poetry.[10]

I can see the temptation to read the sonnet in this way, especially if one is intent upon showing Shakespeare's Christian response to the inevitability of death; as Martin puts it, compared with Horace and Ovid 'the Christian after-life has given Shakespeare's imagination more to embrace'. However, I do not believe that the reader's experience of the sonnet is so simple. John Crowe Ransom was grinding his own axe about metaphor in the sonnets when he observed that this sonnet really only develops the idea of 'the mortality of the common marbles and monuments' and that, with regard to the young man, 'the only specific thing here is something about a gait', but his comments focus our attention upon a weakness in the sonnet's immortalising assertions.[11] To begin with, Ransom is right to point out the sonnet's self-refutation: while it claims to make its subject live for ever it manages to keep him entirely hidden from our view. This is relevant to the whole sequence. The continual claims that poetry preserves and immortalises read oddly when set against the vagueness of its descriptive vocabulary – "fair", "sweet", "lovely", and "beauteous" leave so indefinite an impression that almost any candidate put forward as the historical reality behind the young man can find persuasive support within the collection. In this sonnet there is a little more than merely the 'gait', but nothing distinct: the reader's impression is of a vague Coriolanus-like figure striding over scenes of desolation.

The vagueness of the figure is affected, too, by the sense that he is dead and brought to life by the sonnet. This takes us back to the 'kill to revive' process which began to appear in Sonnet 19. Here, in the first two lines of Sonnet 55, the young man is placed firmly in his tomb. This is not marble, nor a gilded monument, but a poem. And then lines 3–4 qualify this promise of immortality with a glimpse of the young man's actual tomb, the "unswept stone, besmeared with sluttish time". In other words the first quatrain looks forward to two tombs for the young man. One, "these contents", will work much better than the other, "unswept stone", in keeping his memory alive; 'you will shine brighter in here than in there – but you will, of course, be in there as well'.[12]

While the second quatrain extinguishes the young man's life, asserting only the survival of his memory, the third then brings him to life as that purposeful, striding figure marching against death and oblivion. But the bringing back to life is poetic resurrection and poetic animation, a fact emphasised by the contrast between "you pace forth" and "your praise shall . . . find room" in line 10. As in his real life, his poetic life is to be looked at by others, only now the sonnet allows him to be eternally looked at – but the couplet crosses that impression of life by contrasting it with the real resurrection, when bodies rise from their coffins at the last judgement:

> So, till the judgement that yourself arise,
> You live in this, and dwell in lovers' eyes.

By the last line "live" and "dwell" have become strangely undercut; they describe a highly limited form of survival within the poem and lovers' eyes, and without even the sense of freedom and self-determination attainable in Donne's "pretty rooms" built in sonnets. Sonnet 55 promises preservation and immortality, but only on the poet's terms. Most concretely, the prospect of the sonnet as a coffin brings out the poet's desire to contain, control, and confine, which earlier sonnets had prefigured. Sonnet 46, for instance, gave a hint of such a desire in an evocative parenthesis whose immediacy is greater

than the rest of the poem's conventional game with "eye" and "heart": "My
heart doth plead that thou in him dost lie,/(A closet never pierced with
crystal eyes)."[13] The idea is more emphatically presented in Sonnet 48
which laments the poet's failure to lock up the young man except in a place
where he has complete freedom to come and go:

> Thee have I not locked up in any chest,
> Save where thou art not, though I feel thou art,
> Within the gentle closure of my breast,
> From whence at pleasure thou mayst come and part.

And Sonnet 52, as we have already seen, likens the miser's treasure chest and
the wardrobe to the poet's power over his subject.

Of all the immortalising sonnets, 55 is the most confident. Its six 'shall'
verbs convey a certainty of future vision transcending even Sonnet 19's
optimistic claim that poetry is the only possible victorious antagonist of
time. The poet here is a true seer, aloof from the poem and with a vision of
his verse's permanence despite decay, war, and devastation. When the
promise of immortality next appears, in Sonnet 60, it is much more
tentative, coming almost as an afterthought to an universal statement about
time's progress. The sonnet carries on Sonnet 55's sense of inexorable
forward movement, but where that sonnet had envisioned a perpetual
advance of the young man and the poem Sonnet 60 gradually transfers the
advance to time itself, seeing everyone as subject to it; and when poetic
immortality is promised in the couplet it is now seen as something static, a
form of resistance to movement:

> Like as the waves make towards the pebbled shore,
> So do our minutes hasten to their end,
> Each changing place with that which goes before,
> 4   In sequent toil all forwards do contend.
> Nativity, once in the main of light,
> Crawls to maturity, wherewith being crowned,
> Crooked eclipses 'gainst his glory fight,
> 8   And time that gave doth now his gift confound.
> Time doth transfix the flourish set on youth,
> And delves the parallels in beauty's brow,
> Feeds on the rarities of nature's truth,
> 12   And nothing stands but for his scythe to mow.
>   And yet to times in hope my verse shall stand,
>   Praising thy worth, despite his cruel hand.

For those who, like Philip Martin, see Sonnet 55 as the apotheosis of eternising poetry, this sonnet will have 'malformations or inconsistencies of texture' and 'a weak final couplet'.[14] This may be so, but it needs to be said that Sonnet 60 is the finer poem of the two. Where Sonnet 55 dehumanises and depersonalises, creating an immortal puppet, Sonnet 60 describes a general vulnerability where everything, even time itself, is forced to contend forward in sequent toil; both the baby crawling down a corridor of light and time ploughing and mowing are elements in the same process to which there is no exception. The couplet's "and yet" is not so much a promise as a gesture. It proposes immortality, but a heavily qualified one: "times in hope" is an unsure phrase where 'times to come' would have carried absolute certainty, and the final promise of one thing standing out against the movement described in the rest of the sonnet suggests, in its wording, the epitaph on a tombstone.

The most significant change from Sonnet 55 is the transference of interest from the young man to the poet. In 55 the concentration had been entirely on the second person: "you shall shine . . . the living record of your memory . . . Shall you pace forth; your praise shall still find room . . . till yourself arise/You live in this." Now the universal vision of time's progress is a general first person one, "our minutes", the young man being confined to the expression of his value as one element in a couplet which runs through the three persons: "my verse . . . thy worth . . . his cruel hand." The sonnet's moving vision of human vulnerability comes to have little or nothing to do with the young man, for our ultimate perception is of the poet's difficulties in attempting to create a work which will defy the general state of all human things. The work is praise of the young man but the conflict which the couplet presents is between time and the poet. The final phrase "his cruel hand" leads the reader into a remarkable change of focus: the sonnet's argument had seemed to be moving from the general decay of humanity in the second quatrain to the specific decay of the young in the third. There the images are of time's cruel hand at work, transfixing youth's flourish and feeding on its rarity (assuming that the reader sees "nature's truth" as an extension of "youth"). But where the reader expects the couplet to focus on the young man as the quintessence of vulnerable youth he finds instead time's cruel hand opposed to the poet's verse – itself a kind of "hand":

> And yet to times in hope my verse shall stand,
> Praising thy worth, despite his cruel hand.

According to the logic of the sonnet the couplet should be understood to mean something like, 'my verse will survive to praise you despite all that cruel time can do to you'; but the force of "praising" is so great in the final line — the one act of resistance to time's advance — that its primary sense is that 'my verse will continue to praise you no matter how much time tries to wipe it away'. Time's cruelty is defined more by what it tries to do to poetry than by what it does to the young man.

Sonnet 63 picks up the central image of Sonnet 60, that of youth travelling on to age, becoming a king, and then being eclipsed, but fits it into a much less generalised view of time and decay:

> Against my love shall be as I am now,
> With time's injurious hand crushed and o'erworn,
> When hours have drained his blood and filled his brow
> 4 With lines and wrinkles, when his youthful morn
> Hath travailed on to age's steepy night,
> And all those beauties whereof now he's king
> Are vanishing, or vanished out of sight,
> 8 Stealing away the treasure of his spring —
> For such a time do I now fortify
> Against confounding age's cruel knife,
> That he shall never cut from memory
> 12 My sweet love's beauty, though my lover's life.
> His beauty shall in these black lines be seen,
> And they shall live, and he in them still green.[15]

In terms of the kill-to-revive pattern which informs immortalising poetry this a slightly sadistic modification, age-to-rejuvenate — with the subject only being killed in the final lines. The idea of painting in the wrinkles is not only Shakespeare's; it is part of the common stock for all *carpe diem* poets, and other sonneteers take more obvious pleasure in doing it than Shakespeare does here. What is more significant here, in the use of poetry to combat time, is the double time scheme which this sonnet seems to contain — the result, in effect, of the syntactic imprecision of the whole poem. For all of its apparent preparation to make a statement the octave turns out to have no more substance than to be merely a qualification of line 9, an extended description of "such a time" and an explanation for "do I now fortify". More than that, though, its whole premise, both syntactic and in terms of what it says, is nullified by the sestet. The octave proposes that one day in the future the young man will look like the poet does now — aged, worn, close to death — and the reader is at least half aware that the description of the aged figure in lines 2 – 8 is of the poet actually and of the young man only speculatively: as much the poet's lament for his own lost youth as for the young man's potential loss. But then the sestet's fortification image makes all of that seem nonsense, for the fortifying is being done not only for mankind in general but for the poet himself – the "memory" of line 11 is both the world's historical record and the poet's own reminder of what he once knew. In other words, where the octave presents an aged poet and a young subject, the sestet presents the poet still alive and the subject dead – or at least his beauty dead which, for him, is the same thing.

The couplet adds a further twist to the promises of immortality: that it is now primarily the poetry which lives on. The verb "live" is attached to the "black lines", and the final clause, with its verb only understood – "and he in them still green" – conveys not only the young man's dependence upon, but his subordination to, the poetry. The contrast between black and green revives the young man in a limited, stylised way, where the body of the sonnet has graphically aged him and insidiously revived the poet. The sonnet s opening line had presented a melodramatic present contrast cum future parallel between the two, but by the couplet we have come to apply all of the detail about ageing to the young man and, despite the opening "crushed and o'erworn", to see the poet as the vigorous antagonist of time. Again time's cruel hand figures in the sonnet – now as a "cruel knife" – but its cruelty comes from what it attempts to do to the poet rather than the young man, and it is the poet's power to resist which rejuvenates him, not his subject.

Finally the poet's own concern in the confrontation with time comes to dominate the immortalisation process in Sonnets 64 and 65. Sonnet 64 plays a particularly effective trick upon the reader:

> When I have seen by time's fell hand defaced
> The rich proud cost of outworn buried age,
> When sometime lofty towers I see down razed,
> 4 And brass eternal slave to mortal rage,
> When I have seen the hungry ocean gain
> Advantage on the kingdom of the shore,
> And the firm soil win of the watery main,
> 8 Increasing store with loss, and loss with store,
> When I have seen such interchange of state,
> Or state itself confounded to decay,
> Ruin hath taught me thus to ruminate,
> 12 That time will come and take my love away.
>   This thought is as a death, which cannot choose
>   But weep to have that which it fears to lose.

This sonnet fails to do what its imagery promises, that is to stand out against time. The three quatrains seem likely to strike the reader with a sense of *déjà vu*, partly of the imagery of previous sonnets dealing with the battle against time, and partly with the classical stock of poetic claims to immortality.[16] Where the trick is played is in the couplet. The reader's experience of the sequence leads him to expect a couplet like the one which completes Sonnet 60, opposing the familiar vision of time's devastation with the promise or hope of life-giving poetry. Instead the couplet reinforces the vision, and by doing so completes the ageing reversal of Sonnet 63. Where a couplet of poetic immortality would have modified the sense of personal deprivation in line 12, this couplet merely re-emphasises it, leaving the poet, rather than the young man, as the great survivor looking on change and decay without himself changing or decaying, and fearing to love because of the prospect of losing that love.

Against the certainty that the poet, rather than future ages, will be deprived of his love, Sonnet 65 emerges as an entirely personal answer to the ravages of time. Its opening word, "since", looks both backward and forward, as a summary of Sonnet 64 and towards "but" in the second line:

> Since brass, nor stone, nor earth, nor boundless sea,
> But sad mortality o'ersways their power,
> How with this rage shall beauty hold a plea,
> 4 Whose action is no stronger than a flower?
> O how shall summer's honey breath hold out
> Against the wrackful siege of batt'ring days,
> When rocks impregnable are not so stout,
> 8 Nor gates of steel so strong but time decays?
> O fearful meditation; where, alack,
> Shall time's best jewel from time's chest lie hid?
> Or what strong hand can hold his swift foot back?
> 12 Or who his spoil of beauty can forbid?
>   O none, unless this miracle have might
>   That in black ink my love may still shine bright.

Taking up Sonnet 64's fear to have what can so easily be taken away, this sonnet meditates graphically upon possible opposition to time's theft – a fearful meditation, but glorious too in so far as poetry is concerned. The studied vaguenesses of "beauty" in the first quatrain, holding a plea against time's rage, and "summer's honey breath" withstanding time's siege in the second, come to apply to the workings of poetry itself, and not, as we might have expected, to the young man. "Beauty" does exactly what poetry had done earlier in the sequence, pleads a case in law, and like poetry its case is based on the image of a flower; and the rest of the sonnet describes the poet's attempts to hide and protect its subject from time's irresistible onslaught. The only possible answer to the third quatrain's questions is given in the sonnet's final line: time's jewel is best hid in poetry, and only the poet can control and forbid time. It is only a tentative answer — as any predicted miracle must be — and it arises from the fearfulness of the poet's meditation upon time's power. The fear is the same as at the end of Sonnet 64, primarily a fear of deprivation on the poet's part at what he may lose, and hardly at all the young man's fear of losing his looks or his life. In this last sonnet of the immediate immortalisation group he has been depersonalised to the status of an inanimate, if valuable, object — "time's best jewel". That image is carried into the couplet where the quality of brightness may be the only thing to survive, but even this degree of identity is threatened by the reader's uncertainty as to whether "my love shall still shine bright" may not be as poet centred as the rest of the sonnet, with "my love" meaning 'my feelings of love'.

None of these immortalising sonnets contains the elements of opposition between poet and subject which the earlier sardonic sonnets had projected, but they nonetheless describe the poet's victory both over his subject and over time. In them he uses his poetry to assert the power and strength of his emotions, and there is always, carried over from the previous sonnets, the implied contrast of his resistance to change and the young man's fickleness. Indeed, the poet's problems in continuing to love so alterable a lover dominate the next thirty sonnets in the sequence.

5 'The False Heart's History': Rival Values

The poet's victory in the immortalising sonnets is important. Without degrading himself by using sarcasm or sardonic irony he contrives, while asserting his aim to immortalise his subject, to emphasise his sense of his own value. He, not the young man, is the heroic defier of time; and, moreover, he emerges as time's defier without his loyalty to the young man being impaired. The experience of this victory — its demonstration of the poet's energy and, by implied contrast, the young man's helplessness — is needed to prepare the reader for three crises described in Sonnets 66–100, the poet's sense of his own ageing and death, the young man's infidelity, and the rival poet.

The ageing group, 71–74, is a good place to begin examining the poetic strategies of sonnets and groups of sonnets in this part of the sequence since its concern with the depredations of time and the imminence of death links it to the immortalising sonnets, and it exploits further the distinction they helped to make between the poet's and the young man's values.[1] Sonnet 71 I made use of in chapter 1 to demonstrate the capacity of the sonnets to maintain a doubleness of tone and not allow the reader to say for certain whether the poem's superficial selflessness is sarcastic or not:

> No longer mourn for me when I am dead
> Than you shall hear the surly sullen bell
> Give warning to the world that I am fled
> 4 From this vile world with vildest worms to dwell.
> Nay, if you read this line, remember not
> The hand that writ it, for I love you so,
> That I in your sweet thoughts would be forgot,
> 8 If thinking on me then should make you woe.
> O if, I say, you look upon this verse,
> When I, perhaps, compounded am with clay,
> Do not so much as my poor name rehearse,
> 12 But let your love ev'n with my life decay,

> Lest the wise world should look into your moan,
> And mock you with me after I am gone.

I can now add to my earlier comments that it is the possibility of the sonnet's having an ironic edge which protects it from seeming an exercise in self-pity. Without the undertone of contrast between the poet's steadfastness and the young man's fickleness — which on one level is only the contrast between youth and age — so detailed a picturing of one's own obscure death is unlikely to keep a reader's sympathy.[2] Sonnet 72 continues to imagine the poet's death, now linking it to the value of his poetry:

> O lest the world should task you to recite,
> What merit lived in me that you should love
> After my death, dear love, forget me quite,
> 4 For you in me can nothing worthy prove;
> Unless you would devise some virtuous lie,
> To do more for me than mine own desert,
> And hang more praise upon deceased I,
> 8 Than niggard truth would willingly impart.
> O lest your true love may seem false in this,
> That you for love speak well of me untrue,
> My name be buried where my body is,
> 12 And live no more to shame nor me nor you.
>   For I am shamed by that which I bring forth,
>   And so should you, to love things nothing worth.

Like 71 this sonnet balances potential ironies against what would otherwise be suffocating self-pity and hyperbolic modesty. The image of the poet as dead and not worth remembering is set within an opening quatrain which takes up the preceding sonnet's possible ironies: for instance, the idea of one lover being tasked by the world to say why he should have loved is quite ludicrous, except in so far as it reveals the worldliness of that lover; and the strained word order of line 4 encourages the possibility that the young man is not worth the poet, while, of course, it really says the opposite. So, too, the poet's modesty about his verse, ending in the couplet in shame and worthlessness, carries undercurrents of contempt for the process of writing adulatory poetry to an unfitting subject. That insinuation gains more force from the sub-metaphor of the sonnet, which sets up the young man as a poet himself, tasked to "recite" in the opening line, to "devise" a lie in the fifth, and then to "hang praise" and "speak well", all of them the untruthful actions inherent in the poet's task.

Together Sonnets 71 and 72 fix on the young man's actions in an imagined future after the poet's death. The apparent nearness of this event prepares the way for the much celebrated Sonnet 73, in which the poet uses three successive metaphors, one to a quatrain, in order to portray his developing old age and imminent death:

> That time of year thou mayst in me behold,
> When yellow leaves, or none, or few, do hang
> Upon those boughs which shake against the cold,
> 4   Bare ruined choirs, where late the sweet birds sang.
> In me thou seest the twilight of such day,
> As after sunset fadeth in the west,
> Which by and by black night doth take away,
> 8   Death's second self, that seals up all in rest.
> In me thou seest the glowing of such fire,
> That on the ashes of his youth doth lie,
> As the death-bed whereon it must expire,
> 12   Consumed with that which it was nourished by.
>   This thou perceiv'st, which makes thy love more strong,
>   To love that well which thou must leave ere long.[3]

This sonnet is so attractive in its metaphoric structure that it has often been cited as the archetypal Shakespearean sonnet, what Alden called "the finest example of the Shakespearean mode".[4] It may be archetypal in the terms of the ghostly 4:4:4:2 pattern which underlies this kind of sonnet but it actually represents one of the less frequent Shakespearean sonnet structures.[5] Most critical comment on it has understandably concentrated on its metaphoric process – the way in which it helps enact the ageing of the man it describes – but behind the narrowing down from year to day to glowing embers the sonnet does something more, separate from, and to an extent contrary to, its metaphors. This something else is contained in the sonnet's verbs. In the opening line "thou mayst in me behold" is not likely to be interpreted by the reader as anything other than a general statement – an interpretation supported by the breadth of the metaphor which follows. In other words, the reader feels as much addressed as the young man, if not more so; and he therefore takes the statement as the poet's actual opinion of himself. In the second and third quatrains "thou seest" modifies the reader's position only a little. The absence of the auxiliary "may" locates the sonnet as more particularly an address to the young man, but it remains one which the reader can share, as we all share supposedly intimate poems which, while they address themselves to a lover, describe the poet's general state. In the couplet, though, the reader is forced out of the address by the specificity of "this thou perceiv'st"; also, the narrowness of 'perceive' conveys, in retrospect, a stronger and more confined sense into the earlier verbs of 'beholding' and 'seeing', as if to say 'these metaphors, so graphically describing my decline, are the way you see me'. I do not mean by this that the poet does not imagine himself as old, but that by the verb "perceive" he demonstrates his awareness of the young man's attitude to his ageing: the three times repeated "in me" carries the implication that this is not the whole truth about the poet, only a part of the truth which the young man extracts and which ignores a lot. The couplet is pregnant with the irony of prospective legatees at the death beds of rich relatives, the difference in values between the young man and the poet coming in the unexpected "which thou must leave". Ingram and Redpath note the incongruity of the live leaving the dead by glossing "leave" as 'forgo', not 'depart from', but following Sonnets 71 and 72, where it is the young man's version of the relationship, conditioned by the world's demands, which will survive as its record, this reversal of the natural order embodies the different values of the two men. In the young man's view even the most final and unavoidable of partings — the poet's death — is transformed into an act of will on his own part.

The shadowy image of a prospective legatee is taken up again in the final sonnet in the group, number 74:[6]

> But be contented when that fell arrest   .
> Without all bail shall carry me away,
> My life hath in this line some interest,
> 4 Which for memorial still with thee shall stay.
> When thou reviewest this, thou dost review
> The very part was consecrate to thee.
> The earth can have but earth, which is his due;
> 8 My spirit is thine, the better part of me.
> So then thou hast but lost the dregs of life,
> The prey of worms, my body being dead,
> The coward conquest of a wretch's knife,
> 12 Too base of thee to be remembered.
>   The worth of that is that which it contains,
>   And that is this, and this with thee remains.

Ingram and Redpath explain the inheritance metaphor in their note to line 3: 'The metaphor is not that of interest on capital, but of a legal and equitable interest in an estate. Moreover, "My life" is not the owner of this estate, but the property out of which the estate is carved; and "hath" does not express ownership but inclusion (as in "this house has three bedrooms").'[7] The sonnet's argument set up in the first quatrain, is the conventional one that the poet's soul is given up entirely to his lover. In the sonnet's terms that soul is the poem, and after the poet's death it remains the only valuable part of him, his bequest to the young man. But running counter to that argument is a metaphoric development which emphasises the importance of the poet's suffering. Although the metaphor of the first quatrain is a legal one, its introduction by way of "that fell arrest" comes as an incongruous and unexpected prefiguring of his own death. It asserts the physical presence of the poet while describing his death, and this presence carries over into the third quatrain, where "the coward conquest of a wretch's knife" completes the metaphor of his own suffering.[8] It may well be, as editors argue, that the wretch is a personification like Death or Time, but the word's vagueness jogs the reader's memory of the prisoner at the beginning of the sonnet. The dregs of life is despatched in complete obscurity, and, according to the syntax of the sentence, the "wretch", as much as the "body", can be the subject of line 12, "Too base of thee to be remembered". Added to the metaphoric suggestiveness of dark deeds done on orders from above is a continuation of the reversal of normal values which the couplet of Sonnet 73 had introduced. "But be contented" which opens Sonnet 74 may only be glossed with charity as 'do not be upset'. As in the opening line of Sonnet 32 – "my well contended day" – the word is used to describe emotions at death, only this time the contentment is the young man's, not the dying poet's. When the sonnet takes up its shadowy burial service – "the earth can have but earth" – and consolation of the mourners, it reintroduces the idea that even the poet's dying rights have been taken from him: following Sonnet 73's refusal to let him do the leaving Sonnet 74 asserts that the poet's death is the young man's losing of life – "So then thou hast but lost the dregs of life". Finally, the couplet sums up the message of the sonnet; in the words of Ingram and Redpath, 'the value of the living body lies in the spirit which animates it, and, in my case, this spirit is one and the same as my poetry, which will live on with you'.[9] That is an admirable summary of the couplet's meaning, but it still does not fully convey the reader's experience which is of a peculiarly cold ending to the sonnet:

> The worth of that is that which it contains,
> And that is this, and this with thee remains.

The blurring of demonstrative pronouns hardly makes clear the grand meanings which they are expected to carry, and the reader will probably fix on the rhyme words "contains" and "remains" and take into the couplet the sense of a knife at work, cutting the body of the poem and taking out and keeping the valuable contents.[10]

The development from Sonnet 71 to Sonnet 74 is richly ironic in the way in which it sets the poet's values against the young man's and asserts the poet's power over his subject. There is, for instance, no change at all in the young man's attitude to the 'dead' poet: in 71 the conclusion is that he should "not so much as my poor name rehearse", and in 74 the poet is "too base of thee to be remembered". On the other hand, the poetry does increase its survival value: 71 can only raise the possibility of the young man reading it, "if you read this line" and "if . . . you look upon this verse", but 74 is confident of the poem's immortality, it being the soul of the poet remaining with the young man. The ifs of 71 become "when thou reviewest this" in 74, and 71's "remember not the hand that writ it" is transformed into the certainty of "which for memorial still with thee shall stay". The burden of images, too, is transferred from the young man to the poet. Both Sonnets 71 and 72 concentrate on the young man's survival and his actions after the poet's death, but 73 and 74 transfer the reader's attention to the poet himself, with 74 implicitly contrasting the young man's future actions with the poet's self-sacrificial love. The reader experiences a gradually increasing insight into the poet's suffering and the values he maintains during his ordeal, and finds set against that an unchanging certainty as to the young man's emotional depth, which is constantly expressed in sentences of potentially ironic import:

> But let your love ev'n with my life decay (71)
> For you in me can nothing worthy prove (72)
> To love that well which thou must leave ere long (73)
> Too base of thee to be remembered (74)

The contrast in values between the poet and the young man appears within one sonnet a little further on in the sequence, number 77. In discussing Sonnet 72 I noted that it played with the idea of asking the young man to become a poet; this is a strategy which Shakespeare several times uses to reveal the distinction between the poet's conception of things and that of other people (including the reader). For instance, in Sonnet 19 time is given the poet's right to draw lines on the face of his subject, and in Sonnet 26 the poet fails to find the appropriate metaphor and challenges his subject to find a "conceit" which can accept a naked thought. Most editors believe that Sonnet 77 was written to accompany the present of a blank book; and by moving from images of the mirror and the dial to focus on the book, the poet presents his subject with the chance to write himself:

> Thy glass will show thee how thy beauties wear,
> Thy dial how thy precious minutes waste;
> The vacant leaves thy mind's imprint will bear,
> 4   And of this book this learning mayst thou taste.
> The wrinkles which thy glass will truly show,
> Of mouthed graves will give thee memory;
> Thou by thy dial's shady stealth mayst know
> 8   Time's thievish progress to eternity.
> Look what thy memory cannot contain,
> Commit to these waste blanks, and thou shalt find
> Those children nursed, delivered from thy brain,
> 12   To take a new acquaintance of thy mind.
>   These offices, so oft as thou wilt look,
>   Shall profit thee, and much enrich thy book.[11]

In the third quatrain the image of the young man turning poet becomes most clear – he is presented as committing his transient thoughts to the page and, by doing so, giving them an unexpected permanence, so that they become of future interest too. The metaphor which is used sees the writing as children being nursed, a link which connects this sonnet with the common conceit of the poet as a child bearer, especially Sonnet 76, its predecessor, which begins with the question "Why is my verse so barren of new pride?" and goes on to complain that every one of the poet's words "doth almost tell my name/Showing their birth, and where they did proceed".

Before the third quatrain there had been little indication that the poet would cast his mantle over his subject in such a way. In the first quatrain the young man does his characteristic actions, looking in a mirror, looking at a clock (or sundial), and reading a book.[12] In the case of the mirror and the clock the lessons which the young man draws are similarly characteristic: his reflection reminds him of his human susceptibility to wrinkles, and the clock of the waste of his "precious" time. The second and third quatrains then expand upon each of the three images of glass, dial, and book.[13] With regard to the first two it seems as if it is the poet who is giving his own *memento mori* lesson, instructing the young man in the fact that he must eventually die. Only in the third quatrain does it become clear that the whole sonnet is the young man's musings on his own mortality; and then the effect is of a total contrast to the poetic process as we know it in the sonnets – when the poet is poet he looks upon mortal things and muses that even his love is mortal, but when the young man is poet he looks upon mortal things and muses that he too is mortal. The arid self-enclosedness of this vision is mimicked by the sonnet's gradual deterioration. So long as we preserve the illusion that it is the poet's vision, then the metaphors are vivid – mouthed graves and time's thievish progress – but when the non-poet takes over the result is first confusion, in the idea of children being nursed before they are delivered, and then mere poetastry in line 12's wooden metaphor of the delivered children taking a new acquaintance of the young man's mind. The couplet, in rhythm and vocabulary, reproduces the vacuousness of the young man's inspiration: not merely in the idea of his poetry profiting and enriching him – notice the rhythmic weakness of "and much enrich thy book" as a conclusion to the poem – but also in the presentation of the writing of poetry as an "office", i.e. a duty, and, in the terms of the sonnet, an office of the dead.

The difference in values between the poet and his subject is most profoundly treated in the rival poet group, where its frame of reference includes the nature and demands of poetic praise. Before considering that group in the next chapter I want, for the rest of this chapter, to look at two smaller groups of sonnets, in both of which the superiority of the poet's values over the young man's is conveyed by purely poetic means – metaphor, rhythm, syntax, imagery, tone – but without any identifiable loss of poetic decorum. Both groups comprise three sonnets, numbers 88 – 90 and 91 – 93. Sonnet 88 begins the first group, and outgoes almost every other sonnet in its blatant masochism. The idea seems to be that the more the poet hurts himself the more he likes it because the young man likes it more:

> When thou shalt be disposed to set me light,
> And place my merit in the eye of scorn,
> Upon thy side against myself I'll fight,
> 4 And prove thee virtuous, though thou art forsworn.
> With mine own weakness being best acquainted,
> Upon thy part I can set down a story
> Of faults concealed, wherein I am attainted,
> 8 That thou in losing me shall win much glory.
> And I by this will be a gainer too,
> For bending all my loving thoughts on thee,
> The injuries that to myself I do,
> 12 Doing thee vantage, double vantage me.
>   Such is my love – to thee I so belong –
>   That for thy right myself will bear all wrong.

Here the paradoxes of self-wounding are so bizarre that it is not easy to give the sonnet serious consideration. One commentator who does, though, is Martin Seymour-Smith, and his notes bear repetition both for the way in which they demonstrate the sensitivity of response which marks the whole of his edition and, more pertinently, because they forcefully assert an interpretative attitude directly opposed to the argument of this book. In his headnote to the sonnet he says this:

> This sonnet clearly reflects the psychologically peculiar nature of Shakespeare's devotion to the Friend. It has a force far beyond that of a mere 'metaphysical' conceit, and suggests something of the purity of spirit from which Shakespeare derived much of his poetic power . . . Unless we understand that Shakespeare meant this literally — and it does appear, superficially, after all, preposterous — we have little chance of understanding the *Sonnets* as a whole.

And in explanation of the paradox of lines 3 – 4 he adds:

> It is important to realize that Shakespeare meant this literally, and was not saying it to bolster up a conceit. The psychological intention is twofold: not only does Shakespeare intend to love to the bitter end, but also he proposes to demolish the edifice of his own ego by this process of identification with the Friend. Unrequited love becomes an instrument of severe self-criticism, even of self-destruction.[14]

It should be clear by now that one of my purposes in this book is to argue exactly the opposite. If the sonnets can be said to have an 'intention' then it is to maintain and strengthen the ego, rather than destroy it, and this, not purity of spirit, provides the poetic power even in those sonnets where the apparent literal claim is for self-immolation. Had this sonnet existed in isolation Seymour-Smith's case would be strong: despite its constant centering on the poet himself the sonnet firmly declares its intention to destroy the poet's ego. The one qualification which we should make is that the poet still reserves for himself the not inconsiderable powers of poetry: knowing his topic well — "mine own weakness" — he can set down a story which will achieve the effect poets often work for, the winning of glory. In this case, of course, the glory will be all the young man's.

Sonnet 89 continues to promote self-sacrifice by means of further paradoxes:

> Say that thou didst forsake me for some fault,
> And I will comment upon that offence.
> Speak of my lameness, and I straight will halt,

4   Against thy reasons making no defence.
      Thou canst not, love, disgrace me half so ill,
      To set a form upon desired change,
      As I'll myself disgrace, knowing thy will,
8   I will acquaintance strangle and look strange,
      Be absent from thy walks, and in my tongue
      Thy sweet beloved name no more shall dwell,
      Lest I, too much profane, should do it wrong
12   And haply of our old acquaintance tell.
         For thee, against myself I'll vow debate,
         For I must ne'er love him whom thou dost hate.

As well as the poet's self-sacrifice this sonnet continues to present two other ideas central to the previous sonnet—the vindictiveness of the young man's behaviour, and the poet's control over his poetry. In that sonnet the young man's vindictiveness was stressed in the opening quatrain, in the calculated callousness of the first verb, "When thou shalt be disposed", and in the damning phrases "set me light", "the eye of scorn", and "thou art forsworn". Now Sonnet 89 adds the implication that the young man's constant motivation comes from fear of what others will say. The verbs which the opening quatrain uses in relation to him, "say" and "speak", anticipate the poet's not so veiled threat in the third quatrain, that he too is capable of telling damaging stories.[15] The young man's vindictiveness is given full prominence in the second quatrain where "thy will" is sandwiched between – and defined by – the acts of disgracing and strangling. And through it all the poet insists on asserting the powers of his poetry, from the first quatrain's proclaimed intention to comment upon his own offence to the third quatrain's promise to stop writing love poetry. "In" is a useful preposition here. "In my tongue/Thy sweet beloved name no more shall dwell" takes for granted a previous possession: up until this promise the poet's power is so great that his words maintain and contain the young man's name.

The couplet of Sonnet 89 is the logical destination not only of this sonnet but of Sonnet 88 also. Wooden in rhythm and childish in its paradox it sums up the sterile argument of both sonnets – what Seymour-Smith described as superficial preposterousness. The contrast with the next sonnet could hardly be greater, despite the fact that Sonnet 90 immediately takes up the closing word of 89:

      Then hate me when thou wilt, if ever, now,
      Now while the world is bent my deeds to cross,

Join with the spite of fortune, make me bow,
4 And do not drop in for an after-loss.
Ah do not, when my heart hath 'scaped this sorrow,
Come in the rearward of a conquered woe;
Give not a windy night a rainy morrow,
8 To linger out a purposed overthrow.
If thou wilt leave me, do not leave me last,
When other petty griefs have done their spite,
But in the onset come; so shall I taste
12 At first the very worst of fortune's might,
And other strains of woe, which now seem woe,
Compared with loss of thee will not seem so.

The link between this sonnet and its predecessor is one of the most magical in the sequence. At the end of 89 "hate" drops with a conventionally paradoxical thud – "For I must ne'ver love him whom thou dost hate" – but by the end of 90's opening line it has regained all, and more than, its normal intensity. The reason lies chiefly in the way that this line departs so forcefully from the usual practise of the sonnets: one syntactic break in an opening line is rare, but two, as here after "wilt" and "ever", is unique—contrast it with the unbroken mellifluousness of 88's "When thou shalt be disposed to set me light" and 89's "Say that thou didst forsake me for some fault".[16] And the effect is intensified by the next line's opening "now", with the clause which it promises to introduce being held over until line 3.

What happens to the word "hate" imitates in miniature the contrastive effect of Sonnet 90 over 88 and 89. In rhythm, syntax, and, most importantly, metaphor, Sonnet 90 involves the reader completely in a way that the conventional paradoxes of 88 and 89 had failed to do. The sonnet plays a remarkable density of metaphor – submission to a king, billiards, battle, weather, conspiracy – against an equally remarkable simplicity of vocabulary – stock participants like "world", "fortune", "heart", "sorrow", "griefs", and "woe", and mainly plain verbs, "hate", "cross", "join", "drop", "come", "give", "leave", "done", "taste", and "seem". Most importantly, the effect of Sonnet 90 is to assert what the previous two sonnets have tried to destroy, the primacy of the poet's feelings. The succession of imperative verbs emphasises the depth of his vulnerability, his realisation not simply that the young man is likely to be unfaithful, but that he is likely to choose the moment when it will cause most pain. Again it is the opening line which creates the effect, laying bare his vulnerability in its temporal confusion which switches the reader suddenly from "when thou wilt" to "if ever, now". The reader is forced into a confusion analogous to the poet's emotional turmoil: "Then hate me when thou wilt" is the phrasing of stock paradox similar to the statements of Sonnets 88 and 89, leading – one assumes – to a corollary to the effect that the poet will do his best to help the young man in that hate (as in 89's couplet). Suddenly not to get a paradox, but something in phrasing – if not in intention – close to an ultimatum, "if ever, now", moves the sonnet onto a different poetic register. The values which are then projected are the values which the image-conscious young man could never share: they are the primacy of emotion and the acceptance of responsibility for all actions. The very bareness of the couplet, especially the way it manages to give dignity to a final phrase as unpoetic as "will not seem so", points up the fact that there is an ultimate poetic language beyond the reach of metaphor which can describe, to use Seymour-Smith's phrase, 'purity of spirit'.

Sonnets 91–93 are less obviously a self-contained group than 88–90. There are good reasons for including them with the group 94–96 which has an analogous theme, and which shares similar language and imagery; even so, for my argument here the group 91–93 matches 88–90 in developing a conflict of values in two sonnets and then resolving the conflict by means of a distinct change of style in the third. To begin with, Sonnet 91 has a common Shakespearean sonnet structure; it develops an argument through the three quatrains and undercuts it in the couplet:

> Some glory in their birth, some in their skill,
> Some in their wealth, some in their body's force,
> Some in their garments, though new-fangled ill,
> 4 Some in their hawks and hounds, some in their horse;
> And every humour hath his adjunct pleasure,
> Wherein it finds a joy above the rest.
> But these particulars are not my measure;
> 8 All these I better in one general best.
> Thy love is better than high birth to me,
> Richer than wealth, prouder than garments' cost,
> Of more delight than hawks or horses be;
> 12 And having thee, of all men's pride I boast;
>   Wretched in this alone, that thou mayst take
>   All this away, and me most wretched make.

Few of the sonnets in the collection make the reader so secure as this one – and I mean this to apply as much to the poem's form as to its content. The three quatrains are unavoidably poetical. The chiasmus which makes the third quatrain mirror the first allows the same kind of predictability as the reader finds in the quatrains' syntactic structures. The argument is pure idealistic convention: that the possession of his love surpasses any conceivable worldly joy. And the couplet's undercutting is conventional, too, pointing out that the only vulnerability such a blessed person as the poet knows is his fear that the lover might decide to decamp – a case of having all of his emotional eggs in one basket. By the end of the sonnet the reader has no sense that the situation is anything more than poetic convention, with stock claims and anxieties.

Sonnet 92 is linked directly to 91 by way of its opening "but", which introduces the poet's answer to the fear that his lover might leave, and its argument now moves the reader in contrary directions. One is to continue and even strengthen his sense of conventional poetic ideas and attitudes, the other to insinuate real and bitter emotions underlying these stock elements:

> But do thy worst to steal thyself away,
> For term of life thou art assured mine;
> And life no longer than thy love will stay,
> 4 For it depends upon that love of thine.
> Then need I not to fear the worst of wrongs,
> When in the least of them my life hath end.
> I see a better state to me belongs
> 8 Than that which on thy humour doth depend:
> Thou canst not vex me with inconstant mind,
> Since that my life on thy revolt doth lie.
> O, what a happy title do I find,
> 12 Happy to have thy love, happy to die!
> But what's so blessed-fair that fears no blot?
> Thou mayst be false, and yet I know it not.

I should explain in more detail what I mean by this sonnet's contrary directions. One of them is to confirm the convention of Sonnet 92 by stressing first the dependence of the poet upon his lover – "depend" is used twice in the sonnet with much more of its root sense than the word usually bears – and then by extending that dependence to the complete poeticality of stating that one can die for love. The sonnet repeats over and over Rosalind's ultimately fictional statement: "For term of life thou art assured mine/And life no longer than thy love will stay", "in the least of them my life hath end", "my life on thy revolt doth lie", "happy to die". In the other direction, though, the sonnet can not help revealing some of the conflict of values which the stock death threats ought to be meant to hide. The couplet of 91 had left undefined the nature of the young man's decamping; its wording is tied to the possession imagery of the whole sonnet, "that thou mayst take/All this away." In its opening Sonnet 92 does little more than pun on the idea of taking things away — "But do thy worst to steal thyself away" — then, as it progresses it develops a vague but threatening promise of a definition of what the young man will do: "the worst of wrongs . . . the least of them . . . inconstant mind . . . thy revolt." Only in the couplet's "blot" and "false" does the definition clarify itself into infidelity rather than mere departure, and, of course, the couplet raises the prospect not of a future infidelity, but of one going on at the moment and unknown to the poet (note the play on "yet" in the last line). The possibility of this being the case throws the whole sonnet off course; it not only undercuts what has gone before, it exposes it as self-deceiving fiction — and not just self-deceiving, but subject-deceiving too. Firm poeticisms like "life no longer than thy love will stay" and "Thou canst not vex me with inconstant mind" are self and subject flattering lines, for the young man is quite probably inconstant but the poet still lives, and he is vexed. Something of the turbulence generated by the couplet is visible in the third quatrain's uneasy play on "happy", where the word's possible meanings — pleasing, blessed, content, fortunate, lucky, willing — are all simultaneously in action, but all to a great extent cancelling each other out. For instance, "happy title" in line 12, "O what a happy title do I find", is first a pleasing title, but not when the whole line is read, after which it might be either blessed or willing; "happy to have thy love" in line 13 is either an expression of luck or fortune or contentment, and "happy to die" which follows it means either willing to die or lucky to die.[17]

Sonnet 93 marks the final shift in tone as the hypothetical infidelity of 92 becomes established fact:

> So shall I live, supposing thou art true,
> Like a deceived husband—so love's face
> May still seem love to me, though altered new:
> 4 Thy looks with me, thy heart in other place.
> For there can live no hatred in thine eye,
> Therefore in that I cannot know thy change.
> In many's looks, the false heart's history
> 8 Is writ in moods and frowns and wrinkles strange,
> But heaven in thy creation did decree
> That in thy face sweet love should ever dwell,
> Whate'er thy thoughts or thy heart's workings be,
> 12 Thy looks should nothing thence but sweetness tell.
>   How like Eve's apple doth thy beauty grow,
>   If thy sweet virtue answer not thy show.

The contrast between the acknowledged self-degradation of this sonnet and the idealistic love of the three quatrains of Sonnet 91 hardly needs to have attention drawn to it. Through the three sonnets the reader has experienced a progressively bitter joke, where the conventional attitudes of poetic love are demolished by the sordid capacities of this poet's lover. In this sonnet the contrast between ideal and fact is maintained ironically within the very same statements. Three times the sonnet addresses itself to the young man in the terms of sonneteer to mistress, but with an openness of syntax which asks for the reader's agreement with the poet that this master-mistress is a monster of hypocrisy: in line 5 "there can live no hatred in thine eyes" means simultaneously that (poetic ideal) 'you are both beautiful and incapable of any negative emotion', and (the young man) 'you still give the hypocritical impression of love even when you feel hatred'; in line 10 "in thy face sweet love should ever dwell" means (poetic ideal) 'you are born to love perpetually', and (the young man) 'you profess love to everyone all the time'; and in line 12 "Thy looks should nothing thence but sweetness tell" means (poetic ideal) 'your face's constant beauty mirrors your thoughts and feelings', and (the young man) 'whatever you think and feel you make sure that you give the impression of love and friendship.'

In its metaphor, too, the sonnet finds a vehicle for the contest of values. The opening image, "like a deceived husband", is almost ludicrous, as if there were horns on the poet's head, he a husband and the young man his wife. The image is soon dropped and seems to have been only incidental; but in the third quatrain the idea of creation and heaven's decree prepares for a return to the husband – wife motif, coming to a head in the couplet with Eve, the original betraying wife. The poet as unfallen Adam and the young man as both object of temptation and the first tempted is a formidable polarisation, but one which this sonnet encourages; and in retrospect it develops even more clearly the contrast between innocence and experience in Sonnets 91 and 92, in the poet's idealistic beliefs and the young man's actual behaviour.

In Sonnet 93 the poet is trapped in a state of experience, as incapable of escape as the sonnet seems of concluding itself. Here form enacts frustration. The first quatrain initiates the argument by describing the prospective state of affairs where the poet will live in constant self-deception. The next two quatrains elaborate only the one point that nothing can be deciphered from . the young man's expression. No further explanation is given for the poet's planned behaviour, as if the mere fact that the young man has such an unchangingly sweet expression rules out everything but acquiescence to perpetual betrayal. Even at this late stage the sonnet has room in the couplet for some self examination: instead it contains what should be, in terms of its content, a sardonic exclamation, but what turns out to be an expression of admiration:

> How like Eve's apple doth thy beauty grow,
> If thy sweet virtue answer not thy show.

The sardonic quality should come from the rotten inside beautiful outside image of the apple, but the sarcasm is dissipated by the wonder of a beauty which is still growing, and the failure of the poet to pin the adjective "sweet" to its fitting noun in the final line. "Thy sweet show" would have reinforced the whole sonnet's emphasis on the young man's appearance; "thy sweet virtue" proposes a genuinely beautiful essence in the young man's possession.

6 'The Breath of Words': The Rival Poet

Many sonneteers have rivals, but they are usually of the unpoetic kind. Their existence normally allows the poet to contrast his own deserving merit with the undeserved fortune of some insensitive boor – as with Sidney's Lord Rich, for instance. But the contrasts which a rival poet raises are more complicated, for the mere existence of such a figure gives rhetorical generalisations a real point of reference. Consider Sonnet 84 which opens with a rhetorical question typical of the sequence – confusing in its particulars but clear in its general import –

> Who is it that says most, which can say more
> Than this rich praise, that you alone are you –
> In whose confine immured is the store
> Which should example where your equal grew?

Within any other sonnet sequence, or even earlier in this sequence, such a question would stay firmly rhetorical, its main purpose being poetic hyperbole of the 'you are more beautiful than any metaphor can convey' kind. Coming, as it does here, at the end of a group of sonnets which express detailed concern with the stylistic powers of an apparently successful rival, this question replaces hyperbole with professional concern. "Who is it . . . ?" is answerable as 'him', the "alien pen" (Sonnet 78) or "worthier pen" (79), "thy poet" (79), "a better spirit" (80), and the question carries its own unease that the rival *can* outdo the poet in hyperbole, even such hyperbole as lines 2–4 embody where the sense is that the young man's uniqueness means that only he can provide the material suitable for any metaphorical comparison of himself.

The rival poet group covers Sonnets 78–87, but the possibility of there being a rival, or of one emerging, appears several times earlier in the sequence.[1] Sonnet 21, which I discussed in chapter 4, describes rival poets, but there the poet remained secure in the strength of his attachment to his subject in contrast to the superficiality of their attachments: while they are stirred by a painted beauty to their verse, we know from Sonnet 20 that the poet's subject is painted only by nature's hand. Even so, the couplet betrays unease. "I will not praise that purpose not to sell" is a fighting, proverbial defence, but it wilfully disregards the fact that the poet has, by definition, to praise – and, in the terms of the couplet, by definition to sell; a point brought up very soon in Sonnet 24's image of the poet's "bosom's shop".

In another sonnet discussed earlier, number 32 (in chapter 3), the poet has a vision of the state of things after his own death. In a parody last testament he foresees the young man's future contact with better poets – better in style, that is. The second quatrain makes a contrast between the dead poet and his living rivals in terms reminiscent of a husband looking forward to his widow's second husband; "them" are the poet's "rude lines":

> Compare them with the bettering of the time,
> And though they be outstripped by every pen
> Reserve them for my love, not for their rhyme,
> Exceeded by the height of happier men.

The penile overtones of "outstripped by every pen" and "exceeded by the height of happier men" not only convey the poet's sense of his own inadequacy, but they also suggest that the shift from one special poet to a horde of them is a form of – or at the least a symptom of – promiscuity. The hint of sexual impotence occurs in one other sonnet concerned with the writing of poetry. This is Sonnet 76, which comes just before the rival poet group:

> Why is my verse so barren of new pride,
> So far from variation or quick change?
> Why with the time do I not glance aside
> 4   To new-found methods, and to compounds strange?
> Why write I still all one, ever the same,
> And keep invention in a noted weed,
> That every word doth almost tell my name,
> 8   Showing their birth, and where they did proceed?
> O know, sweet love, I always write of you,
> And you and love are still my argument.
> So all my best is dressing old words new,
> 12   Spending again what is already spent:
>   For as the sun is daily new and old,
>   So is my love still telling what is told.[2]

"Still", "always", "ever the same", "daily", and "again" are the important words in this sonnet, supporting the theme of unchanging monotony, the sonnet being controlled almost entirely by verbs in the present tense. Past and future are swallowed up in an unvarying poetic method; and as a vehicle to convey loss of poetic inspiration the sonnet's language and imagery could hardly be improved. The poet's deterioration into complete predictability is described by way of the gradual personification of poetic style in the second quatrain, which runs from abstract sameness in line 5, through well-known dress in line 6, to the faintly comical image of words as children telling everybody who their parent is. The sestet answers the octave's question as to why the poet's work is so predictable, but it does so with imitative monotony, dressing the old anew, spending what is spent, and telling what is told. Even the sun's potent symbolism of death and rebirth is transformed into the mundane experience of its being daily new and old. The reader's problem is that none of these elements rings true: for all of its self-deprecating claims the sonnet is unmistakeably self-assertive, for from the opening lines it implicitly contrasts the poet with all others, mere followers of fashion, and in the second quatrain actually proclaims that writing the way the poet does is the one way to achieve a distinctive personal style. This is not a matter of ironic ambiguity where the reader perceives a discordant line of thought under an apparently self-effacing statement, for there is no line, or even phrase, where the reader might feel the possibility of innuendo – even the sexual-cum-financial play on impotence and poverty in line 12 is open and transparent. The reader, in fact, perceives two distinct and non-contingent sets of values. The poet's centre on his need for fidelity to his subject: from that will emerge his proper style, even if, as is probable, all ends in impotence and rejection. Opposed to this is the set of values which the sonnet implicitly answers, the young man's double requirement that every poem should be in the latest fashion, and that his poet should be capable of providing a perpetual variety of praise.

In the sestet, which answers the octave's question, the poet's values gain complete dominance because of, and not despite, the monotony which I began the discussion of the sonnet by describing. Within the predictabilities of the phrasing the reader perceives a subtle shift in the value of "love". It begins as the word which identifies the young man in line 9 – "sweet love" – but the next line revises its meaning to something parallel to him – "you and love". In the sonnet's last line the revision is completed, so that "love" is now the word which identifies the poet – "So is my love still telling what is told." The effect of the line is a double one. "My love", following an image of the sun in the previous line, leads the reader towards the habitual identification of the young man as the object of comparison, an instinctive response made all the more probable by the reader's memory of lines 9–10, "O know, sweet love, I always write of you/And you and love are still my argument." The instinct is killed, though, by the end of the line, where "still telling what is told" confines "love" entirely to the poet. Retrospectively, too, that sense of "my love" creates a parallel with "my verse" in the sonnet's opening line. "So is my verse still telling what is told" would have effectively prevented the wider emotional ramifications which "So is my love . . ." adds to the sonnet.

The development of Sonnet 76 is inexorable: from a mock technical discussion of the way to write poetry to the conclusion that the poet's fidelity in love forces him into what must seem, to any follower of fashion, a poetic predictability. When the subject to whom the poet writes is so fashion conscious, then the result is poetic impotence to the degree that even so strong an image as the sun loses its symbolic potential. A similar development informs the first three sonnets of the rival poet group: Sonnets 78 and 79 chart, with increasing desperation, the contrasts between the poet's and his rival's style, and Sonnet 80 accepts poetic defeat while asserting a triumph for the poet's values over those of his rival and the young man. First Sonnet 78:

> So oft have I invoked thee for my muse,
> And found such fair assistance in my verse,
> As every alien pen hath got my use,
> 4 And under thee their poesy disperse.
> Thine eyes, that taught the dumb on high to sing,
> And heavy ignorance aloft to fly,
> Have added feathers to the learned's wing,
> 8 And given grace a double majesty.
> Yet be most proud of that which I compile,
> Whose influence is thine, and born of thee.
> In others' works thou dost but mend the style,
> 12 And arts with thy sweet graces graced be;
> But thou art all my art, and dost advance
> As high as learning my rude ignorance.

Unlike 76, Sonnet 78 contains a fair amount of innuendo. One obvious source lies in the first quatrain, in the sexual possibilities of "pen", "use", and "under thee" in lines 3–4, which cannot help but give retrospective double entendres to "invoked" and "fair assistance" in the opening two lines. The second quatrain moves to a different form of sarcasm. Throughout the sonnet the poet's strategy is to present himself as ignorant and untalented,

but lines 5-6 are very close to mock humility in the way they carry
ludicrous secondary images behind their superficial abstractions: the impressions are of loud croakings – "taught the dumb on high to sing" – and
weighty objects in flight – "heavy ignorance aloft to fly." This sarcasm is
deepened by the further hyperbole of the young men increasing learning and
adding majesty to grace; but the word "grace" prepares the way for the
subtlest innuendo of the third quatrain. There line 12 is highly deceptive.
With all the form and language of a compliment, the idea of gracing art with
graces is really only an extension of the preceding line's "dost but mend his
style", and is further diminished by the couplet's counter proposal that grace
should not merely content itself with gracing, but should be "all my art". As
the first quatrain has already made clear, such a hope is already a vain one,
and Sonnet 79 deals with the failure more desperately:

> Whilst I alone did call upon thy aid,
> My verse alone had all thy gentle grace,
> But now my gracious numbers are decayed,
> 4 And my sick muse doth give another place.
> I grant, sweet love, thy lovely argument
> Deserves the travail of a worthier pen,
> Yet what of thee thy poet doth invent
> 8 He robs thee of and pays it thee again.
> He lends thee virtue, and he stole that word
> From thy behaviour; beauty doth he give
> And found it in thy cheek; he can afford
> 12 No praise to thee but what in thee doth live.
>   Then thank him not for that which he doth say,
>   Since what he owes thee thou thyself dost pay.

The link with Sonnet 78 is by way of "grace", which is now the vehicle for
sarcasm in the first quatrain where the idealistic possibilities of "thy gentle
grace" are dissipated bitterly in the next line, in "my gracious numbers".
The sarcasm is maintained by "my sick muse" in line 4, a strange appellation
in the face of the opening line of 78, "So oft have I invoked thee for my
muse." The chief sense of "my sick muse doth give another place" is that the
poet retires to make way for a better poet, but the insinuation is that the
young man has done the replacing. By the second quatrain the sonnet seems
to be returning to the heavy sarcasm of its predecessor, with the
reintroduction of the charge of sexual promiscuity in "thy lovely argument"
and "the travail of a worthier pen."[3] Quite unexpectedly, though, line 7
abandons sarcasm with the almost magnanimous, certainly desperate,

reference to the rival as "thy poet". By the end of the line the reader has been moved from generalised sarcasm to the certain knowledge that allegiances have shifted.

The sestet increases the poet's desperation. In it he attempts to expose the opportunism of his rival, but has to admit that such opportunism works best; and behind it lies the familiar self-sufficiency of the young man which the poet has tried to break into since the opening of the sequence. The poet's claim is that the rival has failed, as any one of 'thy poets' is doomed to do — hyperbolically, since the young man is so far without peer that it is impossible to find a metaphorical equivalent for him, and sarcastically, because the young man's desire is for completely self-centred praise. The sestet glances mockingly at a poem which says that the young man is as virtuous as his virtue, his cheek as beautiful as his cheek — in other words, he alone is him — but the mockery falls apart with the poet's realisation that the rival has found a way of comparing the incomparable, or at the least of giving the young man the impression that he has done so.

The sestet of Sonnet 79 turns the rival's search for apt metaphor into a purely materialistic matter: "He robs . . . and pays it thee again./He lends . . . and he stole . . . beauty doth he give/And found it . . . he can afford . . . what he owes . . . thou thyself dost pay." As if in contrast, Sonnet 80 presents the poet's view of the betrayal from an entirely different metaphorical level, building the poem around a set of nautical images:

> O how I faint when I of you do write,
> Knowing a better spirit doth use your name,
> And in the praise thereof spends all his might,
> 4 To make me tongue-tied speaking of your fame.
> But, since your worth, wide as the ocean is,
> The humble as the proudest sail doth bear,
> My saucy bark, inferior far to his,
> 8 On your broad main doth wilfully appear.
> Your shallowest help will hold me up afloat,
> Whilst he upon your soundless deep doth ride;
> Or, being wracked, I am a worthless boat,
> 12 He of tall building and of goodly pride.
>   Then, if he thrive and I be cast away,
>   The worst was this: my love was my decay.

From the beginning of the second quatrain the image of the young man as an ocean, with his two poets as different kinds of boats, dominates the sonnet very much in the manner of the obtrusive metaphors I discussed in chapter 2.

The obvious way in which this metaphor is elaborated turns the sonnet into a ponderous game: such parenthetical asides as "wide as the ocean is", in line 5, and "being wracked", in line 11, point out to the reader the poet's insistence upon the details of his metaphor, and the metaphor gives rise to a series of only slightly witty puns which describe the young man's superficiality – "wilfully appear" is literally true because the boat is full of Will, like the horse which goes "wilful slow" in Sonnet 51, and "a worthless boat" provides a reverse pun because "worth" had been defined in line 5 as identical to the ocean, and a sunken boat ought, literally, to be 'worthful'. Only in the couplet does the punning become serious, in "cast away" which signals the young man's habitual behaviour towards those he has no more time for. "Cast away" also helps prepare the reader for the sonnet's return, in the last line, to the bitter language of abandonment. The development of the nautical metaphor is aimed at transforming the vision of the young man from one of immense tolerance – as wide as the ocean and able to bear vessels of any and all kinds – to an image of his vindictiveness, as a wrecker and caster away. This is achieved by a poetic impression of logic: the third quatrain seems to mark a conventional development by means of antitheses, the "or" of line 11 apparently introducing a parallel to the antithesis of lines 9 – 10. Instead, however, of contrasting the small support needed to keep the poet afloat with the huge support the rival demands, lines 11 – 12 switch to the system of values within which the young man operates – 'I am wrecked because I am worthless; he rides on because he is tall and proud.' No such development could have been expected from the introduction of the metaphor in the second quatrain, where a defence of the poet's ambition to continue writing to the young man is contained in the reason "But, since your worth, wide as the ocean is/The humble as the proudest sail doth bear"; but by the end of the sonnet "doth bear" has been revised to 'can bear, but can also wilfully destroy.'

To an extent Sonnet 80's opening quatrain prepares the reader for the deterioration of the central metaphor, since that quatrain carries its own poetic deterioration:

> O how I faint when I of you do write,
> Knowing a better spirit doth use your name,
> And in the praise thereof spends all his might,
> To make me tongue-tied speaking of your fame.

The deterioration is not merely a matter of moving from fainting to simply being tongue-tied, although that is part of it. "O how I faint when I of you do write" is a solidly conventional sonnet opening – any follower of

Petrarch might address his mistress in those words — and the reader expects it to be followed by a catalogue of the young man's beauty and the poet's inadequacy to capture it. The rest of the quatrain is, then, rather an anti-climax: lines 2 – 3 imply that the poet faints not because of the vision of the beauty which he has to describe, but because he has a competitor who seems to have more *energia* than him, and line 4 caps it by implying that that this rival poet is mainly motivated by competition too. "Thereof" in line 3 is particularly saucy in the way in which it restricts the application of "praise", making it refer solely to the young man's "name", where we might have expected a wider, less opportunistic, frame of reference.

In the bravado of its metaphor, pursued even to its ship wrecking conclusion, Sonnet 80 embodies a substantial poetic challenge both to the rival and to the young man. Lying behind the whole sonnet is the sense that love poetry is always based on rivalry even if there is no rival poet about, and in the undercutting of the Petrarchan opening line and then the sea metaphor the poet gives plenty of warning to the young man, both of the limits to his vulnerability and of his capacity to retaliate. The couplet repeats this in miniature:

> Then, if he thrive and I be cast away,
> The worst was this: my love was my decay.

Its first line gives the power of making thrive or casting away to the young man, but its second line shows that power to be a delusion, claiming instead that the poet has full responsibility for his own decay — and "decay" is a word whose meaning the previous sonnet had limited to poetic, rather than physical, weakness ("But now my gracious numbers are decayed").[4]

At this point the rival poet group seems to be broken up by a sonnet which has no relevance to it; almost any reordering of the sequence would take out Sonnet 81 and have 82 follow 80, its opening line "I grant thou wert not married to my muse" taking up the complaint at having been cast away. In contrast Sonnet 81 would seem to fit the immortalisation group much better:

> Or I shall live your epitaph to make,
> Or you survive when I in earth am rotten,
> From hence your memory death cannot take,
> 4   Although in me each part will be forgotten.
> Your name from hence immortal life shall have,
> Though I, once gone, to all the world must die.
> The earth can yield me but a common grave,

8   When you entombed in men's eyes shall lie.
     Your monument shall be my gentle verse,
     Which eyes not yet created shall o'er-read,
     And tongues to be your being shall rehearse,
12   When all the breathers of this world are dead,
       You still shall live — such virtue hath my pen —
     Where breath most breathes, ev'n in the mouths of men.

The difference between this sonnet and the earlier immortalisation sonnets lies in its plain, epigrammatic nature, reinforced by the austerity of its metaphorising. William Empson pointed out the peculiar reading experience created by this sonnet when he wrote that 'any two consecutive lines, except 2–3 and 10–11 for accidental reasons, make a complete sentence when separated from their context'.[5] The reader encounters throughout a constant chopping backward and forward, in the manner of the opening lines' antithesis "Or I shall live your epitaph to make,/Or you survive when I in earth am rotten"; and almost no progress is made beyond this antithesis, which includes the survival or death of the poet, the survival or death of the young man, and the survival of poetry ("your epitaph to make"). With some simplification but no real distortion, this pattern traces the development of the argument:

        line   1   I live (you die)
                2   You live, I die
                3   Your memory will not die
                4   My memory will die
                5   Your memory will live
                6   My memory will die
                7   My memory will die
                8   Your memory will live (entombed)
                9   Your memory will live in my verse
               10   My verse will live
               11   Your memory will live
               12   All who are alive today will die
            13/14   Your memory will live in my verse

This adds up to an ironic reconsideration of poetic immortalisation. Sonnets 78–80 had challenged the young man's treacherous preference for the rival poet by developing the retaliatory possibilities of the poet's own verse, and now Sonnet 81 puts the retaliation into action by combining epigram and epitaph. What metaphor there is emerges in the second quatrain, where, following the poet's "common grave", the young man is given a tomb in men's eyes. In the sestet the tomb's monument is defined as the sonnet itself which, like all tombstones, will be read over by future generations. The couplet comes very close to poetic travesty – compare the cod sonnet in *Love's Labour's Lost*, ending "No thought can think . . .", which is not greatly removed from "Where breath most breathes . . ." – but it is saved by its backward glance at line 12's "all the breathers of this world", a sweeping dismissal of the whole generation of poet, rival poet, and young man. The couplet promises a peculiar immortality, a kind of still life – "You still shall live" – contained for eternity inside men's mouths. For the young man the casting away of the poet and taking on of a rival is a matter of ephemeral importance, like maintaining a fashionable wardrobe. Sonnet 81 indicates that poets are not so easily discarded. They have a power which transcends fashion – the power over future life and death. The grimmest threat of all in the sonnet is the pun on "rehearse" in line 11, which combines the prospect of poetic immortality – the young man's existence being repeated verbally through future time – with the threat that in bringing this about the poet is in reality perpetually burying him – to "hearse" over and over again.

Had the reader encountered this sonnet earlier in the sequence he might reasonably have interpreted it as a genuine pledge by the poet to immortalize the young man; and the threats which I have described would, at most, seem covert ones, subordinate to the sonnet's main theme. But seeing it set in the context of the rival poet group the reader is more attuned to the poet's concern with his own vulnerability; and, more specifically, its formal parallels with the preceding sonnet, number 80, encourage him to be suspicious of its phrasing. The opening antithesis, with the first two lines each beginning with "or", continues the alternations of Sonnet 80's sestet, where the antithetical play is similarly signalled by "or" at the beginning of line 11 – "Or, being wracked, I am a worthless boat." In Sonnet 80 the antitheses are between the rival poets, both in the help they are given – "your shallowest help"/"your soundless deep" – and in the difference of quality between them – "worthless boat"/"goodly pride", "thrive"/"cast away". Now the opening of Sonnet 81 moves the antithesis from poet with rival to poet with subject, and the reader's difficulty comes in trying to assess its tone:

> Or I shall live your epitaph to make,
> Or you survive when I in earth am rotten.

Literally, as in my summary of these lines earlier, the choice is between the poet's survival and the young man's: who will live the longer? But such a casual question – as if there were no importance in the choice – can hardly satisfy a reader for whom the sequence has so often emphasised the contrast between the young man's worth and the poet's worthlessness. It may be accepted, however, if the reader carries into the sonnet the casualness of the young man's abandonment of the poet in Sonnets 78–80; in other words, 'whether I live to write your epitaph or whether I die is all one to you.' Taken this way these lines represent the nadir of the poet's treatment by the young man, and the rest of the sonnet exacts retribution for it by actually writing the epitaph. On the other hand, the reader may, remembering the earlier promises of immortality, see the lines as an urgent demand that the poet be not allowed to decay so quickly as Sonnet 80 had predicted, for he still has to fulfil his appointed task of immortalising the young man. If so, then the sonnet's deterioration is all the more menacing: it begins by concentrating on the young man's life and the poet's death and ends by entombing the young man.

The young man's final entombing in the couplet is in men's mouths. That slightly bizarre resting place is more pointedly defined in the phrase "where breath most breathes". In a sense – probably the dominant sense of the line – this conveys a promise of the greatest possible immortality, to be for ever where the breath of life is at its strongest, and it is given greater force by "breathers of this world" in line 12, where men are defined by their most basic action. In contrast, though, the reader has other associations for the word "breath", as the closest thing to nothing, the least noticeable and least distinctive act of a human being. "Breathers of the world" is proleptic: as an equivalent for the simple word 'people' the phrase is mere padding, and its influence on line 14 is to emphasise the insignificance of survival in a place where breath is at its most breathlike. The couplet's lesson is that words are breath, but whether they be 'breath' in the sense of life-giving and sustaining, or 'breath' in their insignificance, is the subject of the remaining sonnets in the rival poet group.

Sonnets 82 and 83 move through a series of possible definitions of words as they are used by the rival poets and the poet himself. The rivals use "dedicated words" indiscriminately, "blessing every book"; their fashion is a "fresher stamp of the time-bettering days", in essence only the "strained touches" of rhetoric. Most damningly, their words have the nature of unnecessary cosmetics, an image introduced in the couplet of Sonnet 82 – "And their gross painting might be better used,/Where cheeks need blood; in thee it is abused" – a contrast with the poet's view of his own words, given in the preceding two lines – "Thou truly fair wert truly sympathized/In true plain words by thy true-telling friend." Sonnet 83 takes up the image of the rival's – or rivals' – cosmetic words, but the contrast which it develops is not, as Sonnet 82 leads us to expect, between one kind of language and another, but between language and silence:

> I never saw that you did painting need,
> And therefore to your fair no painting set;
> I found, or thought I found, you did exceed
> 4 The barren tender of a poet's debt;
> And therefore have I slept in your report,
> That you yourself, being extant, well might show
> How far a modern quill doth come too short,
> 8 Speaking of worth, what worth in you doth grow.
> This silence for my sin you did impute,
> Which shall be most my glory, being dumb;
> For I impair not beauty, being mute,
> 12 When others would give life, and bring a tomb.
>   There lives more life in one of your fair eyes
>   Than both your poets can in praise devise.

Around the middle of the second quatrain the reader becomes aware that the poet is not excusing the inadequacy of his praise, but its non-existence. The temptation, at first, is to regard this as sarcasm – set against the young man's immense need for praise the poet's words will seem hardly to exist – but the third quatrain emphasises so much the poet's silence – "silence", "dumb", "mute" – that it becomes an unmistakable act of will on his part, a refusal to speak. In the terms of 'praise' the sestet is as absolute a statement as even the young man can hope to find: he is so beautiful that any attempt to describe him not merely impairs that beauty, but annihilates it as surely as death will do. As if in contrast to the poet and his rival, the young man is himself a poem, extant, showing and speaking of his own beauty. In a quiet but unmistakeable irony "your poets" in the last line echoes "thy poet" in Sonnet 79. Now the poet and his rival have come together in the face of a greater rival whose poem has no need for words at all.

Both Sonnets 84 and 85 continue to develop variations upon the poet's silence. Sonnet 84 advances the idea that it is undesirable to write poetry to the young man: his very uniqueness – "that you alone are you" is the way the sonnet puts it – makes it impossible to use metaphor; and without metaphor poetry disappears. The only poetry is what the young man contains, as line 9 makes clear in describing what a poet must do to make his style admired everywhere: "Let him but copy what in you is writ." Only the couplet qualifies this vision of total self-sufficiency:

> You to your beauteous blessings add a curse,
> Being fond on praise, which makes your praises worse.

Sonnet 85 continues to develop this idea of there being a host of praisers, and presents the poet ironically as a tongue-tied observer:

> My tongue-tied muse in manners holds her still,
> While comments of your praise, richly compiled,
> Reserve their character with golden quill
> 4 And precious phrase by all the muses filed.
> I think good thoughts, whilst others write good words,
> And like unlettered clerk still cry amen,
> To every hymn that able spirit affords,
> 8 In polished form of well-refined pen.
> Hearing you praised, I say, " 'tis so," "'tis true,"
> And to the most of praise add something more;
> But that is in my thought, whose love to you,
> 12 Though words come hindmost, holds his rank before.
> Then others for the breath of words respect,
> Me for my dumb thoughts, speaking in effect.

Here, in the couplet, the "breath" of Sonnet 81 is put into its proper place, the mere emptiness of words when opposed to the sincerity of unarticulated thought. In many ways this sonnet is a complete simplification of what has gone before: the ludicrousness of the poet's self-representation marks the sonnet as belonging to a run of the mill Elizabethan sonnet sequence, where the poet's strange social behaviour is caused by his being besotted on his mistress. The couplet, too, is entirely fitting. Its demand would be naive at any time, but coming after a group of sonnets which relate the cut-throat world of poetic patronage, where poetic rhetoric is the chief coin, it seems almost bathetic. Through Sonnet 83 and the three quatrains of 84 the poet's silence in the face of the young man's worth had taken on a growing solemnity; then the unexpected sarcastic twist in 84's couplet prepares for a sonnet in which the silence is travestied as much as golden rhetoric had been. Now, in Sonnet 85, the words of the rival and the silence of the poet are placed at bizarre extremes: able spirit against unlettered clerk, tongue-tied muse against richly compiled precious phrase, Amen and 'tis so, 'tis true against the polished thought of a well refined pen. In demonstrating the deadening effect which the young man has upon his poets, either completely silencing them or requiring them perpetually to mint golden words, the sonnet finds a powerful metaphorical equivalent for the illogical extreme of the argument. The idea of the poet using words to demonstrate why words are inferior to thoughts is set against the representation of the young man as a subject who requires more and more precious words, but who is expected, in the couplet, to recognise the value of unspoken thought.

There can hardly be any further development from such complete silence, and the final sonnets in the group, 86 and 87, demonstrate, in radically different ways, the inadequacy of words at a time when silence is the only respectable form of expression. Sonnet 86 is one further, and final attempt at explaining why the poet has been struck dumb:

> Was it the proud full sail of his great verse,
> Bound for the prize of all too precious you,
> That did my ripe thoughts in my brain inhearse,
> 4   Making their tomb the womb wherein they grew?
> Was it his spirit, by spirits taught to write
> Above a mortal pitch, that struck me dead?
> No, neither he, nor his compeers by night
> 8   Giving him aid, my verse astonished.
> He, nor that affable familiar ghost
> Which nightly gulls him with intelligence,
> As victors, of my silence cannot boast;
> 12   I was not sick of any fear from thence.
>   But when your countenance filled up his line,
>   Then lacked I matter, that enfeebled mine.

The details of this sonnet are sufficient to make the normal reader as confused as they make happy the searcher for biographical clues. Since I claim membership of the first group and lack any biographical key to the sequence, my inclination is to fall back happily on Stephen Booth's measured comments on lines 5–12: 'These references to ghostly familiars seem too sinister to describe a rival muse. They sound as though they allude to some specific details about some specific rival poet. . . . The lines remain puzzling and obscure.'[6] The description of these lines as 'sinister' is pertinent to the development of the whole rival poet group. Here, even without our knowing the implications of the spirit tutelage or the visits of the familiar ghost, the general sense of supernatural soliciting is clear. The sonnet's argument is that the poet has been struck down in a way which ought only to be explained by supernatural interference; and while denying the various possible interferences, the poet describes, in reverse, the development of his own present and potential suffering. In the first quatrain he is buried; he is struck dead in the second, sick in the third, and enfeebled in the couplet.[7]

Parallel with this, but in proper order, is a developed belittling of the rival poet – all the more striking after the magnificence of the sonnet's opening image. Even if we connect billowing sails with the breath of words in Sonnet 85's couplet, the idea of a galleon sailing towards a valuable prize invokes admiration both for the power of the rival's verse and for the strength of his aspirations. But this vision is degraded through the second and third quatrains where the rival is first deprived of responsibility for his powers and then seen as a dupe.[8] The couplet returns to the conceit which dominates the rival poet group, that the young man is the great source of poetic inspiration as well as being the only subject for great poetry; but here inspiration is reduced to filling up a line, a phrase chosen to recall the opening line's "proud full sail" and to insinuate the emptiness of the rival's style and the young man's influence. The contrast of the rival's inflated line and the poet's loss of matter is one final expression of the extremes to which both have been driven with such a subject to write to.

The final line of Sonnet 86 – "Then lacked I matter, that enfeebled mine" – comes close to showing enfeebled poetry in action, with the abruptness of its caesura and the forced stress upon "that". The final sonnet in the group, Sonnet 87, demonstrates another kind of poetic enfeeblement:

> Farewell, thou art too dear for my possessing,
> And like enough thou know'st thy estimate.
> The charter of thy worth gives thee releasing;
> 4 My bonds in thee are all determinate.
> For how do I hold thee but by thy granting,
> And for that riches where is my deserving?
> The cause of this fair gift in me is wanting,
> 8 And so my patent back again is swerving.
> Thyself thou gav'st, thy own worth then not knowing,
> Or me, to whom thou gav'st it, else mistaking;
> So thy great gift, upon misprison growing,
> 12 Comes home again, on better judgement making.
>   Thus have I had thee as a dream doth flatter:
>   In sleep a king, but waking no such matter.

As a farewell poem this sonnet is almost an exercise in how not to say goodbye elegantly. The most obvious handicap which the poet sets himself is the rhyming: feminine rhymes best fit a comical poem, or a piece of grotesquery like Sonnet 20, but here they stand at odds with the declared solemn intent of the sonnet. The metaphor, too, is conspicuously ill chosen. Legal and financial imagery dominates several sonnets in the sequence, but never so narrowly as here. The opening lines promise, with the pun on "dear" and the ironic tone of "like enough" and "estimate", a depth which the rest of the sonnet determinedly hides. The reader ends having merely pursued the surface argument – that the poet is too cheap and the young man too dear for one to possess the other – there having been no encouragement to dig deeper than that, and the rhymes having played their important part in supporting the triviality of the metaphor. It is worth emphasising that there is a genuine complexity in the third quatrain, where the young man's "self" seems to be separated from his will – it has the capacity to return of its own accord – but the sonnet's form encourages the reader to ignore the potentially interesting implications of this distinction. The couplet, though, is quite unexpected. Superficially it caps the sonnet's argument by contrasting recollected wealth with present poverty, present-ing them in the radically different images of king and slave. The final word, "matter", recalls the couplet of Sonnet 86, where "matter" is primarily poetic material (the young man's absence took away the poet's subject matter). But here "matter" carries the more general sense of 'substance' or 'value', and it helps complete the ironies of the couplet where the superficial statement 'I (the poet) am a king in sleep, but a slave awake' is paralleled by the innuendo that 'I have had you (possessed poetically and/or sexually) as a king while you sleep, but you are nothing like that when you are awake' – and the innuendo is made the more pointed by the fact that the sonnet's argument has been concerned with the young man's various degrees of consciousness, not being aware of his value when he gave his gift, and taking it back when he becomes properly aware.

Sonnets 86 and 87 demonstrate, as their imagery implies, an enfeeblement and impoverishment of love poetry. In both, the couplets play on sexual frustration: in 86 the rival has his line filled up while the poet lacks matter, and in 87 the underlying image ("had" in sleep) is of a nocturnal emission. The threat at the beginning of the rival poet group had been the prospect of a more talented competitor – one which earlier sonnets in the sequence had foreshadowed – but the greater threat emerges in the nature of the subject of both poets, the self-seeking and ever-demanding young man. In the war between him and the poet the poet's strength had been deployed in the immortalization sonnets: poetry as powerful as the poet's can bury the young man. The young man's response is made here when he reduces that powerful poetry first to silence, and then to a metaphorical degradation worse than silence.

7 'Power to Hurt': The Young Man

The reader's flexibility of response is most strenuously tested when the sequence comes to deal, as it has always promised to do, with the young man's character. In sonnet groups like 67–70 and 94–96 the poet's strategy is to criticise and dissect while he preserves the gestures and expressions of sincere admiration; and this is not simply a matter of providing ironic or parody compliments, for these sonnets go deeper and analyse the actual nature of complimentary poetry. They use its forms of expression, metaphors, and images seriously – almost solemnly, at times – and in doing so reveal the viciousness inherent in the poet-sonnet-subject relationship. Later in this chapter I shall look closely at these two groups of sonnets, but I can begin to illustrate my basic point by first considering a pair of sonnets from earlier in the sequence, Sonnets 27 and 28. Their theme is a typical sonnet one, the poet's absence from his lover. Sonnet 27 describes the poet's inability to find rest, either by day or by night:

> Weary with toil, I haste me to my bed,
> The dear repose for limbs with travail tired,
> But then begins a journey in my head
> 4 To work my mind, when body's work's expired.
> For then my thoughts, from far where I abide,
> Intend a zealous pilgrimage to thee,
> And keep my drooping eyelids open wide,
> 8 Looking on darkness which the blind do see.
> Save that my soul's imaginary sight
> Presents thy shadow to my sightless view,
> Which like a jewel hung in ghastly night,
> 12 Makes black night beauteous, and her old face new.
>   Lo thus by day my limbs, by night my mind,
>   For thee, and for myself, no quiet find.[1]

The primary elements of the sonnet are entirely conventional, including the poet's labour by day, inability to sleep at night, the sanctity of the loved one (here the object of a pilgrimage), and the transcendent power of the loved one's image. The reader is hardly likely to press these matters far, but it is worth noting that the third quatrain is slightly deceptive. It seems to propose some kind of qualification to the suffering described in the octave, for "save that" might well introduce the one contrasting element to what has gone before. It turns out, however, that the jewel-like image of the young man is only one further aspect of night's disquiet. The impression is that to look on such an image must be preferable to looking on darkness, but the couplet makes no such distinction: "thus" refers as much to the third as to the first two quatrains, and "for thee", in the final line, strikes a curious note, as if the conjuring up of the image had been part of a mutual restlessness. Although the image of the jewel in the line 11 has a primarily figurative function, it still carries enough literal weight to leave in the reader's mind the impression of the young man hanging in space in front of the poet. That kind of transport through the night is a physical disturbance of the young man as well as a reflection of the poet's mental disturbance, so that the reader is prepared for the mutual restlessness with which the sonnet closes.

Sonnet 28 completes the description of the poet's restlessness, and, like Sonnet 27, it creates apparently unnecessary difficulties in its third quatrain:

> How can I then return in happy plight
> That am debarred the benefit of rest –
> When day's oppression is not eased by night,
> 4 But day by night and night by day oppressed?
> And each, though enemies to either's reign,
> Do in consent shake hands to torture me,
> The one by toil, the other to complain
> 8 How far I toil, still farther off from thee.
> I tell the day to please him thou art bright,
> And dost him grace when clouds do blot the heaven.
> So flatter I the swart-complexioned night,
> 12 When sparkling stars twire not, thou guil'st the even.
>   But day doth daily draw my sorrows longer,
>   And night doth nightly make grief's length seem stronger.[2]

The sonnet continues the day–night motif of Sonnet 27, but gives it an increased metaphorisation, so that both day and night become fully fledged personifications, ending in the couplet as outright torturers. There the poet is on the rack, being drawn longer by day and having his grief's length strengthened by night. Not only that, but day acts "daily" and night "nightly". These adverbs have a double sense: day not only does its action every day and night every night, but each does it in a way peculiar to itself, day in the fashion of day, night in the fashion of night. Their personification begins openly in the second quatrain, where day and night shake hands, but it is foreshadowed in lines 3–4 by their characterisation as oppressors and enemies of each other. The poet's answers to this pair of tyrants come in the third quatrain, but in a highly ambiguous way. The syntax of the four lines seems designed to slip out of the reader's grasp. For instance, "to please him" in line 9 has two distinct applications: it may refer back to "tell" and be the reason for the telling, or it may be the beginning of the direct speech, qualifying "thou are bright", and giving the reason for that brightness. In the first case "him" signifies the day, in the second it signifies the young man. Line 10 is similarly inconclusive. It may stand as a continuation of the direct speech, with "him" as the young man again, or it may take up the poet's action as a parallel with "tell", with "him" as the day. And lines 11–12 are no clearer: "When sparkling stars twire not" may be the beginning of direct speech to the night, and therefore be a qualification of "guil'st", or it may continue line 11 and explain the condition upon which such flattery is paid. The complications of this ambiguity are numerous. To take one example, "flatter" in line 11 might seem to resolve the difficulty of line 9; i.e. 'So flatter I the night as I pleased the day.' However, not only would that require the reader to undertake a difficult retrospective revision of the earlier line if he had chosen to read "to please him" as a continuation of "tell", but it ignores the possibility that "flatter" might instead be a parallel to "dost him grace" in line 10; i.e. 'So flatter I the night as I did the day grace.'

The complications increase the more one tries to sort the lines out, and it is this deliberate inconclusiveness which allows the poet to achieve his most surprising effect. Any reader of Sonnets 27 and 28 (and most critics) happily accepts these two sonnets as workings out of a conventional theme; but the third quatrain of Sonnet 28 uses the accumulation of conventionalities through the two sonnets – at their most extreme point, where day and night have become personified tyrants – to make treacherously pertinent points about the young man. The direct speech which the poet delivers to day and night, in its very confusion, persuades the reader to see one other addressee. "Thou art bright" and "thou guil'st the even" are typical addresses to the young man – in other words, the quatrain which takes the pair of sonnets to their conventional climax quite unexpectedly exposes the young man's tyrannical desire for flattery. This revelation not only makes the couplet more sinister, but it throws an ironic light backwards upon Sonnet 27's third quatrain. That quatrain is pure praise – the conjured image like a jewel which beautifies and rejuvenates the night. We saw how, despite its transcendence, the image failed to do what the quatrain's syntax indicated it might do, namely give the poet some rest. The third quatrain of Sonnet 28 now helps provide the reason for that failure: such praise is flattery, done to please a tyrant. Perhaps, after all, the two sonnets are as much poems about poetry as they are about being absent from a lover. "Toil" is the word which marks both: Sonnet 27 opens "Weary with toil", and whatever the toil is, its sense is echoed through the octave, in "travail", "a journey in my head", "to work my mind", "body's work", and "a zealous pilgrimage". In Sonnet 28 "toil" is repeated in describing the torture of day and night — "The one by toil, the other to complain/How far I toil, still farther off from thee". In the terms of the sonnets' convention "toil" defines any work undertaken in the absence of the young man, but in the terms of their third quatrains "toil" is specifically poet's work, the day and night search for images of flattery.[3]

Images of flattery recur throughout the sequence, often to be reinterpreted, redefined, or revalued, as the poet relates them to his real friend and their real situation.[4] The group of four sonnets, 67–70, works in this way, with 67 and 68 flattering the young man's beauty and exterior values, and 69 and 70 redefining them through an oblique analysis of his inward state.[5] Sonnet 67 actually opens with a quatrain which promises rich sarcasm and ambiguity, but the rest of the sonnet hardly sustains the promise:

> Ah wherefore with infection should he live,
> And with his presence grace impiety,
> That sin by him advantage should achieve,
> 4   And lace itself with his society?
> Why should false painting imitate his cheek,
> And steal dead seeing of his living hue?
> Why should poor beauty indirectly seek
> 8   Roses of shadow, since his rose is true?
> Why should he live, now nature bankrout is,
> Beggared of blood to blush through lively veins?
> For she hath no exchequer now but his,
> 12   And, proud of many, lives upon his gains.
>   O him she stores, to show what wealth she had,
>   In days long since, before these last so bad.

"Why should" is the basic question of the sonnet; more specifically, "why should he live", the question which opens the first and third quatrains. As it turns out, the question is not to be taken literally, only hyperbolically — but the calculated ambiguity of "with" in the sonnet's opening line does not make this clear from the start. Only the best intentioned reader will instinctively take it to mean 'next to' — i.e. 'why should he live in the same community as infection?' — and reject its other possible meaning of 'containing' infection. That second sense, of course, removes the meaning of "live" from the state of inhabiting to the more basic state of breathing: 'Why does such an infected thing still live?' or, if that is too extreme, 'Why does he allow himself to live in such an infected body/mind, without doing something to cure it?' But even a best intentioned reader will have problems in line 2, where the ironies of a second "with" and the paradox of gracing impiety create innuendoes which can not be avoided; and the rest of the quatrain does nothing to play down the apparent moral objection which the poet feels about his subject's behaviour.

The action of the rest of the sonnet is to transform the apparent hostility of the first quatrain into a joke. The second and third quatrains make it clear, after all, that the best intentioned reader was right, and we should all of us have read the first four lines with our conventional spectacles on: not 'Why should he live at all?', but merely a poetic way of saying how fortunate such a sinful world is to have so pure a creature in it. Reduced to its essentials the sonnet turns out not to be about such moral extremes as infection, impiety, and sin, but about cosmetics instead: in effect, 'Why does the world continue to paint itself when he, who needs no paint, is so inimitably beautiful?' Of course, the question contains its own answer, pointing to the young man's paradoxical fate. The world uses cosmetics in order to try to reach such an inimitable state itself, with the result that the young man must suffer a double anguish. One element of this is described in the first quatrain: by being so beautiful he encourages the infection, impiety, sin, or whatever other word we may use to signify cosmetic painting (or be signified by, for the dependence of the first quatrain upon the second and third may be the other way round; i.e. that cosmetics are the symbols of a sinful world, which, of course, does give the sonnet the moral point it appears to claim in the first quatrain). The second element is that the young man becomes a victim of these impious forces. A strong undertone of the sonnet is that of Nature's blood-sucking of the young man. Thus line 6, "And steal dead seeing of his living hue", describes the action of "false painting": basically it means that their attempts at copying his complexion only result in second rate imitations, but the phrasal compression of the line points to the ambiguity inherent in "steal . . . of", so that their imitation actually drains his cheeks of blood.[6]

Something similar occurs in the third quatrain:

> Why should he live, now nature bankrout is,
> Beggared of blood to blush through lively veins?

> For she hath no exchequer now but his,
> And, proud of many, lives upon his gains.

Here the sense of the sonnet demands that we pause at "live" and relate the rest of the quatrain to nature; but the syntax is not clear, and the reader is tempted to regard "now nature bankrout is" as an isolated qualifying clause, taking the question as "Why should he live . . . Beggared of blood to blush through lively veins?" The couplet finally answers the quatrains' questions, but in a way which increases the young man's victimization:

> O him she stores, to show what wealth she had,
> In days long since, before these last so bad.

He is, it seems, the one valuable asset of bankrupt nature, kept for almost museum purposes.

In a way, then, Sonnet 67's transformation from moral indignation to hyperbolic praise may not be to its subject's liking, since the praise is bound up with implications that the young man is not, after all, so young. Sonnet 68 hardly seems designed to tone down that implication for from its opening line it plays with double entendres of ageing:

> Thus is his cheek the map of days outworn,
> When beauty lived and died as flowers do now,
> Before these bastard signs of fair were borne,
> 4   Or durst inhabit on a living brow –
> Before the golden tresses of the dead,
> The right of sepulchres, were shorn away,
> To live a second life on second head –
> 8   Ere beauty's dead fleece made another gay.
> In him those holy antique hours are seen,
> Without all ornament, itself and true,
> Making no summer of another's green,
> 12   Robbing no old to dress his beauty new;
>   And him as for a map doth nature store,
>   To show false art what beauty was of yore.

It is possible to say that Sonnet 67 never entirely shook off the insinuations of its opening lines. If that is so, then this sonnet makes full redress. It continues, as I have indicated, the undertone of the young man as a victim – one who is being aged by nature – and it sees in his ageing a sign of complete nobility.

Others avoid looking old by using cosmetics; and where Sonnet 67 had characterised cosmetics as the paintings of sin, this sonnet sees them, by way of the wig, as a kind of grave-robbing. In contrast the young man prefers the truth of nature, to live and die as flowers do. So, although a phrase like "the map of days outworn" points to a lined and faded cheek, and although the young man contains "holy antique hours", and although he refuses to make another summer for himself out of someone else's hair, neither he nor the reader should feel defensive or apologetic about it.[7] The result may be exterior decay, but it signifies moral integrity, and that, it seems, is the point of the weighty digression against the fashion of wearing wigs, a typical Shakespearean attack on affectation, and, in implicit contrast, is the typical Shakespearean 'praise of whatever is plain, honest, direct, natural; genuine.'[8]

There are, however, a number of things in this sonnet which might make the reader feel that the digression is not wholeheartedly intended. For one thing, its length in regard to its subject makes it almost a miniature example of a failed objective correlative. I suppose that it is possible to feel deeply about wigs, but such feeling will fail to convince when it comes so soon after a sonnet like 66, which catalogues the real evils of the world, and gives those evils no more than a line each. Here the reader hardly anticipates the sustained diatribe against wigs – that it will be so sustained – before he is half way through it: the first quatrain seem still to be talking about cosmetic paints and to be using "brow" as a general term for 'face'. With a turn of wit the second quatrain takes up the literal sense of "durst inhabit on a living brow", and extends the attack on cosmetics to an attack on wigs, but there it all stops, and the rest of the sonnet, up to the couplet, goes over the same ground, coming up with increasingly bizarre definitions for a wig – the last one being as grass in line 11.

Critical comment on this sonnet has often taken its cue from Malone's 1780 edition and referred the reader to Bassanio's speech in *The Merchant of Venice* III, ii, 72 – 101, to show Shakespeare's concern with the evil of wigs. Putting aside the dubious morality of anything which Bassanio says, it is worth comparing the passages. Both the sonneteer and Bassanio are at their most intense when picturing the wig's previous possessor. The sonnet's idea is more extreme than Bassanio's: "Before the golden tresses of the dead,/The right of sepulchres, were shorn away,/To live a second life on second head" seems to envisage the actual cutting of hair from the corpse to make up the wig. Even so, the effect is not at all gruesome, for "golden tresses of the dead" and "right of sepulchres" provide a rhetorical gloss to overlay the reality of the corpse – as does "beauty's dead fleece" in line 8, where "dead" loses most of its literal weight when offset by "fleece". In contrast Bassanio's words merely see the wig as hair taken from a living person who in course of time has died:

> Look on beauty
> And you shall see 'tis purchased by the weight,
> Which therein works a miracle in nature,
> Making them lightest that wear most of it;
> So are those crisped snaky golden locks
> Which make such wanton gambols with the wind
> Upon supposed fairness often known
> To be the dowry of a second head —
> The skull that bred them in the sepulchre.

The effect is the opposite of the sonnet. The description moves from the beautiful flowing locks to the grave, and focusses finally on the skull out of which the hairs grew. For all of its moral outrage Sonnet 68 avoids any such sense of the skull beneath the skin — instead it remains content with moral generalities. The capping of both descriptions completes the contrast. Bassanio finds a set of images of grandeur and menace,

> Thus ornament is but the guiled shore
> To a most dangerous sea; the beauteous scarf
> Veiling an Indian beauty; in a word,
> The seeming truth which cunning time puts on
> To entrap the wisest

while the sonnet retreats into the vagueness of "holy antique hours" and a couplet which restates the couplet of Sonnet 67, with the added archaism of "yore":[9]

> And him as for a map doth nature store,
> To show false art what beauty was of yore.

My point is that Sonnet 68 is worthy and dull, by design. It completes the expunging of Sonnet 67's opening innuendoes, and repaints the picture of a worthy subject whose untouched exterior is an embodiment of his outstanding integrity; but its character is that of a formal set piece, a poetic opportunity to berate the failings of the age. Its values, though, remain values of appearance, and its greatest achievement is to have completed the conversion of "infection", "impiety", and "sin", which, in the opening quatrain of Sonnet 67, had seemed to usher in at least one sonnet concerned with interior values. Instead Sonnets 67 and 68 together make that moral vocabulary apply merely to the exterior person – those who use cosmetics against him who does not. True, the reader might feel that such exterior matters are pertinent guides to inner values, but the couplet which closes 68 hardly extends the argument in its simple oppositions of false art and nature, and false art and beauty. As it happens, though, Sonnets 69 and 70 move, in contrast, to the young man's inner world. This is Sonnet 69:

> Those parts of thee that the world's eye doth view
> Want nothing that the thought of hearts can mend.
> All tongues, the voice of souls, give thee that due,
> 4 Uttering bare truth, even so as foes commend.
> Thy outward thus with outward praise is crowned;
> But those same tongues that give thee so thine own,
> In other accents do this praise confound
> 8 By seeing farther than the eye hath shown.
> They look into the beauty of thy mind,
> And that in guess they measure by thy deeds;
> Then, churls, their thoughts – although their eyes were kind –
> 12 To thy fair flower add the rank smell of weeds;
> But why thy odour matcheth not thy show,
> The soil is this, that thou dost common grow.[10]

As Sonnets 67 and 68 treated the young man's beautiful appearance, this treats the beauty of his mind. I would expect any reader to make so simple a connection, and to see 69 as an extension of the analysis of the young man's character, half completed in the preceding two sonnets. The one change which might prevent him from doing so is from the third to the second person, from "thus is his cheek" to "those parts of thee" – but the change is, itself, part of the development of the analysis, the movement from "him" to "thee" being a movement from public to private poetry. In 67 and 68 the poet had proclaimed the beauty of his friend, and the integrity which it symbolises. Now Sonnet 69 abandons the claim that a man's exterior can be regarded in such a way; in fact it swings to the other extreme and comes close to implying that a goodly outside must inevitably hide something rotten. Most significantly, though, the sonnet is about expression and observation, tongues and eyes, and as he pursues its argument the reader learns to question the values which Sonnets 67 and 68 had appeared to support.

Sonnet 69's opening quatrain is ominous, holding the promise of some imminent qualification. "Those parts of thee that . . . want nothing" prepares us for consideration of the other parts, not so far analysed, which do want something. Likewise "the world's eye" is an obvious target to be shot down, in the manner of 'what the world sees is this, but what I see . . .' As it happens, the qualifications are made, but not in the anticipated way.

The opening line of the second quatrain is both a summary of what has gone before and an introduction to the more damaging analysis of the young man's interior state:

> Thy outward thus with outward praise is crowned

Like many apparently simple lines in the sonnets its implications are astonishingly various; I shall summarise a few of them here. For a start, "outward praise" is marvellously dismissive, and to be crowned with it introduces a host of stock associations of monarchs besotted on flatterers. More specifically, "outward praise" has its poetic sense, as if it described a particular type of praise, the type which writers (and flatterers) usually give to their subject's exterior. The effect of the line is to put the whole of the first quatrain into a potentially different context, as if it were one example of this kind of praise. Thus, "those parts of thee . . . want nothing that the thought of hearts can mend" is a good example of outward praise — not, of course, to be taken wholly seriously. Similarly, the idea that tongues could be the voice of souls is a definition typical of those which flattering poets must give, to support both their own work and the idea that words are more important than thoughts. I would add, finally, that the first "outward" in the line might equally well be read as an adjective defining "thus" — the outward thus being the one which had opened the previous sonnet in the typical manner of public poetry, "Thus is his cheek the map of days outworn . . ."

By now the reader is well aware that he is in the world of the private poet, and he is prepared for a second quatrain which will contrast the poet's vision with the words of the flattering world and the public poet; but this contrast never happens. Instead the poet stays loyal and presents his subject with a world of eyes and tongues which have not remained content either with what they have seen or with what they have said about that sight:

> Thy outward thus with outward praise is crowned;
> But those same tongues that give thee so thine own,
> In other accents do this praise confound
> By seeing farther than the eye hath shown.

The world's eye does not blind the world, which knows that there are deeper truths than exterior beauty, and men's tongues change accent to contradict their earlier praise of that beauty.[11]

The poet's distinction between himself and the rest of the world is important in the sestet, where it allows him to insinuate criticism while not himself taking on the role of critic:

> They look into the beauty of thy mind,
> And that in guess they measure by thy deeds;
> Then, churls, their thoughts – although their eyes were kind –
> To thy fair flower add the rank smell of weeds;
>   But why thy odour matcheth not thy show,
>   The soil is this, that thou dost common grow.

They, the world, look into the beauty of his mind. The ambiguity there is bound up with the degree of sincerity one can attribute to "the beauty of thy mind". Its apparent contrast with external beauty points to extreme irony, with "look into" taking the sense of close inspection, and holding the implication that such an inspection will reveal the opposite of a beautiful mind. But on the other hand the poet may well claim to intend "the beauty of thy mind" to be taken as literally true. He believes in the young man – unlike the rest of the world – and as he had done in Sonnets 67 and 68 he interprets his external beauty as an indicator of an even more beautiful interior. The opposition between the poet and the world might seem to become explicit in line 11, where the world is characterised as "churls", but "churl" can be, as in Sonnet 1, the tenderest of insults – more an expression of affection than hostility.

The sonnet closes without resolving the matter. The flower image of the last three lines may be understood to complete, in line 12, the churls' opinions, with the couplet marking the poet's final agreement with them. Alternatively, the couplet may not agree with their opposition of fair flower and rank smell of weeds, suggesting instead that the only reason why odour and show are not properly matched is because the young man is too familiar with the world—"thou dost common grow" – and this is, of course, a view which helps the poet insist upon his unique understanding of the young man's value. Once again the poet has done two apparently contradictory things: one is to insist upon his special relationship with his subject; the other is to undermine that subject in the polarised terms of fair outside and stinking inside.[12]

The contradiction is sustained throughout the final sonnet in the group, number 70:

> That thou art blamed shall not be thy defect,
> For slander's mark was ever yet the fair;

> The ornament of beauty is suspect,
> 4   A crow that flies in heaven's sweetest air.
> So thou be good, slander doth but approve
> Thy worth the greater, being wooed of time;
> For canker vice the sweetest buds doth love,
> 8   And thou present'st a pure unstained prime.
> Thou hast passed by the ambush of young days,
> Either not assailed, or victor being charged;
> Yet this thy praise cannot be so thy praise,
> 12   To tie up envy evermore enlarged.
>   If some suspect of ill masked not thy show,
>   Then thou alone kingdoms of hearts shouldst owe.

This sonnet's answer to the attacks of the world revealed in Sonnet 69 is to offer the consolation that such creatures as the young man, by their very nature, will attract slander. Lines 2, 3, and 7, in slightly different ways, define beauty as a state which will always be subject to attack, but there is an important difference between 2 and 3, where the attack comes from "slander" and "suspect", and 7, where it comes from actual vice.[13] That shift of approach has a significant effect on the sonnet since it helps concentrate the reader's attention upon the tantalising implications of the first two quatrains. The opening line, for instance, uses syntactic inversion and a vaguely defined future tense to insinuate the possibility that the "defect" will be found to be something more substantial than merely the fact that the young man has been blamed. "Shall not" also carries strong understones of the poet's power, as if it were an assertion that whatever others may say about the young man, he can supply a full defence. The defence begins in the next line with "ever yet" providing enough romantic flippancy to oppose the world's slander with poetic idealism – and for the rest of the quatrain the poet triumphs. Indeed we might have expected lines 3–4 to support the sonnet's initial implication that there is a defect; instead they merely provide an elaboration of line 2, moving the argument firmly into the province of metaphor, with the crow in heaven's sweetest air. But the prospect of there being a real defect in the young man is taken up again, in the second quatrain. "So thou be good" may be a vague future prescription, in the way that "shall not be thy defect" had been a vague statement about the future in the sonnet's opening line, and its meaning would then be to the effect that provided the young man stays good, then this will happen (this being the promises and threats of the rest of the quatrain). On the other hand, though, "so thou be good" might well betray the poet's doubt about what has already happened – not a future, but a present subjunctive – its meaning being that provided the young man is still good, then this applies to him (the rest of the quatrain describing such a conditional state). After presenting the reader with that puzzle, the quatrain goes on to repeat in substance the excuses for "blame" which the first quatrain had proposed, with the amplification that not only slander, but vice also, is drawn towards beauty. In this respect "present'st" in line 8 is a crafty choice of verb: it contains equally the sense that the young man embodies a pure and spotless youth, and the sense that he deliberately projects an image of purity.[14]

"Prime" is the word which returns Sonnet 70 to the impression of passing time which underlay the cosmetic concerns of Sonnets 67 and 68. "Prime" is the high point of life, looking forward to decline as it looks back to growth, and the sonnet's final quatrain does just this, looking first to the past and then to the future – but in neither case is the issue so clear as in those earlier sonnets:

> Thou hast passed by the ambush of young days,
> Either not assailed, or victor being charged;
> Yet this thy praise cannot be so thy praise,
> To tie up envy evermore enlarged.

Vice and slander have now been inextricably confused with each other, so that the either/or of line 10 presents a double choice: one possibility is 'either you have not been tempted or, if you have, you have overcome it', the other 'either you have escaped without being accused or, if you have been accused, you have managed to get out of it'.[15] That relates to the past. The future is more ominous, resting as it does on the confusion of repetition typical to the sonnets in "this thy praise cannot be so thy praise." Not only "praise" but the demonstrative pronoun "this" is carefully vague – possibly it refers back to the main body of the sonnet, in other words, the young man's past, but equally possibly it looks forward to the next line, meaning something like 'this praiseworthy ability you have to tie up envy.' Probably it works in both ways, but the reader can hardly miss also the common meaning of "this" in the sonnets: 'this poetry which praises you now cannot go on doing so.'

Together Sonnets 69 and 70 hint at depths in the young man's character which are completely contrary to his fair and righteous exterior, the subject of Sonnets 67 and 68. The important matter which unites the four sonnets is the role of the poet in analysing such a character. Sonnets 67 and 68 are public expressions, the poet's statement of values and his exemplification of them by means of the young man's exterior. Sonnets 69 and 70 are personal, heavily ambiguous contrasts of the world's eye and the poet's. From what had been said in 67 and 68 we might have assumed that the world's eye would be most content with cosmetics, while only the young man and his poet appreciate the true value of natural beauty. But 69 and 70 then present us with an ironic reversal of that view. The world's eye sees only too clearly beneath the beautiful exterior, and the poet's task is the opposite of visionary: he has to apply cosmetics to the internal rottenness. Something of this irony informs the couplet of Sonnet 70:

> If some suspect of ill masked not thy show,
> Then thou alone kingdoms of hearts shouldst owe.

Martin Seymour-Smith finds this 'a curiously weak and obscure ending' and paraphrases it in this way: 'If your true beauty were not concealed by the usual ill-repute which goes with beauty, then you alone would be king of all hearts.'[16] By now I think it is fair to say that the reader detects in such couplets not artistic failure or needless obscurity, but rather an embodiment of contradictory impulses, one the resolution to the sonnet's apparent argument, the other a summary of the counter implications of the poet's true feelings. Seymour-Smith's paraphrase admirably accounts for the first of these, but it misses the second. The key is "show", which in his paraphrase is rendered as 'true beauty', and in Ingram and Redpath's as 'true appearance'. Whether beauty or appearance is preferred, in either case 'true' is a difficult epithet to justify as part of the meaning of "show". "Show" as a noun has obvious pejorative connotations - and we would, of course, expect it to mask everything else. Instead "show" itself is masked by "suspect of ill", and underlying the positive interpretations of Seymour-Smith and Ingram and Redpath, we ought to add the poet's relief that such suspicion exists, for otherwise the young man would be uniquely dangerous — own kingdoms of hearts — were it not for the fact that people have been warned about him; with the ultimate irony that this sonnet is one such warning.

In any consideration of the young man's character Sonnet 94 is generally considered a definitive portrait — of the type, if not of the person:

> They that have power to hurt, and will do none,
> That do not do the thing they most do show,
> Who moving others are themselves as stone,
> 4   Unmoved, cold, and to temptation slow —
> They rightly do inherit heaven's graces,
> And husband nature's riches from expense;
> They are the lords and owners of their faces,
> 8   Others but stewards of their excellence.
> The summer's flower is to the summer sweet,

Though to itself it only live and die;
But if that flower with base infection meet,
12   The basest weed outbraves his dignity.
For sweetest things turn sourest by their deeds;
Lilies that fester smell far worse than weeds.

It is typical of the poetic tactics of the sonnets that Sonnet 94 should be, at the same time, one of the most impersonal sonnets in the sequence, and one which seems to speak most directly about the young man's nature. From its first word the primary reference is to "they", and it is never weakened, despite the sonnet's unmistakeable connection both to its immediate predecessor and to its immediate successor, two sonnets which are highly personal in reference. From Sonnet 93 it continues the idea of the unmoved exterior – "Whate'er thy thoughts or thy heart's workings be" – and Sonnet 95 takes up directly the image of the rotting flower – "How sweet and lovely dost thou make the shame/Which, like a canker in the fragrant rose/Doth spot the beauty of thy budding name." The ironic possibilities of Sonnet 94, especially line 5's "rightly" and the apparent inhumanity described in line 7, have long been the subject of critical contention. It seems now to be generally accepted that the sonnet ought to be read ironically, but in stressing the irony we still run the risk of understating the more obvious matter of the sonnet's impersonality, which plays some part in creating the ironic atmosphere, but goes far beyond that in its effect. No other sonnet in the young man sequence, and only one other in the whole collection excludes both the poet and his subject in the way that 94 does – and that one is Sonnet 129, "Th'expense of spirit in a waste of shame." In the young man sequence even the most impersonal of the immortalization sonnets, such as Sonnet 60, includes either poet or subject, or both, in the couplet. Sonnet 1, as befits its function of opening the sequence, has a first quatrain of untypical impersonality, but "thou" in line 5 changes its tone to the one which dominates the rest of the sequence:

From fairest creatures we desire increase,
That thereby beauty's rose might never die,
But as the riper should by time decease
4   His tender heir might bear his memory:
But thou, contracted to thine own bright eyes,
Feed'st thy light's flame with self-substantial fuel . . .

The one other sonnet which maintains a high degree of impersonality is Sonnet 54, and it makes a useful comparison with Sonnet 94:

O how much more doth beauty beauteous seem,
By that sweet ornament which truth doth give.
The rose looks fair, but fairer we it deem
4 For that sweet odour which doth in it live.
The canker blooms have full as deep a dye
As the perfumed tincture of the roses,
Hang on such thorns, and play as wantonly,
8 When summer's breath their masked buds discloses;
But for their virtue only is their show,
They live unwooed, and unrespected fade,
Die to themselves. Sweet roses do not so;
12 Of their sweet deaths are sweetest odours made.
And so of you, beauteous and lovely youth,
When that shall vade, by verse distils your truth.

Even here the reader may detect the personality of the poet behind the first person plural generalisation of line 3, and the couplet, of course, brings the sonnet's argument home to both the poet and the young man.

Like 54, Sonnet 94 moves from generalisation to a supporting – even substantiating – flower image, but there is a difference in the relative weight given to each. In 54 the generalisation about the need for truth as well as beauty is packed into the first two lines while 94's assertion of the rightness of the self-controlled inheriting the earth is allowed to take up the whole of the sonnet's octave. The supporting image then fills the sestet, but in a way which makes the reader more and more uneasy since the anticipated personal reference never arrives. The prospect of the sonnet's eventual pointing to the young man as the self-controlled "they", and the poet as his steward, is held out by the narrowing of reference from "they", "their" and "others" in the octave, to "itself", "it", and "his" (= its) in the third quatrain; instead, though, the couplet retreats to general, plural reference. In other words, like most of Sonnet 54, 94 exhibits itself as an example of poetic generalisation; but unlike 54 it refuses to explain itself. Its achievement is not, as it pretends, description of a character, either individual or general. Indeed few readers could feel secure in explaining just what they had been told in the sonnet, beyond the generalisation that the greater men are the more serious are their crimes: instead, the sonnet is more concerned with demonstrating the primacy of poetic expression for analysis of such a character, for despite the reader's bafflement at what is actually being said he has no doubt about its importance, and the sonnet uses this impression to move him from the level of shadowed metaphor to that of absolute (and crude) metaphor. Shadowed metaphor appears in line 3's comparison of men to stone, which holds through line 4's "Unmoved, cold", but fades away at "to temptation slow", a phrase which can refer only to men, not stones. In the second quatrain the shadowed metaphor is of inheritance, husbanding and governing, but it disappears when put against the idea of being a lord and owner of one's face, with others stewarding one's excellence. In these phrases the reader sees possibilities which the metaphor will not bear — for example, "lords and owners of their faces" includes such ideas as 'they don't blush', 'they don't use cosmetics', 'they are hypocrites who show none of their feelings', 'they possess nothing, except their faces', and 'they are their own men, owing allegiance to no-one'. In contrast the sestet provides one metaphor of growing crudeness:

> The summer's flower is to the summer sweet,
> Though to itself it only live and die;
> But if that flower with base infection meet,
> The basest weed outbraves his dignity.
>   For sweetest things turn sourest by their deeds;
>   Lilies that fester smell far worse than weeds.

Its directness is contained in the poet's plain refusal to aim for variation or elegance or ambiguity, so that "sweetest", in the couplet, repeats "sweet" in line 9, and is given its obvious opposite "sourest"; both the infection and the weed are "base"; and while "flower", in lines 9 and 11, changes to "lily" in the couplet, "weed" stays "weed". The sense rhyme of the octave and sestet — "power" and "flower" — carries the movement from generality to metaphor in miniature, and the palpable metaphoric generalisation of the final line marks a triumph for those poetic techniques which persuade a reader to equate men with flowers, without the poet having to point the analogy explicitly. Kept as a generalisation, the sestet allows the poet complete freedom: he does not, for example, have to explain why it should be the flower's fault that it meets infection, nor need he clarify the apparent contradiction in the couplet's logic, that flowers can perform deeds. Instead, the movement from the octave's obliqueness to the certainty of the sestet's imagery provides relief. In actual argument the use of a metaphor to support a complex case would be intellectually insupportable — the kind of thing which is mocked in parody sermons. Here, though, the poet's role as a spokesman for metaphysical truth allows him to switch to metaphoric irrationality, with the reader happy to welcome such an abandonment of reason.

With Sonnet 94's sestet we are firmly in the province of the obtrusive metaphor, and both Sonnets 95 and 96 continue its exploration. Sonnet 95 first takes up 94's identification of men and plants, and then reintroduces another metaphor familiar from the procreation group:

> How sweet and lovely dost thou make the shame
> Which, like a canker in the fragrant rose,
> Doth spot the beauty of thy budding name!
> 4   O in what sweets dost thou thy sins enclose!
> That tongue that tells the story of thy days,
> Making lascivious comments on thy sport,
> Cannot dispraise but in a kind of praise;
> 8   Naming thy name blesses an ill report.
> O what a mansion have those vices got
> Which for their habitation chose out thee,
> Where beauty's veil doth cover every blot
> 12 And all things turns to fair that eyes can see!
>   Take heed, dear heart, of this large privilege;
>   The hardest knife ill used doth lose his edge.

The opening quatrain is as persuasive as Sonnet 94's sestet, despite its seeming contradiction of the idea that infection leads to a festering stink. Here infection itself, in the form of the worm, is beautified – or, at least, that is the impression we gain. A moment's thought, which the familiar metaphoric vocabulary does not encourage, would show up the metaphor's spuriousness. It is literally and figuratively impossible to make a worm sweet and lovely, or even to make it appear sweet and lovely. All that one can do with it is what line 4 states, namely to enclose it entirely so that it cannot be seen; but by line 4 the reader has fallen for the metaphor – from "make" in line 1 he is persuaded that the young man's powers are miraculous in their capacity to transform the foul into the sweet.

   Later in the sonnet, in the third quatrain, there is another metaphorical sleight of hand, when line 10 casually states that vices chose the young man: a way of denying him any responsibility for his actions. Here, though, the reader is not likely to be so easily taken in as by the sonnet's first four lines since he has had the second quatrain to point the way for him. The third quatrain opens as if it were going to build a second metaphor around the image of a tongue, but that fades into an entirely non-figurative assertion that the young man's "name" – here a synonym for all the sweetness and loveliness of the first quatrain – is sufficient to transform scandal into praise. At least it ought to do that, and it certainly does so for the poet; but the reader gains the opposite impression from the quatrain. One tongue for certain (and probably many more) is making lascivious comments and naming names.[17]

In the light of such scandal to claim, as the poet does, that the mere fact that the young man is involved immediately transforms vice into virtue, is special pleading – more obvious in statement, but of similar unreasonableness to the opening image's beautifying of worms. The second quatrain is not merely an abstract bridging of the flower and mansion metaphors of the first and third quatrains: it directs the reader towards a fuller understanding of the speciousness of the first quatrain's reasoning, and prepares him for the crucial distinction in the third quatrain, between the reality of the young man's infection despite the fairness of his appearance. By line 12 the distinction is quite clear, and the reader readily grasps the implications of superficiality in "that eyes can see". The movement from line 1 to line 12 takes in a subtle but perceptible shift of attention. "How sweet and lovely . . ." at first governs our response, declaring the sonnet to be one of exclamatory praise: not necessarily how sweet and lovely the young man is, but how sweet and lovely is the effect he has upon the ugly facts. By the close of the third quatrain, however, that initial exclamation has turned, in retrospect, from admiration to distaste. And rather than examining the nature of the transformation of ugliness to beauty, as we might have expected from "How sweet and lovely *dost thou make*", the sonnet refuses to budge from its emphasis upon enclosing and covering. The subject of line 12 is "beauty's veil" – and the 'turning' to fair of a veil is only an act of masking, nothing like the transformation which the opening line's "make" had seemed to promise.

In its way, then, Sonnet 95 shows a similar metaphoric strategy to Sonnet 94, the third quatrain being used to cancel all but the most damning implications of the earlier imagery. Like 94, its final destination is a moralising couplet, proverb-like if not actually proverbial, giving the impression that the Shakespearean sonnet form has achieved its full potential by packing into the couplet the pithy lesson learned through the three quatrains:

> Take heed, dear heart, of this large privilege;
> The hardest knife ill used doth lose his edge.

Unlike Sonnet 94's couplet, though, the connection of this one to the main body of the sonnet is unclear. Simply because it is a couplet, and because it sounds like a proverb, the temptation is to take it as a straightforward warning that the young man should not overdo the charm – eventually even the effect of his beauty can pall. The reader's problem, however, is that where the sonnet's momentum is directed towards a summarising conclusion, the actual image of the final line is both new and incongruous.

Where Sonnet 94 had prepared carefully for its summarising line, 95's image of enclosure within a flower and a mansion has no apparent connection with the final line; indeed, very much the opposite applies, since flower petals – the "sweets" of line 4 – and "beauty's veil" are images of fragility, hardly summed up or even given an equivalent in "the hardest knife ill used". Line 13, too, has its complications. It balances threat with affection – "take heed" and "dear heart" – and wraps up both in the vagueness of "this large privilege". The privilege may be either retrospective, summarising the state of affairs described in the three quatrains, or prospective, introducing the final line's proverb.[18] It probably acts in both ways, helping to overcome the drastic change of metaphor, but the poet's unexpected appearance in the line, in the affectionate parenthesis "dear heart", insinuates the identification of "the hardest knife ill used" with the poet himself.[19]

Earlier in the sonnet the reader will have begun to think of the poet's function as praiser of the young man: the opening line of the second quatrain, "That tongue that tells the story of thy days", is to all appearances, the introduction to some comment on the poet's role. Only the further description of line 6, "making lascivious comment", makes it clear that line 5 should not be read figuratively ("tongue that tells" = poet who writes about), but literally as a wagging tongue – and "the story of thy days" is not the young man's history, but only a gossipy account of what he does all day long. Even so, the second quatrain keeps enough residual identification of the tongue with the poet – slightly reinforced by "praise" in line 7 – for the reader to be conscious that he is, in part, reading a sonnet about the poet's function. That function is to enhance his subject's fairness, which, in this case, means participating in the camouflage of vice. The best possible camouflage is metaphor, and in this sonnet metaphor pretends to make shame sweet and lovely: but the pretence is gradually exposed as the sonnet develops, until, at the end of the third quatrain, it becomes openly a matter of disguise. Coming after that exposure, the couplet's threat has been well prepared for – even metaphor's force must inevitably be blunted if it has constantly to be applied to the disguising of vice.

Sonnet 96 is the final sonnet in the group, and it takes up from 94 and 95 both the analysis of the young man's character and the investigation of the poet's role with regard to it:

> Some say thy fault is youth, some wantonness,
> Some say thy grace is youth and gentle sport;
> Both grace and faults are loved of more and less;
> 4   Thou mak'st faults graces that to thee resort.

As on the finger of a throned queen
The basest jewel will be well esteemed,
So are those errors that in thee are seen,
8   To truths translated, and for true things deemed.
How many lambs might the stern wolf betray,
If like a lamb he could his looks translate;
How many gazers mightst thou lead away,
12   If thou wouldst use the strength of all thy state!
But do not so; I love thee in such sort,
As thou being mine, mine is thy good report.

Here the analysis of the young man's character completes, in personal terms, the objective analysis of Sonnet 94. The opening quatrain of 94 had left the reader uncertain as to how he should interpret the immovability of the characters it describes, for set against its potential innuendo is the positive fact that they do not make use of their power to hurt, despite the obviousness of that power – "and will do none" is a phrase which dilutes the negativity of the rest of the sonnet, despite its own negative phrasing. By the end of the third quatrain of Sonnet 96, however, the refusal to hurt has degenerated from the grandeur of "they that have power" to the nature of the wolf who would kill if given the chance. The third quatrain of 96 does not deny the young man's volition as an element in his not hurting many – to that extent the wolf image is misleading, a point made clear in the change from "could", in line 10, to "wouldst", in line 12 – nonetheless, the shift from comparison to a flower to comparison to a wolf is an entirely negative one – no longer a beautiful object which can be infected by others' actions, but now the essence of viciousness.

As well as pursuing the analysis of the young man's nature begun in Sonnet 94 – and, in metaphoric terms, completing it – Sonnet 96 also continues the analysis of the poet's function which underlay Sonnet 95. In this respect it is one of the most capricious in the sequence, each quatrain, and the couplet, playing its own poetic game. The opening two lines disturb the reader's expectations:

Some say thy fault is youth, some wantonness,
Some say thy grace is youth and gentle sport

The echoed "Some say . . . Some say" leads him to expect a carefully balanced parallel, probably on the pattern of the opening quatrain of Sonnet 91:

Some glory in their birth, some in their skill,
Some in their wealth, some in their body's force,
Some in their garments, though new-fangled ill,
Some in their hawks and hounds, some in their horse.

Indeed 96's opening lines do make a parallel, but not the anticipated one, for instead of the second line giving two further suggested definitions of the "fault", they actually define "grace". The effect is to make the reader go back to the beginning of the line, and, in re-reading it, to place an added stress on "grace", in order to emphasise its contrast to "fault". The third and fourth lines follow this by entirely confusing "fault" and "grace":

Both grace and faults are loved of more and less;
Thou mak'st faults graces that to the thee resort.

As in the young man faults and graces are not only indistinguishable, but could not exist without the other, so the reader now finds himself unable to separate, or identify, the two. Thus, in line 3, "more and less" is purposefully vague. If it means 'by the mighty and the poor' (with "of" as part of the phrase), then it is not clear whether mighty and poor love both, or whether, following the order of the phrases, the mighty love the grace and the poor the faults. [20] But if the verb is read as "loved of", then "more and less" has a general quantitative sense — 'to a greater and lesser degree' — with again the vagueness of reference as to whether both graces and faults are loved in this way, or whether grace is loved more and faults less. Line 4 completes the confusion. "Thou mak'st faults graces that to thee resort" has complete syntactic ambiguity: either the young man turns the faults which resort to him into graces, or he turns the graces that resort to him into faults.

One further game which the reader is required to play is with the word "grace". Throughout the quatrain "grace" follows "fault". In line 2 it even comes where "fault" is expected, if the syntactic parallel is to be maintained. Line 3 seems to give "grace" the preference in an elegant reversal of the order of the words in lines 1 and 2, but "fault" is unexpectedly changed to "faults". So, in line 4, "grace" follows suit and becomes "graces", but that change is a more momentous one than from "fault" to "faults". "Grace" has been degraded from line 2, where it has the faintly theological sense of a blessed state, to the mere parallel of "faults", that is, habitual, graceful actions. [21]

The second quatrain plays a different kind of game, the one of the deceitful metaphor, familiar from the first quatrain of Sonnet 95. There the pretence was to make cankers beautiful; here it is to transform a base jewel into a valuable one:

As on the finger of a throned queen
The basest jewel will be well esteemed,
So are those errors that in thee are seen,
To truths translated, and for true things deemed.

Such a transformation is impossible – outside poetry, that is. All gazers at the throned queen know the jewel for what it is, as they know the young man's errors for errors. Translating them to truths and deeming them to be true things are conscious acts on the part of his observers – willing suspensions of desbelief – and not, as the first quatrain would have had it, something dependent upon the will of the young man ("Thou mak'st faults graces").[22] And as if to convey the diminution of the young man's power this quatrain is cruder than the first: the simile built around "As on . . . So are" is more ponderous and more diffuse than the bewildering word game of faults and graces. Then, in pressing home the inability of the young man to control his image, the third quatrain presents an even cruder form of metaphor than mere simile, the form of proverbial expression carried over from the couplets of Sonnets 94 and 95:

How many lambs might the stern wolf betray,
If like a lamb he could his looks translate;
How many gazers mightst thou lead away,
If thou wouldst use the strength of all thy state!

After the festering lilies and the ill-used knife, we are now given the cliché of the wolf in sheep's clothing. The line which introduces it is almost clumsily deliberate – "stern" is a particularly colourless epithet for a wolf – but it appearance is deceptive, since it sets a trap for the reader which is sprung in line 10. "If like a . . ." seems to be introducing the illuminating simile: the wolf could betray lambs if he could act like a . . .? "Lamb" is the unexpected word, and it forces the reader to abandon the idea of a simile, and to read the line as an extraordinarily banal completion of the cliché. Lines 9 – 10 which had promised, with "like", the reviving of a dead metaphor, instead merely emphasise the superficiality of the idea – how many lambs might the wolf betray if it could get to look like a lamb. Then lines 11 – 12 imitate the metaphor of the second quatrain by expending themselves in an incongruous parallel. In essence they have nothing to do with the wolf–lamb cliché, despite the syntactic identity of "How many . . . If like." What we are asked to compare is the wolf dressing up as a lamb with the young man using the strength of all his state: a comparison which obviously does not work. Even to paraphrase "the strength of all thy state" as broadly as Ingram and

Redpath do, with 'all the glamour at your command', only points up the incongruity, asking us to see an association between lambs and glamour.

Sonnet 96 completes the movement from ironic analysis to poetic game which Sonnet 94 had begun. The game, though, is serious, because its object is to move the power to hurt from the young man to the poet. By the end of 96's third quatrain the abstract calculating figure of 94's octave has been turned into a poetic tool—a provider of metaphors of increasing banality, which gradually rob him of power over his actions. Despite "wouldst" in line 12, and the couplet's request "do not so", the wolf's inability to translate himself is the governing final image of the group. In contrast, though, is the poet's growing power, which turns the threatening figure of Sonnet 94 into a figure of sport, with poet leading reader in a deliberate hunt for the telling comparison. The couplet is a final triumph for the poet:

> But do not so; I love thee in such sort,
> As thou being mine, mine is thy good report.

This repeats the couplet of Sonnet 36 word for word, and, in doing so, it mocks that sonnet's preoccupation with the poet's need to part from the young man. There "do not so" was a request for the young man not to reacquaint himself with the poet; that degradation will not help him, because the poet's suffering will be increased by his knowledge that he was responsible for sullying the young man's name. Here the opposite is the case – 'don't lead others astray, because if you do you will ruin my good name.' In 36 "thou being mine" was typical sonnet talk from one lover to another; in 96 it relates to poetic expression – 'already in covering up your behaviour I am driven to clichéd metaphor; any more and my poetic reputation is finished.'

8 'Any Summer's Story': Poet and Lover

For the remainder of this book I shall concentrate mainly upon the final thirty sonnets in the sequence, 97–126, where, after having come through the crises described in Sonnets 66–96, the poet turns inwards in a self analysis which points towards a final self-possession and self-containment. As a result of their describing this process these sonnets are different in character, and almost in kind, from those which have gone before. In one important sense their peculiarity is the natural result of the abandonment of the sequence's declared centre of interest so far – the young man. He, and the love the poet feels for him, fade during this part of the sequence into something little stronger than wistful recollection, with, only very occasionally, a flicker of life to make it seem a part of the present rather than a part of history. From sonnet to sonnet the reader perceives, on the poet's part, the sense of a relationship over and done with, leaving only the scars of remembered emotion; and the atmosphere of things experienced and now only recollected is thickened by the use of images and actions from earlier in the sequence. In Sonnet 99, for instance, the rose makes one more reappearance, but in a narrative poem where its inevitable infection belongs to time past – "A vengeful canker ate him up to death." In Sonnet 110 the poet returns to the idea that he is inextricably bound to the young man, but now that condition is set in the context of a long and weary experience of the world:

> Now all is done, have what shall have no end –
> Mine appetite I never more will grind
> On newer proof, to try an older friend,
> A god in love, to whom I am confined.

Sonnet 120 contrasts the poet's crime for which he is apologising with the young man's earlier crime; and two lines at the centre of the sonnet are pathetically nostalgic in their summary of the way the two men have hurt each other to exhaustion:

> For if you were by my unkindness shaken,
> As I by yours, y'have passed a hell of time. [1]

And in Sonnet 123 the poet once more encounters time as his antagonist, but now from within a world view governed by the brevity and inconsequentiality of all human life, with no exceptions to the rule:

> Our dates are brief, and therefore we admire
> What thou dost foist upon us that is old,
> And rather make them born to our desire
> Than think that we before have heard them told. [2]

In later chapters I mean to show how these sonnets overturn the ideals and assumptions which have dominated the sequence up to this point, but first I can demonstrate that the changes which they embody, although revolutionary, are not unprepared for. Sonnets which occur quite early in the sequence begin to explore the tensions, ultimately irreconcilable, between the poet's need to function as a lover and as a writer of sonnets to, and about, the man he loves.

The tensions appear first in the pair of sonnets, 22 and 23, where there is an early contrast of the poet's feelings and the young man's callousness, all played out in the terms of poetic convention. Significantly, this pair comes immediately after Sonnet 21's scouting of the possibility of there being a rival poet, with the poet concluding it with the pronounced intention not to indulge in empty flattery:

> O let me true in love but truly write,
> And then believe me, my love is as fair
> As any mother's child, though not so bright
> As those gold candles fixed in heaven's air.
>   Let them say more that like of hearsay well;
>   I will not praise that purpose not to sell.

Sonnet 22 fits this pronouncement. It opens with the potential flattery that the young man is synonymous with youth, but by the end of the first quatrain the prospect of his ageing and the poet's death has been introduced, and the rest of the sonnet develops a conceit only obliquely connected to the opening quatrain:

> My glass shall not persuade me I am old
> So long as youth and thou are of one date,

> But when in thee time's furrows I behold,
> 4 Then look I death my days should expiate.
> For all the beauty that doth cover thee
> Is but the seemly raiment of my heart,
> Which in thy breast doth live, as thine in me.
> 8 How can I then be elder than thou art?
> O therefore love, be of thyself so wary
> As I not for myself, but for thee will,
> Bearing thy heart, which I will keep so chary
> 12 As tender nurse her babe from faring ill.
> Presume not on thy heart when mine is slain,
> Thou gav'st me thine not to give back again.

In effect the opening quatrain requires the reader to make a number of successive adjustments, each concerned with getting the sonnet's time-scheme right. The opening line seems to pitch the sonnet into the future, as if it were a wish or a prophecy; and not until the second line is completed does it become apparent, instead, that "shall" is an emphatic present, not a future tense marker. The sonnet's mood has changed from a meditation about days to come to an insistence upon a pose to be adopted in the present, that as long as the young man is young then the poet will refuse to believe that he himself is as old as his mirror tells him he is. The reader will be puzzled, however, because no reason is given for his adopting such a pose, and it is difficult to guess at one. Line 3 does not, as we might have expected, begin to provide an answer: it turns instead to the prospect of the young man's ageing. If anything, the time-scheme becomes more indistinct than before, for "when . . . I behold" may either be a prophecy of the inevitability of the young man's ageing – 'when the time comes that I see you looking old' – or it may describe an habitual action – 'every time I see you looking older'. The reader probably chooses the first option since it fits the sonnet back into the cosy future tense which he had permitted to its opening line, but when he does so line 4 moves him back towards the present, it being more natural to interpret "Then look I" as the marker of an habitual action than as an equivalent to 'then I shall look'.

This is all sonnet manipulation – or, better, reader manipulation – at its craftiest, and it prepares the reader for the exploration of complex themes related to ageing, in particular the perception of its inevitability even in the young, and a lover's attitudes to that perception. And, as if to fulfil these expectations, the second quatrain opens with a line which promises, at the least, the grandeur of generality:

> For all the beauty that doth cover thee

It promises, but the quatrain does not deliver. The reader expects it to develop the observation that the young man's beauty is subject to time's tyranny, or that it will fade and wither like a leaf. Instead the quatrain retreats into a conceit, and, moreover, into a conceit which undermines the poignancy of the first quatrain. It is, in essence, a development of the my heart in yours and your heart in mine convention, taken to the extremes of a swap of personality and individuality – 'I have become you, and you me.' Hence we can understand, in retrospect, the poet's denial of his ageing in the first quatrain, and his perception of the young man's furrowed face – for he, the perceiver, is really the young man, and the young man is really him. At the end of the quatrain he again asks the question which had been posed in the first quatrain, 'how can I be older than you?', but by this time it has sunk into triviality.

This point in the sonnet is most interesting. Being acted out is the inevitable degradation which the conventions force upon the love poet – or, at least, the love poet writing for such a subject as the young man. The first quatrain appears to hide subtle psychological possibilities under its compliment: the unsettled time scheme encourages the reader to contemplate the ways in which old lovers delude themselves into the belief that they can keep pace with the young, while they are constantly reminded of their age – by looking in mirrors, for instance – and also while they have a more than normal awareness that their young master–mistress is showing, or will inevitably show, lines of age. But this early in the sequence such complexities are difficult to sustain, and the sonnet's subject will expect something in the order of the exchange of hearts conceits which he does, of course, get. The prospect now is that the sestet will simply become more involved in the conceit, in the way that Sonnets 24 and 46 pretend to do over eyes and hearts – and in one respect this does happen. The third quatrain has an unusually knotty syntax:

> O therefore love, be of thyself so wary
> As I not for myself, but for thee will,
> Bearing thy heart, which I will keep so chary
> As tender nurse her babe from faring ill.
>   Presume not on they heart when mine is slain,
>   Thou gav'st me thine not to give back again.

The reader's temptations to surrender are great. For instance, the verb in line 10, "As I . . . will", needs expansion: does the reader expand it to 'as I will

look after thyself', or to 'as I will look after myself'? The sonnet's logic
admits either possibility, just as it admits a number of ways of connecting the
next two lines, all qualifying clauses, to the two which have preceded them.[3]
If, however, the reader resists the logical confusion which the convention
encourages, then he will gain from these lines an impression distinct from,
and independent of, their meaning. This is of a contract having been made,
which the poet will keep and which the young man will break. The
quatrain's most striking impression is that the poet is making a heavily
qualified plea, one which emphasises his selflessness and the young man's self-
concern: "which I will keep so chary" set against "be of thyself so wary". It is
a contrast which the couplet underscores. Convention has had its full effect
on the sonnet to the extent that the very real prospect of age and death in the
first quatrain has now become reduced to the typical hyperbole of romantic
poetry, in which hearts are "slain"; but the final line swings back towards
plain speech. Its bare assertion that there was a contract, which is now
irreversible, is a crude simplification of the conceit – the kind of crudity
which the couplet of a sonnet encourages and can get away with – and it
leaves the reader to decide whether he treats it as the culmination of the plea
or as a threat: either, 'this is my reason for asking you to be careful', or, 'you
kill my heart and I have every right to dispose of yours.'

Sonnet 23 is not obviously linked to 22, but, as an anticipation of tensions
which emerge later in the sequence, it brings into the open the conflict
between the roles of poet and lover which stays implicit in 22 (by 'lover' I
mean the poet as lover, not the young man). Its apparent connection is to
Sonnet 21, for where that sonnet had asserted that there would be no empty
flattery, this one makes an elaborate defence for not having produced the
normal range of compliments. One important distinction, though, is that
where Sonnet 21 had been about poetic flattery, Sonnet 23 is about spoken
flattery:

> As an unperfect actor on the stage,
> Who with his fear is put besides his part,
> Or some fierce thing replete with too much rage,
> 4 Whose strength's abundance weakens his own heart;
> So I for fear of trust forget to say
> The perfect ceremony of love's rite,
> And in mine own love's strength seem to decay,
> 8 O'ercharged with burthen of mine own love's might.
> O let my books be then the eloquence
> And dumb presagers of my speaking breast,
> Who plead for love and look for recompense

12   More than that tongue that more hath more expressed.
         O learn to read what silent love hath writ.
         To hear with eyes belongs to love's fine wit. [4]

Rather than seeing the poet in the role of lover this sonnet seems to reverse
the coin and see the lover in the role of poet (again 'lover' does not refer to
the young man). Only through the poetry can his love be appreciated for
what it is, and he only writes because the strength of his feeling renders him
speechless at times when he should be pouring the compliments out. [5] The
corollary to this is that the poetry is no more than a dilution of the emotion —
in the terms of the sonnet, "dumb presagers of my speaking breast". [6]
"Dumb" is unexpectedly literal in its emphasis that only figuratively can
books be said to talk, and it narrows the sense of "eloquence", in line 9, from
the great literary ideal of poetry as a speaking picture, to poetry as a second
best to speech. Thus, while the sonnet's argument is directed towards
persuading the young man to read what the poet has written, it subverts that
argument by admitting that the poetry is only a substitute. The couplet is
particularly double-edged. The reader quite possibly understands it to mean
that the young man must learn to read the poetry properly by using his
imagination to turn the words on the page into spoken words: that is to take
line 14, "To hear with eyes belongs to love's fine wit", as an amplification of
line 13, a qualitative summary of the action of learning to read what silent
love has written. It is tempting, though, to give more substance to the line.
The couplet's structure is, after all, untypical of Shakespeare's practice, with
the two lines forming distinct, self-contained sentences, so that line 14 seems
to mark a new statement, rather than being merely an extension of what has
just been said. [7] In this way the effect is more like that of an antithetical
couplet: in line 13 the poet asks the young man to learn to read his poetry,
and see in it the statement of silent love, but line 14 opposes that with the
impossibility of the young man's ever being able to achieve the more
profound distinction of hearing the poet's love from his silent person.
Whichever way the couplet is read, its implication is that the young man has
neither the capacity not the inclination to understand "love's fine wit." But
so early in the sequence the need to write for such a person is only faintly
questioned, and while the reader takes from Sonnets 22 and 23 the
impression of a superficial, and potentially inconstant, young man, his
deepest engagement is with the poet's attempts to adapt the conventions
inherent in the love sonnet so that he may speak directly to him. If that can be
achieved the hope is that the superficial may be made deep and the inconstant
constant — and this early in the sequence such hopes can still be sustained.
   Sonnet 56 comes in the immortalisation group, immediately after the

promise that the poet's powerful rhyme will outlive marble and gilded monuments of princes. It, too, is a sonnet concerned with time, the first and third quatrains contrasting "today" and "tomorrow", the couplet contrasting "winter" and "summer"; but its argument – the possibility of love's survival beyond a short period – makes the pairing with Sonnet 55 as ironic as any in the sequence:

> Sweet love, renew thy force, be it not said
> Thy edge should blunter be than appetite,
> Which but today by feeding is allayed,
> 4 Tomorrow sharpened in his former might.
> So love be thou, although today thou fill
> Thy hungry eyes, even till they wink with fullness,
> Tomorrow see again, and do not kill
> 8 The spirit of love with a perpetual dullness.
> Let this sad interim like the ocean be
> Which parts the shore, where two contracted new
> Come daily to the banks, that when they see
> 12 Return of love, more blest may be the view;
> As call it winter, which being full of care,
> Makes summer's welcome, thrice more wished, more rare.

This sonnet is one of the most difficult to understand. Part of the reason lies in its place in the sequence: it not only introduces a jarring note into the treatment of time in the immortalisation sonnets, so that the grand personification with his scythe is reduced to "today" and "tomorrow", but it contains the kind of obscurities which we only learn to decipher in the latter part of the young man sequence. If this sonnet came at the very end, say between Sonnets 125 and 126, then the reader would feel fairly confident about identifying "sweet love" as it is normally glossed by editors, i.e. the spirit of love, and would accordingly read the sonnet as the poet's address to himself. Where it stands, though, it causes insoluble problems. If "sweet love" really is the spirit of love, and not the beloved, then it would be logical to interpret "love" in the second quatrain, addressed in exactly the same way, also as the spirit of love – in which case, requesting the spirit of love not to kill the spirit of love makes no sense at all. But any attempt to make "love" in line 5 a change of reference, so that now the beloved is being addressed, runs into the difficulty that it makes the image of the second quatrain – one of feeding the eyes until they wink with fullness – an improbably grotesque wish for the young man (improbable in terms of the sequence's careful avoidance of any incongruousness in his description).

In fact it is impossible to know who the sonnet is addressed to, whether the beloved or the spirit of love, and if the latter, whether that spirit is in the beloved or in the poet or in both. Additionally there is the difficulty of knowing the level at which the sonnet is pitched. Hilton Landrey interprets the opening two lines as if "appetite" meant specifically sexual appetite: 'apparently, the friend's sexual appetite has begun to displace his love for the poet, hence Shakespeare urges a renewal of the strength of the friend's affection.'[8] Support for this comes from the sexual undertones of erection and flaccidity which run through the octave, in, for example, "blunter" and "sharpened", "fullness" and "dullness". These are, however, only undertones, and it is possible to interpret the major image of the octave as appetite in the sense of eating — what, in fact, it claims to be — rather than mere sexual appetite. I say 'mere' to emphasise the difference this involves. As a contrast between love and sexual appetite the octave is entirely conventional; indeed Landry's sentence quoted above turns it into pure cliché. But in the contrast between love and appetite for food there is a more complex metaphor, both encouraging and denying the similarity between the two. Love is unlike appetite in its constancy and unchangeability, or at least it should be, but it is similar, the sonnet implies, in man's perpetual craving for it.[9]

The sestet clears up nothing. Instead of analysis or clarification it offers metaphor. Of course the offer is directed at the sonnet's addressee, whether that be the spirit of love or the actual beloved, but it is the reader who is ultimately addressed. What he experiences in "Let this sad interim like the ocean be" is a retreat from the problems which the octave had raised, into pure poeticising.[10] He may see Hero and Leander in the "two contracted new", or some vaguer image of two lovers whose contact with each other is frustrated: in either case he is being shown that the poet can and will manipulate his poem even to the point of imposing upon the most fraught of situations the stuff of romance. But the poet takes care, too, to let the reader know that this is a conscious, deliberate act of poeticising. The couplet's almost offhanded "As call it winter . . ." brings into the open the secondary possibilities of the ocean metaphor. Through lines 9–12 the reader's major impression of "let this sad interim like the ocean be" is that it means what it says figuratively: 'either I, or you, or both of us, or the reader as well for that matter, think of the interim as if it were an ocean.' However, the strangeness of the request to take up a new metaphor at this point in the sonnet is sufficient for the reader to carry through the quatrain some uneasiness. "As call it winter" comes at just the right time to reinforce this feeling; and it makes line 9, in retrospect, take on the more calculating sense of 'let me find a metaphor which will describe this sad interim in a way which suits my purposes.' At this stage in the sequence the poet's purposes are to camouflage what is wrong, and a vague Hero and Leander suits them admirably.[11]

Only late in the young man sequence is the camouflage discarded. It is possible to see it happening to one of the sequence's favourite metaphors in the group of three sonnets, 97–99. These sonnets contrast absence and presence – absence from the young man being like a winter even when it is actually summer, for summer is only to be found where the young man is. Sonnets 97 and 98 play with figurative and actual seasons: figurative seasons are in the poet's feelings and they are deliberately set in contrast with the real seasons outside. Thus the opening quatrain of Sonnet 97 describes the poet's feelings, but in a metaphor so graphic that it persuades the reader to set the sonnet in winter:

> How like a winter hath my absence been
> From thee, the pleasure of the fleeting year!
> What freezings have I felt, what dark days seen!
> What old December's bareness everywhere!

This winter, though, is only figurative, as the next line makes clear:

> And yet this time removed was summer's time

and this sense of reality never quite leaves Sonnet 97, even though the rest of the second quatrain, and the whole of the third, describe the way in which, to the poet, even the produce of the summer had been transformed to "hope of orphans, and unfathered fruit".[12] The distance between the third quatrain and the couplet demonstrates very clearly the sonnet's schizophrenic separation of fantasy and reality. Fantasy gradually takes over the third quatrain to the point where the young man controls all summer, and without him even the birds do not sing:

> Yet this abundant issue seemed to me
> But hope of orphans and unfathered fruit;
> For summer and his pleasures wait on thee,
> And thou away, the very birds are mute.

That last image is the height of poetic idealism, and the couplet does not attempt to cap it. Very much the opposite, it pulls the carpet from under the metaphor by admitting that in the real world the birds do sing, and, more importantly, the poet does hear them:

> Or if they sing, 'tis with so dull a cheer,
> That leaves look pale, dreading the winter's near.

The concession to romance is that what birdsong there is seems ominously to promise winter, but that hardly counteracts the surprise of "Or, if they sing . . ."[13]

Sonnet 98 works the opposite way. It opens in reality, "From you have I been absent in the spring", and closes in fantasy, "Yet seemed it winter still." The movement into fantasy is followed through the poet's mind, in his refusal to involve himself in the things of summer. In the sestet both the lily's white and the rose's vermilion are pictured as mere shadows of the young man:

> Nor did I wonder at the lily's white,
> Nor praise the deep vermilion of the rose;
> They were but sweet, but figures of delight,
> Drawn after you, you pattern of all those.
>   Yet seemed it winter still, and, you away,
>   As with your shadow I with these did play.

Taken together, then, the two sonnets trace a pattern of fantasy into reality, then reality back into fantasy — metaphorical winter followed by actual summer, actual spring followed by figurative winter. Out of this circle one image in particular has emerged, that of the poet playing with flowers, and it becomes the governing image of Sonnet 99, the one fifteen-line sonnet in the sequence:

> The forward violet thus did I chide:
> Sweet thief, whence didst thou steal thy sweet that smells
> If not from my love's breath? The purple pride
> Which on thy soft cheek for complexion dwells,
> 5 In my love's veins thou hast too grossly dyed.
> The lily I condemned for thy hand,
> And buds of marjoram had stol'n thy hair;
> The roses fearfully on thorns did stand,
> 9 One blushing shame, another white despair;
> A third, nor red nor white, had stol'n of both,
> And to his robbery had annexed thy breath;
> But for his theft, in pride of all his growth
> 13 A vengeful canker ate him up to death.
>   More flowers I noted, yet I none could see,
>   But sweet or colour it had stol'n from thee.

Perhaps no sonnet in the whole collection, the final two excepted, tests the reader's patience so much as this one. Tucker Brooke, in his 1936 edition, described the three sonnets, 97—99, as being 'written as if the poet's heart was not much in them', so it is no surprise to see Martin Seymour-Smith giving this sonnet as succinct a dismissal as anything written by Shakespeare has ever had: 'a poor sonnet which, however, follows on directly from 98'. [14] In contrast, though, Stephen Booth gives this sonnet copious annotation, and, in typical manner, he indicates his response to the tone and matter of the whole sonnet in an apparent afterthought to his comments on the word "ate" in line 13. He first explains why he prefers to print the modern form "ate", rather than keep the Quarto's spelling "eate", because 'to retain the old spelling here is to create a quaintness rather than report one.' He then adds the following in parentheses:

> Retention of "eate" is particularly misleading here because the childlike redundancy of "ate him up to death" has genuine coyness, a nursery-tale ring, that a reader allowing for quaint archaisms can lose. This poem – perhaps intentionally – sounds like a parody of its kind; it is grossly uneconomical; the speaker sounds like someone who is 'pouring it on', and, in this line, he sounds conscious of the listless, stale perfunctory nature of such an exercise in traditionally appropriate fancies; in short, he sounds contemptuous of the role he is playing and of himself for playing it. [15]

Readers who prize Shakespeare's sonnets for the few obviously great sonnets the collection contains, and to whom many of the rest are unfinished or eccentric excrescences, will probably consider this the worst kind of literary criticism, taking everthing as grist to its mill and converting tedious poetry into a serious analysis of tedium. But the reader for whom Booth is writing is the one who wishes to make sense of the whole collection rather than plunder it for individual excellence, and for him Booth's description of the tone of the sonnet helps explain why the effect of reading Sonnets 100—126 should be so different from reading the earlier young man sonnets. [16] Sonnet 99, in its completion of the group 97—99, forms the bridge between two worlds of metaphor and imagery. It returns to the rose, the great informing image of the sequence from its very beginning, and acts out the reduction to hollowness of that image and, with it, the hollowness of all love poetry addressed to the young man.

It is crucial for the development of the sequence that the exposure of such poetry's listless, stale, perfunctory nature – in Booth's words – takes place in a sonnet whose essential conventionality should be able to mislead even sensitive readers into thinking it just another Petrarchan exercise. How close the sonnet is to the stock in trade of other Elizabethan sonnet sequences may be seen by comparing it with one of Henry Constable's *Diana* sonnets. The comparison was first made by Massey, in 1872, who saw in it one of the few possible sources of a Shakespeare sonnet:

> My lady's presence makes the roses red,
>> because to see her lips, they blush for shame:
>> the lily's leaves, for envy, pale became,
> 4   and her white hands in them this envy bred.
> The marigold the leaves abroad doth spread,
>> because the sun's and her power is the same:
>> the violet of purple colour came,
> 8   dyed in the blood she made my heart to shed.
> In brief, all flowers from her their virtue take;
>> from her sweet breath their sweet smells do proceed;
>> the living heat which her eye beams doth make,
> 12   warmeth the ground, and quickeneth the seed:
>> The rain wherewith she watereth these flowers
>> falls from mine eyes, which she dissolves in showers. [17]

Any reader considering the two as single poems, unattached to sequences, is as likely to prefer Constable's version of the tradition that the poet's beloved is the source of all flowers' beauty, as he is Shakespeare's. The opening conceit of Constable's sonnet is more immediately attractive than anything in Shakespeare's sonnet. It manages, with no loss of elegance, to have its cake and eat it too, asserting first that roses are so red and lilies so white because they take their colour from his lady's presence — but the taking of the colour is, respectively, blushing with shame and growing pale with envy, because their colour lacks the intensity of her colour; and from this comes the corollary that, in relation to her, roses are not red and lilies are not white, although it needed the reader's knowledge of the redness of roses and the whiteness of lilies to provide the basis for the metaphor. Also, the whole sonnet is both self-contained and, as far as a poem can be, logical. Its purpose becomes clear at the end of the second quatrain when Constable sees her creation of the violet's purple as the result of his bleeding heart, and the sonnet ends on that note with a couplet which sets the whole flower metaphor within the life-giving showers which she forces from his eyes. In other words the poetic logic is that nature's beauty is drawn from her greater beauty and the poet's suffering. The sonnet depends upon total stasis: any realisation on the poet's part that his lady may not be so absolutely beautiful, or any movement she makes to alleviate his pain, would wreak havoc upon nature — and since nature cannot be reversed to the degree that roses cease to be red and lilies white, it is impossible for her to pity him.

Shakespeare's sonnet provides nothing so neat or self-contained. Taken out of the collection it is an oddity, with no apparent purpose, let alone argument. It opens with the poet's chiding of the "forward violet" for stealing its beauty from the young man. This is quoted verbatim, and then lines 6–9 give, in reported form, his criticism of other plants for the same fault — but as the list moves on to roses the sense of spoken criticism slides into an unspoken·noting of their weaknesses:

> The lily I condemned for thy hand,
> And buds of marjoram had stol'n thy hair;
> The roses fearfully on thorns did stand,
> One blushing shame, another white despair

"I condemned" carries its force over to "had stolen" — that is, 'I condemned the lily for having stolen the whiteness of your hand and the buds of marjoram for having stolen the beauty of your hair'[18] — but by the time "did stand" is reached it has faded into plain description. Finally the sonnet focusses on a third rose, neither red nor white, which had taken its qualities both from the other roses and from the young man's breath, and which had been eaten by a canker worm in punishment for that. The couplet adds nothing beyond noting that all other flowers which the poet had seen had likewise stolen their beauty from the young man. In effect the sonnet makes no progress, apart from replacing the poet's speech to the flowers with his mental noting of them; otherwise it begins with, has at its centre, and ends with the flowers' thefts: "Sweet thief, whence didst thou steal . . . And buds of marjoram had stol'n thy hair . . . But sweet or colour it had stol'n from thee."

My argument is that Sonnet 99 uses its conventional predictability to enclose a final and quite damning criticism of the young man by way of the most well worn metaphor in the sequence. Part of the criticism, as Booth points out, emerges from the poet's realisation that his poetry now amounts to 'pouring it on'. I will go further than that, though, and point to the reader's response to the fate of the final flower, the (apparently) pink rose which is consumed by a vengeful canker. According to the sonnet's logic this flower is being punished for having stolen from the young man and the other flowers; the reader appreciates this intellectually, but responds instinctively to the image of a canker devouring a rose and identifies the rose with the young man. The instinct is, of course, the result of the sequence's conditioning, where the example of the devouring cankerworm is constantly held up as the young man's probable fate if he goes on the way he has been doing. Other things in the sonnet help make the contra-logical identification of the young man and the rose. One is the singling out of the rose as distinct from, and parasitical upon, the other roses: that it has stolen from them also counteracts the sonnet's presentation of all flowers as thieves, by showing most of them now as victims of theft. There is also the effect in line 11 of the vague verb "annexed" — "And to his robbery had annexed thy breath" — which makes it seem as if the young man had participated in the theft.[19] Finally, and most effective of all, there is the sleight of hand which transfers the sonnet's address from the flowers to the young man, the result, indirectly, of its unique fifteen-line structure. The most obvious candidate for an extraneous line is the opening line, for "thus did I chide" introduces, or seems to introduce, a fourteen line sonnet made up of the poet's complaint to the flowers. "Sweet thief", which opens line 2, teases the reader. He knows from the first line that it is an address to the violet, but to accept this he has to disregard his instinct to apply it to the young man — an instinct conditioned by the sequence's almost formulaic use of "sweet" to describe him, and the Petrarchan habit of calling a lover some such name as 'thief' or 'murderess'; and the rest of the quatrain (assuming that to be lines 2—5) encourages the reader not to abandon that instinct. The violet is described in the language normally applied to the young man, and in a syntax which eventually makes it impossible for the reader to decide whether the violet has taken its colour from him, or whether he has robbed the violet.[20]

The sleight of hand comes in the second quatrain: "The lily I condemned for thy hand" continues the complaint, but in reported speech. Now the addressee is the young man. "My love's breath" and "my love's veins" have become "thy hand" and "thy hair", and, in line 11's mirroring of line 3, "thy breath". The result of all this is a reader's response on two levels. Logically he sees the canker-worm as the young man's agent of revenge; but instinctively he sees it bringing to pass the act threatened for so long in the sequence, when it destroys beauty's rose which should have been immortal.

It is worth returning to the Constable sonnet and making one further comparison between it and Shakespeare's Sonnet 99. Both poems take their central conceit and their images from the same convention, even to the point that Shakespeare's sonnet seems to echo phrases of Constable's, but these similarities hide the great metaphorical gulf which separates the two. Constable's sonnet, for all of its conventionality, contains an assertion of beauty and beauty's influence. It projects a world of natural beauty whose colour and perfume is taken from the poet's lady as naturally as life is taken from the sun:

> The marigold the leaves abroad doth spread,
> because the sun's and her power is the same

In Shakespeare's sonnet the vision of the young man's influence on the natural world is the opposite. "Sweet thief", in line 2, is as apparently gentle an address to a flower as any Petrarchan poet might deliver to his mistress, but the sonnet gradually drifts away from that, towards a tone of moral concern. The relationship between the young man and the natural world is life giving only in the sense that the host is life giving to the parasite. Whether, in the end, the canker-worm wreaks its vengeance on behalf of the young man, or the poet, or the natural world, is impossible to decide: but what Sonnet 99 has done is to take its metaphor seriously, a major event in the development of the young man sequence. In its logic line 13 describes the death of a flower — " A vengeful canker ate him up to death" — and this is the most powerful vision of death so far in the sequence.[21] In contrast to the sonnets which have gone before, where death has either implicitly or explicitly appeared as time's assistant, a figurative being, this is an actual, imaginable, observed death — part of a narrated incident whose occurrence is no less moving because its constituents, the rose and the canker, have been the constituents of the most familiar metaphor of the sequence.

9 'Sweets Grown Common': The Reversal of Roles I

When the reader begins Sonnet 100 the opening lines will seem so familiar that he can probably predict both the development of the sonnet's argument and the ways in which it will portray the poet—young man relationship. "Where art thou, muse, that thou forget'st so long/To speak of that which gives thee all thy might?" appears to return to the theme of sonnets like 83 and 85, where the poet admits to "having slept in your report" and bewails his "tongue-tied muse" which forces him to think good thoughts rather than write them. And the sonnet's development fits so much into the pattern of those earlier sonnets that the reader's sense of having seen it all before puts it in danger of being one of the least interesting in the sequence, a mere plodding through a well known routine. In beginning this chapter with a discussion of it, I do not intend to avoid this element so much as to introduce the possibility that its predictability is deliberate, a necessary first step in a group of three sonnets whose purpose is to shift the reader away from a stereotyped response to the poet—young man relationship, and towards seeing it in a different kind of metaphoric context.

This is Sonnet 100:

> Where art thou, muse, that thou forget'st so long
> To speak of that which gives thee all thy might?
> Spend'st thou thy fury on some worthless song,
> 4   Darkening thy power to lend base subjects light?
> Return, forgetful muse, and straight redeem
> In gentle numbers time so idly spent;
> Sing to the ear that doth thy lays esteem,
> 8   And gives thy pen both skill and argument.
> Rise, resty muse; my love's sweet face survey
> If time have any wrinkle graven there;
> If any, be a satire to decay,
> 12   And make time's spoils despised everywhere.
>   Give my love fame faster than time wastes life;
>   So thou prevent'st his scythe and crooked knife.

Many things conspire to make the reader give only half of his attention to this sonnet. It is, from the start, explicitly conventional: the separation of the poet from his muse, and his address to it as a separate being, is an almost dead metaphor — the more so here, as each quatrain begins with a renewed nod in its direction. The whole sonnet is a metaphoric self exhortation to begin writing poems to the young man again, but the address to the separate being of the muse turns it away from self analysis — i.e. 'why cannot I write such poetry anymore?' — to empty rhetoric, and the rhetoric becomes emptier as the sonnet develops. It does not need a particularly cynical reader to greet lines 7—8 with disbelief, for too many sonnets have already dealt with the young man's failure to respond for us to believe that his ear esteems the poet's lays. Nor does anything in the third quatrain seem likely to engage the reader's sympathies: like the rest of the sonnet, it relies upon automatic responses to formulas from earlier in the sequence, with time no sooner spoken of than he graves wrinkles and takes spoils, a process leading inevitably to his scythe in the couplet. Any attempt to ignore the stock images and focus instead upon the actual meaning of the quatrain only leads to a greater disenchantment; the muse is asked to look again at the young man's face, and, in response to the merest wrinkle, he should then be a satire to decay, taking as his subject the whole of time's spoils. This is the ultimate Petrarchan conceit, where one flaw on the loved one's face is equivalent to global destruction.

The reader who came to Sonnet 100 with the impression that the muse is a dead metaphor is hardly likely to have had his mind changed by the end of the sonnet. The couplet's plea for the muse to act in defiance of time seems merely a more detached, less impassioned way of affirming poetry's immortalizing powers than in such earlier sonnets as 19 or 81, where the claim is put directly, in the first person. But the muse is not so easily killed off, and the next sonnet, number 101, not only maintains the fiction of the poet addressing his muse, but has embedded within it the muse's answer to the poet:

> O truant muse, what shall be thy amends
> For thy neglect of truth in beauty dyed?
> Both truth and beauty on my love depends;
> 4 So dost thou too, and therein dignified.
> Make answer, muse, wilt thou not haply say,
> Truth needs no colour with his colour fixed,
> Beauty no pencil, beauty's truth to lay;
> 8 But best is best, if never intermixed?
> Because he needs no praise, wilt thou be dumb?

> Excuse not silence so, for't lies in thee,
> To make him much outlive a gilded tomb,
> 12   And to be praised of ages yet to be.
>   Then do thy office, muse, I teach thee how
>   To make him seem long hence as he shows now.

To say that this sonnet has the muse's answer embedded in it is one way of describing lines 6–8, but needs to be qualified, since it is not so much the muse's answer as the poet's suggestion of what that answer might be. Indeed, these lines provide an interesting problem for the modern editor: does he put them in inverted commas, or leave them as they stand in the Quarto where, of course, no such convention applied? Ingram and Redpath do the former, following, they claim, "nearly all modern editors"; Seymour-Smith and Booth leave them as they are. The difference is not insignificant. Ingram and Redpath claim that the commas "give added life to the lines" – by that I take them to mean that the commas make the lines seem the muse's direct speech, thereby turning the sonnet into an actual confrontation between two separate entities, the poet and the muse. Without the commas the conflict remains an imagined one. [1] In either case the lines mark a momentous change in the sequence, for they bring into the open the counter poetics which up to this point has only been implied. If the muse's answer, or suggested answer, be taken seriously – and the rest of the sonnet indicates that it expects to be – then it dismisses all of the poetics of praise which has underpinned the sequence so far. Truth and beauty are defined in terms of total self-sufficiency, and, furthermore, any artifice applied to them can only do harm, since best only stays best "if never intermixed". [2] This is distinctly different from Sonnet 21's refusal to overpraise, where the poet promised, instead, "to truly write". Now, no writing at all can be the only true response.

To return to the punctuation; if we take lines 6–8 as the muse's direct speech, then we leave the poet some room to manœuvre, and line 8 takes the opportunity presented by the muse's use of "needs". For the muse, "needs" contains an innuendo: "Truth needs no colour" is part definition of truth, and part implication that the young man is not representative of truth because he so clearly wants to be praised. The poet, though, ignores the innuendo, and uses "needs" only passively. The fact that the young man is perfect, and therefore needs no praise, is no excuse for silence, and the sestet proposes a purpose for poetry which transcends mere present praise – it can make him "be praised of ages yet to be". If, however, we read lines 6–8 as the poet's suggestion of what the muse's answer might be, then the sestet's proposal is more tentative. The sonnet becomes an interior battle, a piece of self persuasion in which the poet first attempts to analyse the reasons for his inability to write any more about the young man, followed by the urging of one greater motive for writing which should override those reasons. But that greater motive is doomed by its return to the idea of "praise". Lines 10–11 raise the possibility of real immortality – "for't lies in thee/To make him much outlive a gilded tomb" – but 'outliving' turns out to be merely a matter of being praised by future ages, and "praise" has already been contaminated by its use in line 9 to sum up the whole action of artifice in lines 6–8.

The reader has two possible ways through the second and third quatrains. Whichever he takes, or even if he takes both, he is left at the end in a state of doubt. If the sonnet is read as a purely internal conflict, then the third quatrain leans heavily against any prospect that the poet will write in praise of the young man again, or any kind of poetry of praise for that matter. If he accepts the fiction that there is a separate muse with whom the poet is in battle, then the couplet signals the poet's loss of that battle:

> Then do thy office, muse, I teach thee how
> To make him seem long hence as he shows now.

This is, of course, the poet writing without a muse; and without that guidance, the words he chooses betray his attitudes: "seem" and "show" carry too great a weight of deception and affectation. As synonyms for 'be' and 'is', which is how they function here, they represent the very kind of cosmetic praise which the muse has already sworn to have no part in.

Sonnet 102 finishes the group. It abandons completely the fiction of the muse, but makes clear its connection to Sonnet 101 immediately, by taking up "seem" and "show":

> My love is strengthened, though more weak in seeming;
> I love not less, though less the show appear.
> That love is merchandised, whose rich esteeming
> 4 The owner's tongue doth publish everywhere.
> Our love was new, and then but in the spring,
> When I was wont to greet it with my lays,
> As Philomel in summer's front doth sing,
> 8 And stops his pipe in growth of riper days.
> Not that the summer is less pleasant now
> Than when her mournful hymns did hush the night,
> But that wild music burthens every bough,
> 12 And sweets grown common lose their dear delight.
>   Therefore, like her, I sometime hold my tongue,
>   Because I would not dull you with my song.

"Seeming" and "show" do more than make the immediate connection with Sonnet 101, they also force the reader to recognise, if he had not already done so, the implications of those words at the end of that sonnet. At the beginning of this paragraph I wrote that Sonnet 102 abandons completely the fiction of the muse. That is true in so far as there is not here the appellation "muse", or the vocative address to that figure which occurs three times in both Sonnets 100 and 101. In a more covert way, though, this sonnet is much more the muse's than the other two. We saw how, in Sonnet 101, the poet had answered the muse's reasons by slightly twisting his use of the word "needs". In effect Sonnet 102 opens with a similar trick, only in answer to the poet himself. At the end of 101 "seem" and "show" were the poet's words, meant by him to convey only their surface meaning, and aimed at the muse as an indication of what he should be doing. Sonnet 102 is the answer, and since it is the muse's turn to speak it seems reasonable to assume that it is her answer, or, more plainly, her poem. And to a muse who believes that truth needs no colour nor beauty no pencil, then the deceitful implications of "seem" and "show" need to be picked up and exposed immediately.

For us to go on and read Sonnet 102 as the muse's poem — with "you" therefore meaning the poet, not the young man — is unnecessary, and probably wrong. From the beginning of Sonnet 100 the reader knows, to the extent that the muse is a dead metaphor, that the proclaimed existence of that figure is an act of fiction, and its sustainment through Sonnets 100 and 101 he understands to be one way for the poet to analyse his failure to write. Two sides of his personality are identified and put into conflict with each other: through 100, and for most of 101, the lover makes the running and the artist reacts. Finally, in 102, the artist takes control and the lover disappears from view.

This change of emphasis is a development which I think is sensed by every reader of Sonnet 102. I say sensed because the main metaphor of the sonnet works hard to cover up what is actually being said: the nightingale, especially in his tantalising mythical guise as Philomel, and the wild birds at song, provide an unexpectedly vivid set of images, the more so since they come directly after two sonnets where the imagery has been either muted or formulaic.[3] I shall explore this metaphor in a moment, but my immediate point is that the reason for the poet's silence — or near silence — which the metaphor leads up to, is quite different from the one given at the beginning of the sonnet. The opening quatrain seems only peripherally to be concerned with love poetry. It fixes firmly on the idea that the true lover does not make a display of his love, and the mercantile image of lines 3 – 4 seems designed to recall the couplet of Sonnet 21:

That love is merchandised, whose rich esteeming
The owner's tongue doth publish everywhere.

Let them say more that like of hearsay well;
I will not praise that purpose not to sell.

By the couplet of Sonnet 102, however, the reason for the poet's silence has
been radically changed from this positive, dignified ideal, to the merely
pragmatic response of an unappreciated poet; like the nightingale the poet
has stopped singing because there are too many other songsters about:

Therefore, like her, I sometime hold my tongue,
Because I would not dull you with my song.

Coming at the end of this group of three sonnets, the couplet is a particularly
ironic thrust, echoing mockingly the idealism of Sonnet 100's "Sing to the
ear that does thy lays esteem"; and in the phrase "I would not", it contains
only the barest pretense of respect for the young man, hardly hiding its
contempt for the person who can make no distinction between the
nightingale's song and the song of other birds, and who is likely to be soon
bored with all song.

If, as I believe, Sonnet 102 marks a moment of change in the sequence
where the values of the poet begin to take over completely from the values of
the lover—worshipper, then the metaphor of the nightingale is very
important. Its climax comes in the third quatrain where the nightingale is
presented as a creature in complete control of its song, as well as with
knowledge of its overwhelming excellence.Its uniqueness is, of course, the
poet's as well: "As Philomel" in line 7 and "like her" in line 13 indicate the
similitude between the two, but were it only to be similitude the reader
might be able to avoid the full force of the projection of the poet's values
through the figure of the bird. Instead, the third quatrain transforms the
simile into a metaphor, forcing upon the reader some perception of the
indivisibility of the poet and the nightingale. To show how that happens, I
shall have to begin with the octave:

My love is strengthened, though more weak in seeming;
I love not less, though less the show appear.
That love is merchandised, whose rich esteeming
4   The owner's tongue doth publish everywhere.

> Our love was new, and then but in the spring,
> When I was wont to greet it with my lays,
> As Philomel in summer's front doth sing,
> And stops his pipe in growth of riper days.

Here Philomel does not appear until line 7, and then only as one element in a simile; but its appearance breaks up one pattern which the sonnet has already established — that of two line descriptions of different states of love ("My love . . . That love . . . Our love"). In compensation it seems to introduce a different form of symmetry, lines 7−8 giving reasons for the state of affairs described in lines 5−6, just as lines 3−4 give reasons for the state described in lines 1−2. The only difference between the two halves is that where lines 3−4 supply a metaphorical explanation, lines 7−8 stay on the more superficial level of the simile. However, line 8 is slightly unexpected. The reader anticipates that the nightingale simile will present merely another way of putting what lines 5−6 have just said — i.e. 'how well I sang to you in the past' — but instead of such nostalgia he gets a return to the declared matter of the sonnet: not, 'when I sang to you in the past it was like the nightingale singing in spring', but instead the much more pertinent 'I have stopped singing to you just as the nightingale stops singing in summer.'

So far the simile is in hand, and the reader's mental adjustments still allow him to keep the bird and the poet apart. The rest of the sonnet makes this much more difficult, for, instead of dropping the nightingale simile, it intensifies it:

> Not that the summer is less pleasant now
> Than when her mournful hymns did hush the night,
> But that wild music burthens every bough,
> And sweets grown common lose their dear delight.
>> Therefore, like her, I sometime hold my tongue,
>> Because I would not dull you with my song.

The complexities of line 9 would probably need a page to analyse. Put simply, they are that the line forces the reader to confuse the poet and the bird. On one level the sonnet seems to be returning to the matter in hand, taking up the poet's figurative summer as a continuation of his earlier "spring" in line 5, but on another level it continues the nightingale simile by beginning to give the reasons for the bird's silence. "Now", at the end of the line, is both the sonnet's now — the actual period of the poet's weaker seeming love — and the nightingale's now — the riper days when she stops her pipe. [4] The rest of the sestet makes play of the confusion between the two:

it allows the poet to portray himself as the unique songmaker, silenced only by his contempt for would-be rivals, with the couplet showing his greater contempt for the young man who has no ear for his music.[5]

In essence this group of three sonnets has begun to break down the schematized roles which the earlier part of the sequence had done so much to establish. The opening of Sonnet 100 lulls the reader into expecting another series of variations on the theme of the poet's muse being unable properly to praise the young man; but by the end of Sonnet 102 such rules no longer apply. The poet has used the muse to assert his, rather than his subject's, uniqueness and independence, and after such poetic subversion the reversal of roles, in which the poet is the sinner and the young man the victim, becomes, if not inevitable, then at least comprehensible and acceptable. Sonnets 117–121 deal directly with that reversal, culminating in 121's outspoken self-justification "No, I am that I am, and they that level/At my abuses reckon up their own"; but before we come to the brutality of that group, four earlier sonnets, 109–112, analyse more indirectly the causes and effects of the change of roles, and the possible poetic strategies for coping with it.

Most critical attention has been directed to Sonnets 109–112 – especially Sonnets 111 and 112 – for their possible autobiographical allusions: Shakespeare the dramatist bewailing his public means and public manners, with his nature subdued to what it works in, like the dyer's hand. This is obviously a matter of importance in any consideration of Shakespeare the man, even if for a study like this of the development of the sequence as a work of art, its interest is more incidental than central; but that generations of critics and readers have felt the need to explore such potentially autobiographical elements at this point in the sequence is useful support for my argument that this is the place where roles are reversed, with the poet emerging as the explicitly central figure, and the young man fast fading into a victim's obscurity.[6] Nothing could be a clearer measure of the change than the way Sonnet 109, which begins the group, takes up a major theme of the sequence, the poet's absence from the young man, and makes it quite obvious that the absence has been of the poet's choosing and under his control:

> O never say that I was false of heart,
> Though absence seemed my flame to qualify.
> As easy might I from myself depart,
> 4   As from my soul, which in thy breast doth lie.
> This is my home of love; if I have ranged
> Like him that travels I return again,

> Just to the time, not with the time exchanged,
> 8   So that myself bring water for my stain.
> Never believe, though in my nature reigned
> All frailties that besiege all kinds of blood,
> That it could so preposterously be stained
> 12   To leave for nothing all thy sum of good—
> For nothing this wide universe I call,
> Save thou, my rose; in it thou art my all.

This sonnet signals its insincerity in several ways. One is the degeneration of "all" in the sestet — "All frailties . . . all kinds of blood . . . all thy sum of good" — so that the couplet's final claim that the rose is the poet's "all" has a more than conventionally hollow hyperbolical ring. Another sign that the poet is writing what he no longer feels is the unusually cramped rhyming through the second and third quatrains: in the second the rhyme stays fixed to the same vowel — ranged, again, exchanged, stain — and the third repeats it in "reigned" and "stained". Finally, "preposterously" is a word which would obtrude in any sonnet, and here its effect runs counter to the poet's argument which is itself the preposterous thing, not, as the sonnet would have it, the young man's accusation. In the context of the second quatrain, to be preposterously stained would be a fair summary of the poet's action as he presents it — where the metaphor of travelling from home seems to convey his admission of infidelity. But in the final three lines the poet retreats from that admission, and replaces it with the emptiest of conventional confessions, that to have paid attention to anything else in the universe, other than the beloved, has been a crime. "This wide universe" is a much more acceptable accomplice than an actual person.

So far I have been describing the sonnet's retreat into insincerity after the apparent beginnings of a confession in the second quatrain. It might be objected, though, that the confession is couched in such vague terms, with so much verbal casuistry, that I am overstating its importance.[7] My answer must be that the second quatrain surprises the reader sufficiently for him to be alert to all of its possible ramifications. Consider, after all, the effect of the first quatrain—the way in which it strikes a reader familiar with the claims and appeals of the sequence up to this point:

> O never say that I was false of heart,
> Though absence seemed my flame to qualify.
> As easy might I from myself depart,
> As from my soul, which in thy breast doth lie.

It is an entirely unexceptional appeal, resting its case on the stock image of the poet's soul locked in the lover's breast, and the one response the reader is unlikely to have is to restrict its reference to the actual moment of speaking, the present. Indeed, although the first two lines admit both a present sense and a future sense – either 'don't say that I have been false although my absence seems to have given reason for it', or, 'don't ever say that I am false although my absence might seem to give reason for it' – the image of the third and fourth lines points the reader towards the future alone.[8] The poet's soul lodged in his lover's breast goes hand in hand with promises of eternal fidelity. The more surprising, then, is the second quatrain's location in time:

> This is my home of love; if I have ranged
> Like him that travels I return again,
> Just to the time, not with the time exchanged,
> So that myself bring water for my stain.

Now the future is ignored and the sonnet firmly located in the present and immediate past – not 'I will never be unfaithful', but 'I have not just been unfaithful although it may seem as if I have.' And by the time the reader reaches the end of the quatrain, and the speciousness of the claim that merely having returned on time will cleanse the stain, then the opening line might well be reinterpreted purely literally – not 'I have not been unfaithful', but 'don't say that I have been unfaithful'. If so, then it is not a substantially greater jump for the reader to interpret the couplet literally:

> For nothing this wide universe I call,
> Save thou, my rose; in it thou art my all.

Not 'I hold the universe to be nothing', but 'I call the universe nothing.'

If in Sonnet 109 the poet's admission of his sin is generally implied rather than stated, Sonnet 110 sets out to give a confession in full. The couplet of 109 had insisted upon a complete spurning of the world, so it comes as a jolt to move immediately to a sonnet whose opening question returns the reader to a consideration of public demands upon the poet, and their effect upon his love. This is Sonnet 110:

> Alas, 'tis true, I have gone here and there,
> And made myself a motley to the view,
> Gored mine own thoughts, sold cheap what is most dear,
> 4   Made old offences of affections new.
> Most true it is, that I have looked on truth

> Askance and strangely. But by all above,
> These blenches gave my heart another youth,
> 8   And worse essays proved thee my best of love.
> Now all is done, have what shall have no end–
> Mine appetite I never more will grind
> On newer proof to try an older friend,
> 12   A god in love, to whom I am confined.
>   Then give me welcome, next my heaven the best,
>   Even to thy pure and most most loving breast.

So unexpected is the return to the poet's public life that the reader begins to suspect here, more than anywhere else in the sequence, the presence of something like the metaphysical dramatic mode, with the poem set out as an argument in response to an imagined interlocutor.[9] Between 109's "thou art my all" and "Alas, 'tis true" the telling objection has been voiced: 109's poetic panacea will not be enough to cleanse the stain, and Sonnet 110 offers a set of fresher excuses.[10]

Fresher excuses they may be, but in the end no clearer – unless the reader is prepared to abandon the suspension of common-sense which the sonnet convention demands. At the heart of this sonnet, so cold-blooded a reader will find lines 7–8 transparently crude – "These blenches gave my heart another youth,/And worse essays proved thee my best of love" – the poet's main excuse for his infidelity being that it has rejuvenated him, and, by implication, made him a better lover for the young man. Wrapped around these lines, though, is a series of phrases and images which might be held up as models of vagueness – how to say nothing, while giving every impression of having admitted, confessed, and acknowledged guilt. The poet admits to having made himself "a motley to the view" (line 2), a phrase which conveys the sense of having made a fool of himself in public, but nothing more specific than that; and the sonnet continues to communicate the tone of guilt without the substance: "Gored mine own thoughts" (3), "sold cheap what is most dear" (3), "Made old offences of affections new" (4), "I have looked on truth/Askance and strangely" (5–6), "these blenches" (7), "worse essays" (8), "Mine appetite I never more will grind/On newer proof" (10–11). It is not simply that none of these phrases makes the reader any clearer about the nature or extent of the guilt, but that the very act of confession – the declared purpose of the sonnet – is betrayed. Instead of poetic rhetoric being used to dignify the relationship between the poet and his beloved, it degrades it: guilt becomes a matter to be clouded with words, persuasion away from the truth. And from this, perhaps, comes the contrary effect of line 12, "A god in love, to whom I am confined". Within the sonnet's

argument, both literal and metaphorical, this is a conventionally hyperbolical compliment. The young man is a god – whether a god who happens to
be in love, or a god of love, is a pleasing ambiguity – and the poet is bound
to serve him alone, as if he were a repentant sinner who, as the sonnet had
earlier described, had served false gods but now realises the value of
monotheism. In contrast, though, is the depressing effect of the rhyme word
"confined", which makes the poet's love seem imprisonment, especially
when set against the life and novelty of the rejuvenating infidelity which
informs most of the sonnet. As if to tilt the balance towards the second
response, the couplet rings with innuendo:

> Then give me welcome, next my heaven the best,
> Even to thy pure and most most loving breast.

"Next my heaven" puts the god in love in his second best place, and "most
most loving" reduces the sonnet to doggerel – and I shall pass over the
appropriateness of the epithet "pure" for the young man. But knowing the
sonnet's subject as we do by now, we may judge that doggerel will probably
keep him more happy than would poetry; and the opening of the next
sonnet, number 111, indicates that the poet's arguments in 110 have worked.
The poet, it seems, is not guilty since he is principally the victim of fortune:

> O for my sake do you with fortune chide,
> The guilty goddess of my harmful deeds,
> That did not better for my life provide
> 4 Than public means which public manners breeds.
> Thence comes it that my name receives a brand,
> And almost thence my nature is subdued
> To what it works in, like the dyer's hand.
> 8 Pity me then, and wish I were renewed,
> Whilst like a willing patient I will drink
> Potions of eisel 'gainst my strong infection;
> No bitterness that I will bitter think,
> 12 Nor double penance, to correct correction.
>   Pity me then, dear friend, and I assure ye,
>   Even that your pity is enough to cure me.

In discussing Sonnet 110 I wrote about the cold-blooded reader who will see
at the heart of that sonnet two crude excuses for the poet's infidelity –
rejuvenation and appreciation by contrast. I ought to have added that this
reader will probably be struck by the idea that both of these excuses are

particularly apt indications of the reversal of roles between the two men at this point in the sequence. The young man's youth, his need to spread his charms around (while stopping short at procreative intercourse) and to taunt the poet with his infidelity, have been common themes of sonnets throughout the sequence. Now, by the end of Sonnet 111, even the most charitable reader will have begun to appreciate the change: the poet rather than the young man has become the public creature, and the young man rather than the poet is forced to make excuses for his lover's infidelities instead of openly accusing him. Nonetheless, the poet is still the poet, the man who pulls the strings of the sonnet, so that our perception of the young man as a victim is, at the same time, keener and more frustrating, than our earlier perception of the poet in that role.

I had better expand that distinction a little. In a sonnet earlier in the sequence where the victim does the speaking – Sonnet 34, for instance – the very fact that there is a conventionally formed poem tempers our response. The poet complains; we receive his complaint sympathetically, but we are always aware of his control over what he says, so that the couplet of purely conventional self humbling does not hide from us the probability of sarcastic retaliation:

> Ah, but those tears are pearl which thy love sheeds,
> And they are rich, and ransom all ill deeds

In Sonnet 111, though, the victim is not allowed to speak – his speech is merely summarised in the first line, and although we may not be sure of exactly the place where it happens, we are aware that the poet has taken over and has turned that speech the way he wants it.[11] At the end of the first quatrain, "public means which public manners breeds" is persuasive to the eye and ear, as are many of the lines in the sequence which depend upon immediate repetition of a word, but neither the reader's intellect nor his moral sense will be taken in by it.[12] And it is not merely a passing idea, but is given two separate images in the following lines, the branded name and the dyer's hand. This is the point where it is useful to be able to fall back upon autobiography, with Shakespeare the player not so much lamenting the fact that the stage has such a bad name as he is lamenting his having to work in such a sordid profession – an attractive way of getting around the speciousness of the sonnet's reasoning, since it is not difficult to demonstrate that players were held in contempt, and that an aspiring gentleman whose talents led him into that kind of work might well find this an irksome and unfair blow of fate. I shall not waste space on trying to dissuade supporters of that interpretation from making central what is only peripheral; instead I will argue that, if anything, it makes the poet's position even more unsupportable. So far, in Sonnets 109 and 110, we have seen being developed an admission of infidelity. Sonnet 110 had played with the idea that such weakness on the poet's part is equivalent to going public, the first quatrain combining the two typical public figures, the jester and the pedlar, but with the reader always aware that these were metaphorical parallels. [13] Quite coolly, Sonnet 111 takes the metaphor literally: the poet's public life has led to his public deeds. Actually it is not public deeds but "harmful deeds" which the sonnet announces its intention to excuse, but even that phrase is a weak summary of the catalogue of vague but serious faults which 110 had listed; and by the second quatrain this sonnet has turned from an examination of the poet's infidelity to self pity at the kind of environment which he has to live and work in. To return to my earlier formulation, our perception of the young man as the victim is both keener and more frustrating than our earlier perception of the poet in that role—keener because we come to see him as the most pathetic of victims, one who cannot even speak for himself, but more frustrating because it is almost impossible for the reader to maintain his sense of the poet's fault through the octave of Sonnet 111: his attention is directed towards pity for the poet in his public role, probably all the greater if he finds himself feeling sympathy for one of nature's gentlemen forced to sink his hands into the pitch of theatre life.

The second half of the sonnet twice calls explicitly for pity:

8   Pity me then, and wish I were renewed,
    Whilst like a willing patient I will drink
    Potions of eisel 'gainst my strong infection;
    No bitterness that I will bitter think,
12 Nor double penance, to correct correction.
      Pity me then, dear friend, and I assure ye,
      Even that your pity is enough to cure me.

Anyone searching for examples of Shakespeare's failures in sonnet writing will be strongly tempted to make these lines the plum. Lines 8–12 depend more on an instinctive verbal repetition than on making sense, and the couplet is spectacularly weak. [14] It would be superfluous of me to argue that the botching is intentional: my general case that the young man sonnets form a carefully designed sequence takes for granted that such effects are planned. Assuming that the reader will give Shakespeare the benefit of the doubt, then the effect of these lines' obvious improverishment is to force into the open the collusion between the reader and poet, at the expense of the young man. The wish to be "renewed", in line 8, is a vague one, part religious and part medical, and the role it leaves for the young man has just that degree of sententiousness, part doctor of divinity, part doctor of medicine. For the reader, the effect of that comparison comes close to burlesque, given the probable nature of the poet's actual sin and disease — and the poet's quaffing of vinegar only adds worse to bad.[15] The poet, in fact, is casting his roles with great care. He is now no longer sinner, but victim; the young man no longer complainer, but spiritual guide, the poet's only possible saviour. Such roles are plainly ridiculous, but the reader's complicity is willingly given, and what started in Sonnets 109 and 110 as shifty confession, ends in Sonnet 112 as defiance and self-justification:

> Your love and pity doth th' impression fill,
> Which vulgar scandal stamped upon my brow;
> For what care I who calls me well or ill,
> 4   So you o'er-green my bad, my good allow?
> You are my all the world, and I must strive
> To know my shames and praises from your tongue;
> None else to me, nor I to none alive,
> 8   That my steeled sense or changes right or wrong.
> In so profound abysm I throw all care
> Of others' voices, that my adder's sense
> To critic and to flatterer stopped are.
> 12   Mark how with my neglect I do dispense:
>   You are so strongly in my purpose bred,
>   That all the world besides me thinks y' are dead.

So far as the world goes, past cure past care. In 111's couplet only the young man could clear the poet of his infection. Now the cure is described in metaphorical detail as the ultimate cosmetic operation, the filling in of a scar; and when that is done the poet has no care for what the world says or thinks. We are, of course, in familiar territory in this sonnet, with the lover cast as the poet's whole world, and the sense that the rest of the world looks with a critical eye upon their relationship. What is unfamiliar, though, is the use of this self denying convention for the purposes of self-justification. Scattered through the sonnet are (gradually diminishing) acknowledgements by the poet that he might have done something wrong — "vulgar scandal", "well or ill", "my bad, my good", "my shames and praises", "right or wrong", "to critic and to flatterer" — but they are submerged in the language of romantic self-denial — "for what care I who calls me", "You are my all the world", "I must strive/To know . . . from your tongue", "None else to me, nor I to none alive", "In so profound abysm I throw all care." Or at least that will seem to be the language of self-denial to the reader who has experienced the sequence so far; but within the group 109–112 it emerges as self-justification. All comes to a head in "neglect", in line 12, a line which explicitly introduces the couplet:

> Mark how with my neglect I do dispense:
> You are so strongly in my purpose bred,
> That all the world besides me thinks y' are dead.

Is it neglect of the world or neglect of the young man which the couplet excuses? The impossibility of choosing between the two measures the success of the poet's strategy, a success which has been strangely supported by editorial indecision over the couplet. In the Quarto text the couplet seems to mark the final turn of the screw: not, as the reader might anticipate, 'you are so much a part of my life that I consider the rest of the world to be dead', but 'you are so much a part of my life that the rest of the world thinks you are dead'. Understandably, this has been too much for a number of editors, who prefer the anticipated sense, and emend line 14 to "That all the world besides methinks are dead."[16] It is comfortable to have the Petrarchan ending, but not really necessary. As the Quarto stands, the couplet completes the first stage of the reversal of roles. Now the poet is the sinner who is excused both by himself and by his self-denying lover; the young man is the lover who lives in complete obscurity except for the reflected glory of the poet.

10 'To Constancy Confined': Present Time

In Chapter 12 I shall discuss the treatment of time in these last sonnets, in particular their design to show the poet, not the young man, as the potential victor over time. Before that, and partly in preparation for it, I am devoting this chapter to the group of three sonnets, 105–107, each of which, in different ways, focuses on the poet's position in the present and his memory of the past. For reasons which should become clear, I shall begin with the central sonnet of the group, number 106:

> When in the chronicle of wasted time
> I see descriptions of the fairest wights
> And beauty making beautiful old rhyme
> 4 In praise of ladies dead and lovely knights,
> Then in the blazon of sweet beauty's best,
> Of hand, of foot, of lip, of eye, of brow,
> I see their antique pen would have expressed
> 8 Even such a beauty as you master now.
> So all their praises are but prophecies
> Of this our time, all you prefiguring,
> And for they looked but with divining eyes,
> 12 They had not still enough your worth to sing;
>   For we which now behold these present days,
>   Have eyes to wonder, but lack tongues to praise.[1]

Up to this point in the sequence the remembrance of things past had been a vital part of the poet's consciousness, but usually subordinated to the demands of present and future time with the young man. At least that is the declared intention of a poem like Sonnet 30, where the sessions of sweet silent thought, and the sighs and wailings which they provoke at the memory of dead friends, are removed by thinking of the young man. Sonnet 106 is not so acutely personal, in that it meditates upon poetry of the past rather than past friends, but its similarity to Sonnet 30 is marked both in its plot – a solitary meditation upon time past – and in its "When . . . Then" syntactic structure. Where it differs is in its failure to come to any resolution. Sonnet 30's comfort in the mere act of thinking upon the young man proclaims the idea of progress: time has now brought a final, all-embracing conclusion. Sonnet 106, in contrast, first promises the same kind of progress as is found between the Old Testament and the New, but frustrates its promise in the couplet.

As well as Sonnet 30, this sonnet recalls at least one other in the sequence, Sonnet 59, which it seems to be answering. Sonnet 59 had proposed, hypothetically, that nothing really changes – "If there be nothing new, but that which is/Hath been before . . ." – and, following that hypothesis, it raised the question as to whether the new world is better able than the old to find words to praise its most wonderful creature:

> O that record could with a backward look,
> Even of five hundred courses of the sun,
> Show me your image in some antique book,
> 8 Since mind at first in character was done,
> That I might see what the old world could say
> To this composed wonder of your frame;
> Whether we are mended, or where better they,
> 12 Or whether revolution be the same.

Few commentators have found much to say for the sonnet's attempt to answer its own question in the couplet:

> O sure I am the wits of former days
> To subjects worse have given admiring praise.

This seems so unconvincing – and unconvinced – that it has prompted Ingram and Redpath to describe it as an intentionally ironic understatement, 'otherwise the ending would be ineffably banal.'[2] Whether or not it is ironic, the couplet encompasses the whole of Sonnet 106, where the poet muses on the work of former wits and the admiring praise which they have given to inferior subjects. The major difference, now, is that the poet speaks from certainty: he knows that those former poets were always reaching to describe perfection in spite of the imperfection of their subjects. This insight into the poet's fate is one of the reasons for the reader's greater awareness of the poet's presence in Sonnet 106, than in either 30 or 59. In 59 "That I might see what the old world could say", and "O sure I am . . .", seem more or less automatic first person references; and in 30 "I summon up remembrance of things past" has already been metaphorically contextualised by "sessions", and itself leads into a sonnet where the poet's personality is hidden behind the imagery. In Sonnet 106, though, the reader shares the poet's meditative process. At first, "I see description of the fairest wights" seems the same kind of automatic first person as in Sonnet 59, especially in the archaic context of "fairest wights", but when the verb "see" recurs in the second quatrain, it has a slightly changed sense, from mere observation to actual understanding.[3] The first quatrain's opening "When" makes us anticipate the second quatrain's "Then", but the necessary verb is held up for two lines – not 'Then I see', but

> Then in the blazon of sweet beauty's best,
> Of hand, of foot, of lip, of eye, of brow,
> I see . . .

The familiar "When . . . Then" structure often requires the reader to tread a careful line between simultaneity and consequence – between 'when I see this, at the same moment I see that', and 'after I have seen this, then I see that.' Here, however, the reader's forced wait for the verb points him towards consequence, as if a train of thought were carried through the initial sight and all of its details, ending in an understanding of what that sight means – and its meaning here is bound up with the poet's own experience as a reader. The octave is his response to, and interpretation of, the poetry of the past: from the sonnet's beginning that response is inseparable from the poet's sense of its pastness. Not only the archaism of wights and knights, but the opening line's half romantic, half resigned "chronicle of wasted time" makes the atmosphere one of loss, and nostalgia for that loss.[4] The line which rounds off the quatrain, "In praise of ladies dead and lovely knights", is insidiously disturbing. "Dead" is the word which does the damage – I suppose that poems in praise of ladies dead might, in one sense, be funeral elegies, but I doubt whether many readers consider the elegiac to be the primary meaning here. "Ladies dead" is a phrase which conveys, as simply as possible, the huge distance which separates the poets of the past and the poet of the sonnets: his subject is alive and breathing, theirs are dead and cold – and the phrase's contamination extends to its parallel, "lovely knights", which would normally be a romantic cliché, but which now takes on the pathetic perspective of the romantic figures of the past turned to dust.[5]

Sonnet 106 shows the poet to be a particularly biased reader of poetry, his sense of its pastness making his response to it entirely reductive. The second quatrain carries over the morbidity of "ladies dead" into its catalogue of beauty, but now the reader's sense that those beautiful descriptions of hand, foot, lip, eye, and brow, are only pathetic reminders of the past, is pitted against the poet's reading of them all as a prefiguration of the young man. I doubt whether he carries many readers with him, and I doubt too whether he intends to, for what he is describing is strictly personal, his own meditation coming from his own sense of the fragility of the present moment. The impossibility of holding on to the present has dominated the sequence from its beginning: its declared aim, in keeping alive beauty's rose, has been to hold in perfection the very moment of the young man's prime – something which procreation and poetry promised to do, but which now seems impossibly idealistic. For any poetry to survive as more than antique work, it needs to be reinterpreted now, and, in this case, "now" is the moment when the young man masters his beauty – leading to the effortless conclusion here, that "all their praises are but prophecies/Of this our time, all you prefiguring." At this point in the sonnet readers make the kind of tactical retreat which they have become expert at doing: 'we must allow the poet his convention, and here he makes use of both Christological and typological conceits to affirm the uniqueness of his subject' is their judgment, thereby indicating their own good sense in not giving way to the hyperbole, but merely giving it a balanced critical – and in our case, historical – acceptance. But this response is something which the couplet identifies and acknowledges:

> For we which now behold these present days,
> Have eyes to wonder, but lack tongues to praise.

In the couplet's first line "now" reappears, and seems only to be a line filler – for who else beholds these present days, other than people 'now'? The answer is two other sets of readers: those in the past who see them as it were through a glass darkly, and those in the future who will see them in the same way as the poet sees the poetry of his past, the product of an antique pen.

Sonnet 106 is, finally, a series of frustrations. Past, present, and future perpetually check each other, with the poet's attempt to describe the perfection of his subject doomed to take its own place in the chronicle of wasted time. The chief frustration is voiced in the couplet. The young man provides the ideal subject for prophetic poetry, but no prophet has appeared.[6] Furthermore, one implication of the couplet, in its generalised "we", is that the times themselves do not permit such a poet; but the reference is also a personalised one, with "behold" and "have eyes to wonder" completing the "I see . . . I see" refrain of the first two quatrains. In this respect the sonnet is a bridge between Sonnets 105 and 107, and marks the centre point in a poetic reassessment of time, in which the poet's obsessive concern with his one all-transcendent subject gives way to a poetry of universal prophecy. The difference between Sonnet 105 and Sonnet 107 is immense: 105 is self-contained, works within the confines of its three-in-one conceit, and uses it to explain why the poet's work, as a whole, must be so monotonously confined; 107 has proved to be the most open-ended in the collection – full of vague but apparently meaningful phrases, it has teased a century of commentators by its refusal to make its incertainties assured, and it closes with images of a triumphant, ever-fresh poetry.

Clearly any attempt to read the sonnets seriously must eventually grapple with the magnificent incertainties of Sonnet 107. My way of approaching it is to try to assess the degree to which it is experienced as the poetically logical conclusion to the two sonnets which precede it. So, before considering the link which connects it to Sonnet 106, I must first point out what it is that connects Sonnet 105 to 106. The link between them is the deification of the young man. In 106, as we have seen, the deification is primarily literary: the poetry of the past and its visions of beauty's best are all prefigurations of the young man's unique beauty, in the same way as the Old Testament prefigures the New.[7] Sonnet 105 also has a literary context, but it is related more pointedly to the poet's love for the young man:

> Let not my love be called idolatry,
> Nor my beloved as an idol show,
> Since all alike my songs and praises be
> 4 To one, of one, still such, and ever so.
> Kind is my love today, tomorrow kind,
> Still constant in a wondrous excellence;
> Therefore my verse to constancy confined,
> 8 One thing expressing, leaves out difference.
> Fair, kind, and true, is all my argument,
> Fair, kind, and true, varying to other words;
> And in this change is my invention spent –
> 12 Three themes in one, which wondrous scope affords.
>   Fair, kind, and true, have often lived alone,
>   Which three, till now, never kept seat in one.

It is not difficult to see why this sonnet should have failed to attract much critical discussion: even so sensitive a reader of the sonnets as Stephen Booth discounts it as seriously intended, describing it as a 'playful experiment in perversity'.[8] But it is possible to take the sonnet seriously, as Martin Seymour-Smith does in his explanatory note. This is how he concludes it:

There is an almost doxological deliberateness about this particular sonnet which suggests that what Shakespeare really meant was: 'I realize that, because of what is bad in your character, some people might call you a false God. But my love owes to you a deliberate celebration of those qualities of kindness, beauty and truth which you do in reality possess. My love's duty is to concentrate upon these qualities even in the teeth of the evidence.'

This interpretation is in no sense intended as a paraphrase; but it does account for the peculiar dogmatic and liturgical quality of the sonnet.[9]

There might not appear to be any common ground between those who see Sonnet 105 as a mere exercise of wit and Seymour-Smith's perception of an almost doxological deliberateness in it; but both of these extremes do at least share the negative role of playing down the sonnet's basic concern, which is with the writing of love sonnets. There is no doubt that the opening quatrain is more a game of wit than anything else: as Booth puts it, 'the wit . . . derives from the false logic resulting from the speaker's studiously inadequate understanding of idolatry . . . although all polytheism is idolatrous, it does not therefore follow that any and all monotheisms are orthodox as the speaker here pretends.'[10] I would add to this that underlying the wit is a matter of real concern to the poet, namely the effect that writing to such a subject has upon his poetry: the substance of the quatrain is that to vary his writing any way – from "fair, kind, and true", as the sonnet later makes clear – is impossible. And the second quatrain makes the equation between subject and poem exact: just as he is unchanging, so must the poet's verse be. That is, and continues to be, the argument of the sonnet; but by this point the reader is beginning to pick up distinctly subversive implications. A verse which is so confined that it only expresses one thing and leaves out difference is sterile and predictable – to use Seymour-Smith's word, more doxology than poetry – and in the third quatrain these implications are pinned to particular words, "spent" and "affords". The idea of spending poetic invention recalls Sonnet 76's "Spending again what is already spent" (which also rhymes with "argument"). There poverty and impotence underlie the financial and sexual meanings of the word: both reappear in this sonnet, where the plain passive – "And in this change is my invention spent" – emphasises the sterility of so confined a verse. More ironic is "wondrous scope" in the next line, "Three themes in one, which wondrous scope affords." It clearly echoes "wondrous excellence" in line 6, and if we are content with the sonnet's declared one for one equation of the young man and the poem, then it is fitting that the same epithet should describe both. Just as the young man's constancy is wondrous, his uniqueness actually containing three separate themes, so will poetry dedicated to him have wondrous variety of description at its command. But "affords", set against a spent invention, contradicts that and encourages the reader to treat the whole line as irony. After all, three themes in one has just been poeticized at the beginning of the quatrain, and the result hardly bespeaks wondrous scope: "Fair, kind, and true is all my argument,/Fair, kind, and true, varying to other words." The couplet takes up the refrain, but to even worse effect:

> Fair, kind, and true, have often lived alone,
> Which three, till now, never kept seat in one.

Booth's comment on the last line is particularly pertinent: 'The line is nearly prose; whether by accident or design, its rhythmic awkwardness suggests the difficulty of retaining three in one.'[11]

Sonnet 106 follows by extending the poet's confinement (and the reader's) to cover not only his own verse but all other poetry. Every attempt to paint beauty's best was, it seems, a prefiguration of the young man, and now the confinements of time are added to Sonnet 105's confinement of the poet's verse to the unyielding constancy of its subject. Then Sonnet 107 unexpectedly, but not unreasonably, breaks out of the multiple confinements — not unreasonably, in that the movement from the poet's religious servitude to the world's religious servitude in Sonnets 105 – 106, if it is to be developed any further, can only end apocalyptically; but the change is unexpected since 107's apocalyptic vision contradicts both the sterility of "fair, kind, and true" and the despair of 106's couplet:

> Not mine own fears nor the prophetic soul
> Of the wide world dreaming on things to come
> Can yet the lease of my true love control,
> 4   Supposed as forfeit to a confined doom.
> The mortal moon hath her eclipse endured,
> And the sad augurs mock their own presage,
> Incertainties now crown themselves assured,
> 8   And peace proclaims olives of endless age.
> Now with the drops of this most balmy time
> My love looks fresh, and death to me subscribes,
> Since spite of him I'll live in this poor rhyme,
> 12   While he insults o'er dull and speechless tribes.
>   And thou in this shalt find thy monument,
>   When tyrants' crests and tombs of brass are spent.

I do not have to argue strongly for the word "apocalyptic" to describe this sonnet, since I doubt whether any reader can miss its eschatological power. Partly it is a matter of phrasing and imagery – "things to come", "confined doom", "Incertainties now crown themselves assured", "endless age", "death to me subscribes" – but more important is the sweep of the whole sonnet from the sombre to the sublime. We have become so familiar with the discussion of potential historical significances in the sonnet than we may tend to treat it more as a document than a poem. The trouble with this approach is that it spoils the actual experience of reading the sonnet: not only is the grandeur of its vagueness lessened by having phrases such as "mortal moon" pinned to specific persons or events, but such particularisation encourages the reader to see the sonnet as something emerging from a settled viewpoint – for instance, relief at the defeat of the Armada, or at Elizabeth's recovery – when it is really a sonnet of much less certainty than that. The experience of reading it, rather than reading about it, is to feel insecurity and uncertainty through the first two quatrains, until the assertion of line 8, that "peace proclaims olives of endless age" – and I mean 'insecurity and uncertainty' to apply primarily to the sonnet's plot.

Sonnets are not like plays, whose endings begin at the first line. Shakespearean tragedy, for instance, is normally unmistakable tragedy from the opening scene, and where it is not, as in *Romeo and Juliet*, then the audience is given explicit direction as to the way matters will develop. A sonnet requires much less investment from the reader, so it is possible, and often desirable, for the poet to lead him one way, and then force him to change direction either part of the way through or at the end. But some sonnets require more than normal investment, and there the reader is likely to feel uneasy if he is not sure what it is that he is investing in. Sonnet 107's investment is bound up with the syntax, rhythm, and vocabulary of the opening lines. Its opening phrase demands the reader's full acquiescence: "Not mine own fears" is unmistakably the opening of a long, grand sentence – an opening of rhetorical immensity. The one other sonnet which opens like it is 55, "Not marble, nor the gilded monuments/Of princes . . .", and its direction and purpose is clear from the moment we reach the verb "outlive" in the second line. But in 107 the rhetoric seems to become more and more ambiguously qualified, so that while the meaning of the first quatrain, reinforced by its syntax and rhythm, is that the poet's love transcends both his own and the world's limitations, the reader is burdened with a vocabulary which conveys fear and threat – "fears", "things to come", "lease", "control", "supposed", "forfeit", and "confined doom", and there is also the action of "yet" in line 3, "Can yet the lease of my true love control", which makes it difficult to avoid taking the inference that so far the poet's love is transcendent, but it must eventually fall under the control of his fears and the world's prophecy.[12] Lines 5—7 supply further ambiguities:

> The mortal moon hath her eclipse endured,
> And the sad augurs mock their own presage,
> Incertainties now crown themselves assured . . .

"Mortal moon" is a disturbing conjunction, with its recollection of the Book of Revelation, where the imminent apocalypse is foreshadowed by the vision of the moon turning to blood — the more so, if we consider Hotson's argument, made with the aim of tying the line to the defeat of the Armada, that "hath . . . endured" is an uncertain verb when applied to an eclipse, since it can mean either that the moon has survived it, or that she has succumbed to it.[13] The next two lines have their own menace. The sadness of the augurers might be the result of their doomladen prophecies having failed to come to pass, or it might describe their sadness at having their prophecies of triumph fail — auguries can be good or bad, and the line's ambiguity comes from its description of the prophets as "sad", and not the things which they had prophesied. "Incertainties now crown themselves assured" also moves the reader two ways at once: the impression is that all incertainty has now been cleared up, but the hint of a personification of Incertainty — of a whole tribe of them, in fact — leads to a view that things are more uncertain than ever: everything is now ruled by incertainty. Only at line 8 does the reader find his own certainty about the purpose of the sonnet: "And peace proclaims olives of endless age." It is, it emerges, a poem of triumph, the song of a man who has won. "Now" is the moment when peace can proclaim its own eternity, and "now", as lines 9—10 put it, the poet's love looks fresh. To that extent the negative possibilities of lines 1—7 have been cleared away for the poet, who, as the rhythm had indicated, was certain from the start. For the reader, though, the experience of those lines is not so easily wiped away, and he is likely to approach the sestet with the impression that the poet's confidence is forced. Interestingly, Stephen Booth arrives at a similar judgement from a discussion of the first two quatrain's lack of specificity: 'all in all', he writes, 'the first eight lines both present grounds for and completely undercut the informed optimism of the last six.'[14]

The one unspecific which I want to concentrate on is the word "love" which occurs once in the octave and once in the sestet. In each case, lines 3 and 10, the reader is encouraged first to interpret it in its primary meaning in the sequence, that is the young man. In line 3, "Can yet the lease of my true love control", his instinct is to read "true" as if it were potentially ironic, when set against the poet's fears and the wide world's prophecies being unable to control his true love's lease. Editors normally gloss "lease" as something equivalent to 'allotted time', but the reader is not likely to be so certain of its meaning straight away, and will hold in his mind other possibilities which make it potentially applicable to the young man, such as 'permission to stay', or even a pun on 'leash'.[15] However, line 4 tips the balance when true love is "supposed as forfeit to a confined doom". The possible meaning of lines 1 – 3, that whatever the poet or the world does it cannot stop the young man erring, can not fit line 4, and the reader accepts "my true love" as a description of the poet's feelings instead. "Love" in line 10 works in the same way: "My love looks fresh, and death to me subscribes". "Looks fresh" is so much more typical of a person than a feeling that the reader almost automatically assumes the line to mean that at this idyllic time the poet's lover looks as fair as he has ever looked to him. The second half of the line causes a jolt: it will hardly bear the kind of emphasis on "to me" which will make it a parallel to the first half of the line; i.e. 'At this idyllic time he is young again and I have conquered time.' Again the reader has to abandon the young man as the line's referent, and set up in his place the poet's feelings.

This analysis of the way "love" works may seem unnecessarily laboured, but I pursue it this far because it epitomises the whole action of Sonnet 107. In this sonnet the poet's confinement to the young man – and all poetry's confinement, according to Sonnet 106 – is finally broken. The reader experiences the break in a number of ways: a new and alarmingly vague set of images, a release from the oppression of time which the previous sonnets have so sterilely supported, and, in relation to "love", a growing sense of the poet's apocalyptic, universal vision. As readers of the sonnets we expect the intrusion of the young man. In lines 3 and 10 "love" first encourages our expectation, and then shuts the door on it; and the third quatrain, quite remarkably, asserts the poet's triumph over death and survival in his own rhyme:

> Now with the drops of this most balmy time
> My love looks fresh, and death to me subscribes,
> Since spite of him I'll live in this poor rhyme,
> While he insults o'er dull and speechless tribes.

The young man does finally get into the sonnet, in the couplet:

> And thou in this shalt find thy monument,
> When tyrants' crests and tombs of brass are spent.

The formula recalls the couplets of the immortalising sonnets, notably 55 and 60, but the impact here is distinctly low-key. "And" introduces the idea of the sonnet as a monument, but makes it seem as if it were an appendage to the poet's survival rather than the culmination of it; and there is, also, an implied contrast between the poet's triumph and the young man's enduring monument, in effect between life and death. In this respect the poet's claim that he will live "in this poor rhyme", echoed in the couplet's "in this", is tantalising. It recalls earlier hints of the poem as a container, especially a tomb, for the young man, but now the contrast is between the poem as his tomb and the poem as the poet's room, the confine within which he lives. Also the adjective "poor" has a double effect. In one sense it is a conventional understatement, a pretended humility which actually makes the achievement all the greater, that something so puny can outlive tyrants and defy time. The convention, though, is undermined by the possibility that "poor" may apply literally. For the reader with memories of Sonnet 55's "powerful rhyme" it comes as an unexpected epithet for immortalising poetry, all the more so in its extreme contrast with the grand claim of the previous line that death subscribes to the poet. In effect, the poet's survival is a limited, confined one. It may be the best possible when compared to the fate of dull and speechless tribes, but in absolute terms it is impoverished — and Sonnet 107 expends the greater part of its energy on the absolute, a vision of the whole universe, in which the dull and speechless tribes are the penultimate element, and compared to which love poetry has small significance. This subordination of love is the apocalypse of the sonnets.

11 'Policy in Love': The Reversal of Roles II

Close to the end of the young man sequence a group of five sonnets, 117–121, demonstrates explicitly and unambiguously the reversal of roles between the young man and the poet. In a significant way it stands as the sequence's emotional climax, and, in Sonnet 121, presents one possible conclusion to it. It ought to be unnecessary for me to emphasise the importance of a group of sonnets in which the poet openly patronises the young man, for its effect upon the reader is revolutionary, bringing at last into the open what for so long had been the subject of innuendo and implication – but it is hardly an exaggeration to say that while Sonnet 121 has received some detailed critical comment, the group as a whole has been generally neglected.[1] This is a pity, because as much as any other group in the sequence these five sonnets make the reader put into practise the whole of his craft of sonnet reading. Each sonnet compels attention to every phrase, and leaves at its finish a strong dissatisfaction, the feeling that something vital to the poem's meaning has still not been absorbed.

These are vague formulations, and I can only begin to give them critical respectability by looking in this chapter at the actual sonnets. This is Sonnet 117:

> Accuse me thus: that I have scanted all
> Wherein I should your great deserts repay,
> Forgot upon your dearest love to call,
> 4 Whereto all bonds do tie me day by day;
> That I have frequent been with unknown minds,
> And given to time your own dear purchased right;
> That I have hoisted sail to all the winds
> 8 Which should transport me farthest from your sight.
> Book both my wilfulness and errors down,
> And on just proof surmise accumulate;
> Bring me within the level of your frown,
> 12 But shoot not at me in your wakened hate,

> Since my appeal says I did strive to prove
> The constancy and virtue of your love.

A possible, indeed a probable reason for this sonnet's neglect is that it comes immediately after 'the most universally admired of Shakespeare's sonnets'. Worse than the mere act of succession, it seems to act as a perverse echo of "Let me not to the marriage of true minds." Stephen Booth, whose description of Sonnet 116 I have just quoted, describes this sonnet as 'something like a pun' on its predecessor, and, in a typically concise paragraph, he sums up the peculiar relationship of the two sonnets. Sonnet 117, he writes,

> . . . picks up on 116's topics (e.g. constancy, departure, accusation, proof, value, writing, ties between people, measuring worth), its metaphors (e.g. navigation, trials at law, the range of weapons . . .), and its language (e.g. "minds" and "unknown" in 116.1,8 and "unknown minds" in 117.5; "error" in 116.13 and "errors" in 117.9); but 117 uses them to entirely different effect (in 116 the speaker is grand, noble, general, and beyond logic; in 117 he is petty, particular, and narrowly logical). Note the phonetic and ideational relationship between the fourth lines of the two, the repetition of "alter" in 116 and "all" in 117, and the strikingly urgent likeness and correspondingly urgent difference between the two couplets.[2]

I would add to this one further contrast between the two sonnets which helps create their 'punning' relationship, and which I intend to use as my starting point for a discussion of Sonnet 117. This is that where Sonnet 116 is an entirely poet centred sonnet, 117 only pretends to be. Behind 116's grand assertions of the nobility and constancy of true love there is a powerful self dramatisation. The first person pronoun only appears three times in the sonnet, almost incidentally in the opening line – "Let me not" – and then not again until the couplet:

> If this be error and upon me proved,
> I never writ, nor no man ever loved.

but despite this paucity – or possibly even because of it – the reader can hardly avoid seeing the poet behind the generalisations, turning his own predicament into a matter of universal significance. It is, after all, a basic Shakespearean response, so that in moments of greatest crisis his characters transform their personal experience into a vision of the general state.[3]

In Sonnet 117, however, the surface is overwhelmingly personal: the sonnet is a prolonged piece of self justification, using the first person pronoun twelve times, and belonging to a recognisable type of confession which attempts to disarm by its very frankness. But this impression is deliberately misleading, for it turns out that the poet only uses his confession in order gradually to remove himself, and his sin, from our attention. In the sonnet's first half it seems as if we are, finally, about to get an open declaration of what the poet has done – not that we necessarily need it for its information, but the very act of declaring it will provide satisfaction for our moral sense – and, of course, some idea of his reasons for having done it. The promise develops with the growing clarity of the metaphors: "I have scanted all . . . Forgot upon your dearest love to call . . . I have frequent been with unknown minds." As the sonnet unwinds, though, the poet's presence dissolves into metaphor and pun – a ship and a target, and one who is entirely Will full – and in his place, and much more to the poet's point, comes the figure of the young man, with the sonnet finally acting as a character sketch of him in his newly subservient role: "your great deserts . . . your dearest love . . . your own dear purchased might . . . your sight . . . your frown . . . your wakened hate . . . your love." In support, too, is the subdued legal metaphor which runs through the sonnet: part of its action is to change the young man from a neglected lover complaining justifiably at his treatment into an almost caricatured magistrate figure. "Accuse me thus" the sonnet begins, and "accuse" seems, for the octave, to carry the strength of justifiable anger. But in the octave there are also indications of what is to come, in "your dearest love . . ./Whereto all bonds do tie me day by day" and "given to time your own dear purchased right", and the sestet clarifies these hints by echoing "Accuse me thus" with two further legal imperatives, "Book . . . down" and "surmise accumulate" (on "just proof"); and in lines 11–12 the full legal process is supported by the image of the young man sitting in full-scale judgment with all the righteous indignation of the law. But the righteous indignation of the law is quite a different thing from the justifiable anger of a lover, and by having brought about that change the poet is able to counter a mere matter of criminality with an appeal in the couplet:

> Since my appeal says I did strive to prove
> The constancy and virtue of your love.

This couplet is so vicious because it contrasts the reader's expectations with the sonnet's actual achievement. From its opening line it had promised a confession of sins, and indeed it gives as frank a one as could be hoped for, with almost no sense of the poet's seeking excuses for his infidelity.[4] Its frankness makes the couplet's excuse the more ridiculous: it defends the catalogue of errors with the argument that all had been committed with the purpose of testing the young man's fidelity; and if it might seem difficult to add to the heartlessness of such a defence, then a consideration of the way in which the couplet reinforces the sonnet's legal metaphor should clear away that illusion. A little earlier I described how the poet gradually refines himself out of his poem. The couplet marks the end of this process, the poet being replaced by a piece of paper – not 'I appeal that . . .', but "my appeal says . . .", as if it were a stock defence to a stock charge: 'my form of words to answer your form of words is that all my crimes were committed for the higher purpose of revealing your worth.'

The detachment of the poet from his confession is a reminder that it is a poet who is being judged, and a poet is one whose words of truth must never be tied to his actual behaviour – 'poetic license' bears more than its most obvious meaning. In great part the ease of the confession comes from its juxtaposition with Sonnet 116. In form, the couplet's rhyme is substantially the same as 116's couplet – "prove"/"love" – and in content "the constancy and virtue of your love" is almost an epitome of what 116 had proclaimed. But with all its ease it remains a cruel joke, the poet's most extreme and coldest assertion of his superiority.

The next two sonnets retreat from 117's cruelty, and concentrate upon making the poet's excuse by way of the more conventional poetic devices of wit and paradox. Sonnet 118 announces itself, in its opening similes, to be a consciously poetic working out of the reasons why:[5]

> Like as to make our appetites more keen
> With eager compounds we our palate urge –
> As to prevent our maladies unseen,
> 4   We sicken to shun sickness when we purge –
> Even so, being full of your ne'er-cloying sweetness,
> To bitter sauces did I frame my feeding;
> And sick of welfare found a kind of meetness
> 8   To be diseased ere that there was true needing.
> Thus policy in love t'anticipate
> The ills that were not grew to faults assured,
> And brought to medicine a healthful state,
> 12   Whick rank of goodness would by ill be cured.
> But thence I learn and find the lesson true,
> Drugs poison him that fell so sick of you.

Here the poet takes his appeal a stage forward from the couplet of Sonnet 117. Instead of offering the disingenuously simple excuse that he had sinned in order to prove his lover's fidelity, he now presents a defence based on fear and insecurity. I suppose that 117's couplet could be assigned to the same cause – one only tests a lover one has fears about – but its expression shows more mockery than anxiety. Here, in Sonnet 118, the tone is anxious, one carefully structured, apparently logical explanation for the poet's "policy in love t'anticipate/The ills that were not." The premise of the whole sonnet is that it is an human instinct to anticipate ills, and, in attempting to forestall them, to use apparently unnatural means – hence the two similes in the first quatrain, the "eager compounds" to stimulate the appetite and the purges to ward off illnesses.[6] As with most similes, it does not help the reader (or the commentator) to push them too far, except that the poet himself seems intent on doing so; and the result is a sonnet which never breaks free from its initial constraints, and probably is not intended to. By the end of the opening quatrain the reader has a stronger than normal sense of the way the sonnet will develop. The first simile might have promised an expansive treatment of the idea that sexual attraction needs constant stimulation, but the quatrain refuses to complete the simile: it postpones the apodosis, beginning instead a second, very different simile.[7] I say very different to emphasise the fact that although the two have things in common – both, for instance, involve the making of preparations, literally and figuratively – they represent crude polarities of experience. The "eager compounds" are specially framed for the gourmet to gourmandize, while the purgatives are emetics which achieve the opposite effect.

The reader is aware, therefore, that the sonnet has two separate lines of argument to pursue and, if possible, to tie together. Of course the awareness is only tentative, for no Shakespearean sonnet needs to be the victim of its own beginning unless the poet chooses it to be – but such a choice is made here in the peculiarly limited second quatrain:

> Even so, being full of your ne'er-cloying sweetness,
> To bitter sauces did I frame my feeding;
> And sick of welfare found a kind of meetness
> To be diseased ere that there was true needing.

The limitations are principally formal. The quatrain unimaginatively completes the two similes, following the order of their appearance in the first quatrain, two lines of appetite succeeded by two lines of sickness, so that by line 8 the reader feels himself to be locked into a highly formal exercise of wit. Added to this, though, is a sense of incompleteness, the idea that the similes have not really been made. A simile is normally the bluntest of metaphorical weapons: "like as" or "as", particularly at the beginning of a poem, promises an explicit statement in the way that metaphor does not. So, when Sonnet 37 opens "As a decrepit father takes delight/To see his active child do deeds of youth", we expect, and receive, the explicit parallel that father equals poet, decrepit equals ill treated by fortune, active child equals the young man, and deeds of youth equals (if ironically) his worth and truth: "So I, made lame by fortune's dearest spite,/Take all my comfort of thy worth and truth." In Sonnet 118 we get no such explicitness. The two similes are circular, so that "eager compounds" is merely echoed by "bitter sauces", and "we sicken" by "to be diseased". Now any editor worth his salt annotates "bitter sauces" to point out to the reader that this is actually a way of describing the poet's infidelities, and it is normally glossed as referring to the people with whom he has been unfaithful. [8] My feeling is that these glosses are there because the editors fear that readers will not automatically make such an equation. Of course the gloss is probably the rightest one for the man whose job it is to explain the sonnet, but a reader ought to feel that the identification of sauce with a person is obtrusive to the point of perverseness. The poet has chosen to pursue an euphemistic argument − the more obviously euphemistic in that it uses the simile, one of the more explicit rhetorical forms − and to explode the euphemism may be morally respectable, but it wrecks the experience of reading the sonnet. The second quatrain depends upon the reader's refusing to ask the pertinent questions: how can one be full of never cloying sweetness? [9] Who, or what, are the bitter sauces? What was the feeding? How can one be sick of welfare? And does line 8, "To be diseased ere that there was true needing", mean that there would inevitably have been a time of disease even if the poet had not done what he has done? And if so, how does the poet know? I say that the quatrain depends upon the reader's refusing to ask these questions: it is a little more complicated than that, because the reader knows that the principal reader of the sonnet is the young man − note the effect of "your" in line 5, which contrasts with the generalisations of the opening quatrain − so that his refusal is, in great part, an awareness that the young man will refuse to ask the questions which the poet dangles in front of him.

The sestet then achieves what the sonnet has always promised to do, by tying together in line 12 the similes of appetite and medicine, assuming, that is, that "rank of" means primarily 'gorged with': [10]

> Thus policy in love t'anticipate
> The ills that were not grew to faults assured,
> And brought to medicine a healthful state,

Which rank of goodness would by ill be cured.
But thence I learn and find the lesson true,
Drugs poison him that fell so sick of you.

But the reader's satisfaction at seeing the two similes united is likely to be offset by his resentment at the sestet's insistence upon maintaining the paradoxical wit of the octave. For a brief space – one and a half lines, in fact – the sonnet seems to promise the possibility of straight talking. By that I do not mean anything so crass as an outright description of the poet's misbehaviour, but some such statement in the manner of Sonnet 116 which subordinates metaphor to the demands of personal truth. "Thus policy in love t'anticipate/The ills that were not . . ." seems to anticipate this development: it has the shadow of another metaphor, from statecraft, but at the least it signifies a breaking away from the limited terms of the two similes. However, the break does not last. "Ills", in line 10, the reader might initially take to be political ills, if he senses the possible development of the "policy" metaphor. More probably, he will take them to be primarily the infidelities of a lover, from "policy *in love*". This is, of course, their literal meaning, but as the sestet develops it is clear that the literal meaning must be subordinated to the old illness metaphor. "Faults" maintains the illusion that the metaphor is not all important, but this soon gives way with "medicine" and "healthful state" – note the way the political metaphor gets entirely swallowed up by the medicinal one – and "by ill be cured". Finally, the couplet's wit depends upon the reader's total acquiescence to the logic of the metaphor, at the expense of any common-sensical, leave alone truthful, assessment of what has happened between the poet and the young man.

Sonnet 118 uses one weapon of love sonnetry, the paradoxical simile. Where it had been used often in the sequence with at least the superficial intention of defending the young man and wittily explaining away his behaviour, now it explains away the poet's. The next sonnet in the group, number 119, uses another familiar weapon, the exclamation, to the same end:

What potions have I drunk of siren tears,
Distilled from limbecks foul as hell within –
Applying fears to hopes, and hopes to fears,
4   Still losing when I saw myself to win!
What wretched errors hath my heart committed,
Whilst it hath thought itself so blessed never!
How have mine eyes out of their spheres been fitted
8   In the distraction of this madding fever!

> O benefit of ill, now I find true
> That better is by evil still made better;
> And ruined love when it is built anew
> 12   Grows fairer than at first, more strong, far greater.
>   So I return rebuked to my content,
>   And gain by ills thrice more than I have spent.

One function of exclamation is to make hyperbole acceptable; and the octave of this sonnet presents a catalogue of excessive ills and suffering. Critical debate is usually taken up with the nature of the fault which is being described here, if described is not too restrained a word. "Siren tears" mentions a female of sorts, a hint which has been gratefully taken to indicate Shakespeare's acknowledgement that his feelings for the young man have been swamped by the desire for heterosexual adventures. But this has been countered by the argument that "siren" is, after all, in the singular, and essentially only a figurative female, while the shape of limbecks is indubitably phallic – a signification probably strengthened by their being "foul as hell within."[11] Both sides of the argument reflect the reader's real problem with such a sonnet: quite simply, how literally – which is tantamount to saying how seriously – can one take it? And here the question is complicated by the possibility of considering the sonnet by itself, or of reading it as part of a group of sonnets. By itself it might survive as a genuine attempt at self analysis: first two quatrains of contrition and self disgust, followed by a sestet of *felix culpa* intensity. As one sonnet in a group dealing with the poet's sin, its argument develops too easily for it to register either contrition or self analysis. Martin Seymour-Smith is one editor who has a strong sense of the sequence's development, but here he provides only a straightforward account of the sonnet, including this paraphrase of the third quatrain:

> 'Oh, how I have benefitted from my purely lustful exploits! For now I have discovered that a love which was more than merely lustful, though it had its lustful element, has been purified. A love relationship that has been ended, and then re-created in this way, is worth far more than it was at first.'[12]

Like all paraphrases this is forced to simplify and flatten out the sonnet's latent ambiguities – for example, in line 10, "That better is by evil still made better" has a sense directly subversive of Seymour-Smith's rendering of the lines, and, consequentially, of the quatrain's whole argument. As well as the idea that having experienced, and overcome evil, makes a pure love even purer, the actual phrasing of the line makes the alternative unavoidable, namely that love can only be improved by infidelity. But let us assume as readers that we ought to make a positive effort to keep out such ambiguities: after all, the kind of hyperbole which the octave contains of foul limbecks and eyes popping out of the head encourages us to approach the sonnet as if it had no such subtleties. If we fall in with the tone of the first eight lines, then Seymour-Smith's rendering of the third quatrain is appropriate. First comes the pain and torment, then the ov~rwhelming relief that not all has been lost; indeed, that something has actually been gained from all that suffering. This is where the problem lies, though, since as part of a group of sonnets such hyperbolic protestation seems grotesque. Sonnet 116 had described the unaltering nature of true love. In opposition to that Sonnets 117 and 118 both describe the poet's infidelity: the first a cynical confession, the second a witty analysis of it. Now 119 asks the reader to disregard what has gone before, both 116's claim that to alter is to destroy love, and the implication of 117 and 118 that the fatal alteration has been made. And in contrast to 118's presentation of a calculating, almost philosophical infidelity – "policy in love" – 119 presents a frenzied, hysterical infidelity, making it the sonnet which most closely anticipates the excesses of Sonnet 129's analysis of "lust in action".

It is tempting, therefore, to criticise Seymour-Smith's interpretation of the sonnet, and especially his paraphrase of the third quatrain, from the view that although he might have got the literal meaning of the lines right, he still fails to grasp the tone of the sonnet – the whole thing is a burlesque which he takes too seriously. Stephen Booth, who usually leaves his view of the tone of a sonnet to emerge from his comments on individual parts of it, is unusually direct about this one. In discussing its alchemical imagery he points out that the last line, "And gain by ills thrice more than I have spent", introduces a note of avarice, and

> although it can be considered simply to refer to the necessity of using natural gold in the alchemical process and to the vast multiplication of wealth that theoretically ensued, its tone is that of a successful confidence man; that tone acknowledges the most salient fact both of popular alchemy . . . and of the speaker's mock-serious defence of his infidelities: both are transparent frauds.[13]

I think that the problem here is genuinely insoluble. Either one detects Booth's confidence man and sees through the whole contrivance, or one accepts Seymour-Smith's interpretation of the sonnet as a vision of the re-creation of pure love. Concentration on the sonnet's incidentals only makes the problem more obvious, not its solution. I have already mentioned the possibility of reading line 10's idea of making better even better by way of evil in an entirely subversive way. Slightly different, but equally a matter of interpretation of the sonnet's tone, is the verb "fitted" in line 7 – "How have mine eyes out of their spheres been fitted". Its use here matches no similar recorded use of the verb 'to fit' in Elizabethan English, although contemporary readers would have had as little trouble as a modern reader does in absorbing the new sense (i.e. 'forced by fits') while recognising its novelty. What he would also have noticed, and what the modern reader misses, is the visual pun on 'benefited': in the Quarto text the line reads "How haue mine eies out of their Spheares bene fitted." The pun makes little sense, though, until the third quatrain, where "benefit of ill" turns out to be the real subject of the sonnet. In this way "been fitted" is a link between the bizarre imagery of the octave and the emotionally restrained language of the sestet; and, amusingly, the link is made at the point where the frenzy is at its greatest, with the poet's eyes popping out of their sockets.

Well, how does the reader respond to such a link? To us the very existence of the pun is probably enough to allow us to damn the third quatrain as too contrived to reflect genuine emotion; but that response ought to be set against the Elizabethans' use, and Shakespeare's in particular, of the 'worst' puns in the most intensely emotional moments.[14] I labour the point because it seems clear to me that the sonnet does change gear in the sestet, so that lines 11–12, if extracted from the rest of the poem, return to the sublime tone of Sonnet 116:

> And ruined love when it is buit anew
> Grows fairer than at first, more strong, far greater.

Partly the effect lies in the slide from "ruined" to "built anew" to "grows fairer"; "ruined" seems first to follow from the sonnet's earlier imagery, and to be purely human in reference; "built anew" retrospectively subdues the human to the image of a building; that, in turn, is transformed by "grows fairer", which raises the image of stately trees while it gives new force to the human image of "ruined" by repairing the spoilt beauty of the human form. Then the irresistible simplicity of "more strong, far greater" helps unite the cluster of images in the two lines, of noble mansions, stately trees, and the human form divine.[15]

How justifiable such a response may be to the language of the sestet of Sonnet 119 is, as I have said, a problem; and one which the reader ought not to avoid, because the last two sonnets in the group, 120 and 121, seem to build upon this newly emerged simplicity and directness of language. The problem is heightened at the very opening line to Sonnet 120, but before I look at that poem I should explain what I mean by describing the language in this way. It would be nonsense to claim that the sestet of Sonnet 119, for the first time in the sequence, presents a language of simplicity and directness. In fact, as I have indicated in discussing lines 11 and 12 of Sonnet 119, the simplicity is actually very artful, coming from a subtle fusion of metaphors, which gradually gives way to the directness of "fairer . . . more strong, far greater". Nevertheless, the sestet's language is in marked contrast to the octave's "siren tears", "limbecks foul as hell within", "wretched errors" committed by the heart and eyes fitted "out of their spheres". More than that, it stands in contrast to the two preceding sonnets, where 117 uses metaphors of veiled and not so veiled cynicism, to be replaced by 118's paradoxical wit. And the reader will have noticed the contrast because by the sestet of 119 he should be aware that here, more than in any other group in the sequence, he is following a complex narrative.[16] He does not yet know how it will end, but he appreciates the need for its continuation beyond Sonnet 119. So far the group has continued three successive responses by the poet to his infidelity: they form a complex narrative because although they are all unmistakably relations of what is past and over, they represent different states of awareness. Thus 117 has the bravura and cynicism of a man preparing to commit the act, 118 the perplexity of one who can not understand why he is doing what he is doing, and 119 the contrition and developing sense of redemption of one who only now appreciates what he has done to himself. But Sonnet 117 had opened the group by addressing the young man, and it is the response of the addressee which the narrative now takes up in Sonnet 120:[17]

> That you were once unkind befriends me now,
> And for that sorrow which I then did feel
> Needs must I under my transgression bow,
> 4 Unless my nerves were brass or hammered steel.
> For if you were by my unkindness shaken,
> As I by yours, y' have passed a hell of time,
> And I, a tyrant, have no leisure taken
> 8 To weigh how once I suffered in your crime.
> O that our night of woe might have remembered
> My deepest sense, how hard true sorrow hits,
> And soon to you as you to me then tendered
> 12 The humble salve which wounded bosoms fits!
>   But that your trespass now becomes a fee;
>   Mine ransoms yours, and yours must ransom me.

Stephen Booth has a masterly analysis of this sonnet in his edition, and any further discussion of it is likely only to be annotation upon his commentary. After an exhaustive summary of the way in which the couplet's oblique relation to the sonnet matches the whole sonnet's forcing of the reader 'to perceive two natures in one thing and/or engage him in trying to maintain his awareness that different things are not the same', he concludes with this summary of the whole sonnet's effect:

> the poem makes two separable but still intertwined statements and does not effectively mediate between them: 'I feel your pain because my own was once as great'; and 'I do not feel your pain because my own was once as great.'[18]

This is the heightening of the reader's problem which I mentioned a little earlier. Beginning at Sonnet 117, the narrative has required the reader to absorb two potentially incompatible emotions. One is the sense of guilt and remorse at the poet's infidelity, the other his assertion of the necessity of, and justification for, his behaviour. In 117 and 118 the incompatibility remains only potential; in 119 it governs the structure of the sonnet, making an almost schizophrenic contrast between frenzied remorse, in the octave, and sublime intention, in the sestet. Here, in Sonnet 120, the incompatibilities are, as Booth says, unmediated: on the one hand there is the complete empathy which only one who has suffered can feel for another who is suffering; on the other the cynicism of one who has been oppressed at the sight of his oppressor's suffering. In his discussion of the sonnet Booth writes of the reader experiencing a number of crises. Perhaps the first of these comes in the opening line, with "befriends".

"That you were once unkind befriends me now" takes up the simplicity and directness of Sonnet 119's sestet. The language, like the sentiment, could hardly seem plainer: "once" is opposed to "now" — 'Once you were unkind to me, now I am to you, and because you were once unkind to me I can more easily understand why I am so unkind to you now.' That seems to be the import of the line, but already it is becoming clear that the simplicity and directness hides more complexity than does an opening line of declared metaphor, such as "Like to make our appetites more keen" or "What potions have I drunk of siren tears". Here "befriends" demands some interpretation, possibly along the lines my paraphrase has suggested, to explain why the memory of a past indignity should give the poet cheer to remember it now. The reader may reasonably be content to let his interpretation hang fire, waiting for the sonnet to give the reason for the memory's being a befriending one; but if he does so he has to wait until the couplet for a reason to be offered, since lines 2–12 ignore the comfort implicit in "befriends" and concentrate entirely on the mutual suffering. By line 4 "befriends me now" seems to have been a false start — the first quatrain has ignored the idea of consolation and has developed instead the image of the poet bowing under a weight of transgression — but few readers of the sonnets are likely to treat "befriends" as an aberration. If it were a verb like 'consoles' or 'supports' it might easily be passed over, but 'friend' is potent both as word and idea in the sequence, and the verb offers too many punning opportunities for a reader to leave it hanging. The pun most likely to be suspected is almost a grammatical one, taking the 'be-' form literally in its making a verb out of a noun, and understanding it to mean 'turns me into the friend now' (the Quarto prints it as "be-friends").[19]

How far the pun will be taken changes during the opening quatrain:

> That you were once unkind befriends me now,
> And for that sorrow which I then did feel
> Needs must I under my transgression bow,
> Unless my nerves were brass or hammered steel.

At its most extreme the pun might promise a sonnet of the sadistic order of Sonnet 117 — 'now the tables are turned and you will suffer as I did when you were the friend' — and the second line looks to be moving towards some such crudity as it seems to use "for" in the direct sense of exchange ('And in exchange for that sorrow . .'); only the remainder of the quatrain readjusts it to its primary sense of 'because of'.[20] With the concentration upon the poet's present feelings in lines 3 and 4 the idea of roles being reversed fades into the more sympathetic vision of identical experience between the poet and the young man. Both have oppressed and both have suffered, and the poet's remorse for having oppressed is given the visible action of the one who is oppressed, bowing under the weight of it.

But notice too the way the apparently ornamental imagery of line 4 works. The addition of "hammered steel" to "brass" seems to have been made only for the sake of elegant variation, but the reader actually registers it as a contra-logical consequence of "bow" in line 3, as if it were now bowing under a hail of blows. In other words, the emphasis is primarily, in terms of the imagery at least, on the poet's suffering, so that although the sonnet may be delineating parallel, shared experience, it does so purely through the poet. In line 5 the young man is "shaken" — a link of a kind with "bow" and "hammered" — but only in hypothesis. The real, indisputable shaking was the poet's, as lines 5–6 make pointedly clear:

> For if you were by my unkindness shaken,
> As I by yours . . .

And in a strange way, later in the sonnet, there is a peculiar justification for "hammered steel". In line 10 the poet asks why he had not remembered "how hard true sorrow hits" — had he done so, he would not have been such a tyrant to have been so thoughtlessly unfaithful. The reason why, though, is continued in the first quatrain: simply, the blows of true sorrow make nerves of hammered steel. In that sense the apparently incidental imagery of the sonnet contains the justification for the poet's apparently remorseless behaviour.

I do not claim that the reader makes such a judgement in the calculated way in which it is set down here, but that he is continuously aware of a stream of images whose implications run counter to the argument or confession he is reading. Lines 7 and 8 provide him with comparable intuitive qualification to the sonnet's line of argument:

> And I, a tyrant, have no leisure taken
> To weigh how once I suffered in your crime.

The meaning of these lines is registered as an intensification of the poet's self-condemnation: 'I am a tyrant not to have stopped to consider the degree to which I had suffered when you were unfaithful to me.' However, I doubt whether any reader merely and simply registers only that meaning, for there seems to be embedded in the movement "tyrant . . . leisure . . . to weigh" a counter argument which implies, first, that the poet is no tyrant, and second, that his behaviour has some justification. To take the first point: "And I, a tyrant, have no leisure taken" supplies an instinctive paradox, since the nature of tyrants is to take leisure, especially when it comes to weighing up the crimes of others against them.[21] In saying 'weighing up' here, I am anticipating the second point in the counter argument which rests on the image of balancing crime against crime. Of course, the primary meaning of "weigh" in the line "To weigh how once I suffered in your crime" is simply 'to consider'; but the quatrain had opened with the sense of suffering weighed against suffering — "if you were by my . . . As I by yours" — so that it becomes impossible for the reader to keep the scales image out of the line; and once the image is admitted so is the implication that the poet's crime is a justified repayment of the suffering he had endured.

In the couplet Sonnet 120 returns to its beginning and explains why the young man's unkindness should now "befriend" the poet:

> But that your trespass now becomes a fee;
> Mine ransoms yours, and yours must ransom me.

If the reader has allowed the implications of the imagery, which I have been describing, to subvert the poet's confession, then the couplet is decidedly hollow, an echo of the financial imagery of Sonnet 119. I think, though, that even the charitable reader who receives the sonnet as a frank confession of ingratitude and infidelity must allow that it is, in an important way, contaminated by its emphasis on the poet's suffering. In this respect the sonnet forms a contrast to the poem which began the group, Sonnet 117. That sonnet declared itself to be concerned with the poet and his behaviour, but its effect throughout was to turn the reader's attention from the poet to the young man. The opposite happens here. In describing the narrative structure of this group I introduced this as the anticipated sonnet which describes the experience of the oppressee, in other words the young man. But 'in other words' does not apply, and Sonnet 120, for all of its apparent concern for the young man, leaves the reader with the impression of how much the poet suffered in the past. "'Y' have passed a hell of time'', in line 6, is possibly the most poignant statement in the sequence, but its poignancy comes not from an imaginative sharing of the young man's suffering, but from its force of personal recollection as it completes the line which begins "As I by yours". Something analogous emerges from the movement from first person plural to first person singular in the compressed syntax of lines 9–10:

> O that our night of woe might have remembered
> My deepest sense, how hard true sorrow hits.

"Our night of woe" is a typical sonnets phrase: impossible to pin down to any specific time or place, but grandly suggestive of a range of potential meanings.[22] Most forcefully, it brings to a climax the comparison between the sufferings of the poet and the sufferings of the young man, as the whole bitter experience is condensed into one short period of shared suffering. Immediately, however, the climax becomes peculiarly the poet's, isolated within his memory and his deepest sense – and the final image of the quatrain forces the experience of the two men further apart as the poet remembers the humble salve which the young man had applied to his wounded bosom.[23]

Sonnet 120 never loses its concern with the young man's suffering, but as part of the group of sonnets which begins at 117 its greater significance lies in its completion of the poet's self analysis: in his past suffering he finds justification and motive for his present behaviour – and by that I do not only mean his "crime" of infidelity, but also his greater crime of having taken over the friend's dominant role, of having become independent. There is, after all, a calculated callousness in the couplet, as if the suggestion that one bad deed cancels out another were a sufficient substitute for the humble salve which the poet ought immediately have tendered to the young man:

> But that your trespass now becomes a fee;
> Mine ransoms yours, and yours must ransom me.

Perhaps the most powerful word here is "now", which imposes present values upon past experience. The past contained true sorrow, but now that memory has deteriorated into a purely material thing, the matter is one of fair exchange. This breaking free from the pain of the past is a strong, if still implicit, statement of independence. The sonnet which completes the group, number 121, makes that statement explicit:

> 'Tis better to be vile than vile esteemed,
> When not to be receives reproach of being,
> And the just pleasure lost, which is so deemed,
> 4   Not by our feeling but by others' seeing.
> For why should others' false adulterate eyes
> Give salutation to my sportive blood?
> Or on my frailties why are frailer spies,
> 8   Which in their wills count bad what I think good?
> No, I am that I am, and they that level
> At my abuses reckon up their own;
> I may be straight though they themselves be bevel.
> 12   By their rank thoughts my deeds must not be shown,
> Unless this general evil they maintain –
> All men are bad and in their badness reign.

The problems of understanding this sonnet have been debated at length by a series of editors and commentators.[24] In the past few years their tone has become increasingly desperate. Thus Ingram and Redpath comment on the couplet: 'Most commentators either burke the issue or offer unsatisfactory explanations which give the poem a weak ending. We tentatively offer the following interpretation as possible . . .'; Martin Seymour-Smith on the opening quatrain: 'These lines, which provide an example of poetic precision unparalleled by few save Shakespeare himself, defy accurate paraphrase – as the many attempts of commentators show. However, the essential meaning is . . .'; Hilton Landry on the whole sonnet, after having summarised various general views of it: 'There is, of course, something to be said for all these summary views . . . but any critic must stand or fall on his interpretation of the details of this difficult sonnet.'[25] Even Stephen Booth, whose edition shows a constant willingness to grapple with multiple layers of difficulty in the sonnets, seems to hang back on Sonnet 121, and only in one sentence in his comment on the biblical overtones of line 9 does he allow a general sense of the sonnet's import to emerge. There he sympathises with those critics who have expressed irritation at the forcing of 'a solemn assumption of divine authority' upon the poet's "I am that I am", but, he adds, the echo with Exodus 'is unmistakeably present and does make the speaker sound smug, presumptuous, and stupid'.[26] Booth makes no more of this impression – indeed, the rest of his commentary takes the sonnet, and therefore the speaker, quite seriously – but the way he describes the poet here makes light of the strenuous efforts of generations of commentators, and the defensiveness of those cited earlier in this paragraph. My instincts are to side with 'smug, presumptuous, and stupid', and I am not sure that these instincts are as far removed from the experience of reading the sonnet as they are opposed to the attempts to force a meaning upon it which editors and critics feel compelled to make. Partly my instincts have been reinforced by having made these same attempts in vain: the more one explores it, the more the sonnet takes on the identity of an extended platitude, like trying to force a coherent personality upon the aphorisms of Iago. This should not really be a surprise, since from its opening line the sonnet declares itself to be a cliché; and if the reader is prepared to give some intellectual or moral weight to the assertion that it is better to vile than to be considered vile, then the second line removes all such substance by stating the conditions for that assertion: "When not to be receives reproach of being". I do not think that this line actually conveys anything more than is inherent in the opening line's opposition of being vile and being thought vile, but its effect is to emphasise the speaker's state of mind as a combination of self-righteousness and self-pity, a state of mind which the reader continues to perceive, despite the complex vagueness of the rest of the sonnet. In effect, it becomes a series of self-justifying questions and assertions set up in defence against real or imagined persecutions.[27]

Sonnet 121 forms one possible ending to the young man sequence; not, as it turns out, the real end – there are five sonnets still to come – but the end to one vital movement of the sequence, the reversal of roles between the poet and his subject. As a possible final sonnet it is both depressing and degrading, an anti-climax with a vengeance, as if the poet had become so 'be-friended', to take up 120's pun again, that he has absorbed the attitudes and philosophy of the young man when he had been at the height of his infidelity. Throughout the sequence the poet has reproduced, in his portrait of the young man, either by explicit denunciation or by sarcastic innuendo, the very views which, in this sonnet, he takes so much pride in announcing as his own. The decay is both general and personal. It seems to be the common opinion that the third person plural reference in the sonnet — "others", "their" and "they" — indicts the whole world as spies and adulterate watchers. But I would add that behind the plural also stands the very singular third person reference of the young man, who appears as "they" earlier in the sequence, in Sonnet 94 for instance, making Sonnet 121 a quite venomous finale to a group of sonnets which began "Accuse me thus . . ." Now neither the world nor the young man may make any approach to the poet, let alone accuse him of anything, unless they subscribe to the couplet's philosophy, that "All men are bad and in their badness reign."

From "vile" to "bad" the sonnet's terms are almost entirely negative, only the enigmatic "just pleasure" and "think good" provide relief from the catalogue of vileness which runs through the sonnet: "vile", "vile esteemed", "reproach", "false", "adulterate", "sportive", "frailties", "frailer spies", "wills", "count bad", "abuses", "bevel", "rank thoughts", "general evil", "bad", and "badness".

Psychologically this state of mind might be a fitting end to a relationship which began in subservience, as if the final assertion of independence required the poet's jettisoning of all values. Aesthetically, though, it smells of decay. Sonnet 121 is a singularly barren poem in the sequence: like the barren young man, its emphasis is on being rather than acting. Its lack of depth in language or imagery is signalled in the opening lines, where "to be" is required to carry the burden of the argument. Being, without the desire to act, had always been the young man's prerogative.[28] Now, being, in its purest state, with no image to support or qualify it, is the poet's self-definition — "I am that I am" — and now his deeds may not be shown to the world or to the young man.[29] It is probably impossible to wrestle out of the sonnet any comprehensible justification for the poet's self-elevation. It exists for its function, to act as the final sonnet in the series of groups which narrate the role reversal of the poet and the young man. Within the confines of that relationship the reversal is completely negative: the self regarding young man, impervious to the poet's needs or the world's values, has been replaced by a self regarding poet, impervious to the young man's needs or the world's opinions. That sterile view comes dangerously close to being the sequence's final statement about love poetry.

12 'Necessary Wrinkles': Time and the Poet

I closed the last chapter with a depressingly sterile vision of the poet's independence. At the end of Sonnet 121 the poet's self-definition is directed not by a sense of his own worth, but in relation to a world where men are falsely valued. "'Tis better to be vile than vile esteemed" is a deliberately perverse statement: the rest of the sonnet exposes its irony by relating it to a society in which those who do the esteeming are the ones with vile natures.[1] But so much of the sonnet's force is spent on the frailties of the society that the poet's strength exists only in contrast – and a peculiarly hesitant contrast, at that. The gist of "I may be straight though they themselves be bevel" is that the world should not judge the poet by its own values, no matter how similar to theirs his actions might appear; which is, in part, an acknowledgement that the poet's external behaviour is as typical of the society he contemns as he claims his internal vision is untypical.

If this were the only point of reference by which to judge the poet's self presentation in these last sonnets, then it would be tempting to see his independence as a form of spiritual self-destruction. There are, however, a number of sonnets which embody a change in the poet's attitude towards time, and these provide a more positive and powerful internal vision than do the sonnets which I looked at in the previous chapter. The relationship between the poet and the young man remains time-bound to the end, so that even the reversal of roles between the two fails to give the poet the freedom to create a poetry which will transcend the vile world's values. Out of that time, though – in the context of all time – the sterile contrasts of "straight" and "bevel" disappear. The sonnets I shall discuss in this chapter act in contrast to those which describe the end of the relationship, giving a broader, more humane vision; and it is with this vision that the sequence reaches, if not a triumphant, at least a positive end.

The first of the final sonnets on time is Sonnet 100. I have discussed it before, in chapter 9, as the first sonnet in a series of groups which describe the change of roles between the two men, but there I had little to say about the poet's attitude towards time as it appears in the sonnet:

> Where art thou muse, that thou forget'st so long
> To speak of that which gives thee all thy might?
> Spend'st thou thy fury on some worthless song,
> 4   Darkening thy power to lend base subjects light?
> Return, forgetful muse, and straight redeem
> In gentle numbers time so idly spent;
> Sing to the ear that doth thy lays esteem,
> 8   And gives thy pen both skill and argument.
> Rise, resty muse; my love's sweet face survey
> If time have any wrinkle graven there;
> If any, be a satire to decay,
> 12 And make time's spoils despised everywhere.
>   Give my love fame faster than time wastes life;
>   So thou prevent'st his scythe and crooked knife.

I described this earlier as a sonnet of deliberate predictability: it uses a series of stock elements to lull the reader, in preparation for the subversive effects of Sonnets 101 and 102. One of those elements is time, who, as many times earlier in the sequence, is no sooner mentioned than he graves wrinkles and takes spoils; and the merest wrinkle to be observed on the young man's face is, in good Petrarchan fashion, the signal for a meditation on global desolation. Without retreating from that view of the sonnet I would like to modify it by pointing out that in one particular way, in its attitude to time, it does contain a presentiment of something new in the sequence. In bald summary I can describe this as the beginnings of an acceptance that while the primary purpose of poetry is to give the young man eternal fame, this goal is only attainable by describing the wrinkles on his face – and describing them means accepting them.

Early in the sequence the wrinkled face had been only a threat, a state so far removed from the present perfect fairness of the young man that even while voicing it the poetry carried its implicit admission that the threat had little power. Later the wrinkled face is more of a reality, but the poet detaches himself and the reader from its pathos by using it for sarcastic or satiric effect. In Sonnet 77, for instance, the rhythmic woodenness of the octave relegates the *memento mori* effect of the glass and dial to a mere commentary on the young man's blinkered vision, and prevents the reader from feeling sympathy for the man who sees his beauty beginning to fade:

> Thy glass will show thee how thy beauties wear,
> Thy dial how thy precious minutes waste;
> The vacant leaves thy mind's imprint will bear,

4   And of this book this learning mayst thou taste.
     Time's wrinkles which thy glass will truly show,
     Of mouthed graves will give thee memory;
     Thou by thy dial's shady stealth mayst know
8   Time's thievish progress to eternity.

The sestet hints at some kind of pathetic irony in comparing the young man's written thoughts to children, thereby reminding him and the reader of the warnings of the procreation group, but all pathos is wiped out in the couplet's return to the stiffness of expression of the octave:

     Look what thy memory cannot contain,
     Commit to these waste blanks, and thou shalt find
     These children nursed, delivered from thy brain,
12 To take a new acquaintance of thy mind.
      These offices, so oft as thou wilt look,
      Shall profit thee, and much enrich thy book.

In Sonnet 100, in contrast, the young man's wrinkled face in the third quatrain is the one image of pathos in the poem. Here the detachment of poet and muse acts paradoxically to reveal the poet's concern, with the repetition of "if" at the beginning of lines 10 and 11 emphasising, in its careful hypothecation, the poet's knowledge that there are wrinkles on the face:

     Rise resty muse; my love's sweet face survey
     If time have any wrinkle graven there;
     If any be a satire to decay,
12 And make time's spoils despised everywhere.

The double "if" forces the reader to readjust his understanding of the request to the muse. At first the poet asks the muse to rise – the final act in the sonnet's demand for the muse to appear and redeem his wasted time – and find out whether the young man's face has any wrinkles on it. But that is a fairly pointless request to a muse, and line 11 provides the real point of asking the muse to stir herself: not for the mere passivity of observing wrinkles, but to oppose the wrinkling process by becoming a satire to decay. The quatrain orders her to observe and describe; and only through that process will be achieved the couplet's promise of 'preventing' time:[2]

     Give my love fame faster than time wastes life;
     So thou prevent'st his scythe and crooked knife.

The chief direction of Sonnet 100 is towards the next sonnet, where the separation of poet and muse is given a different emphasis, but the sestet's admission of a new realism with regard to time is taken up quite unexpectedly in Sonnet 104. I say unexpectedly, because its opening quatrain seems to prepare the reader for a return to the conventional attitude that the young man can never grow old — but its opening phrase, "To me", turns out to be an important qualification:

> To me, fair friend, you never can be old,
> For as you were when first your eye I eyed,
> Such seems your beauty still. Three winters cold
> 4 Have from the forests shook three summers' pride,
> Three beauteous springs to yellow autumn turned
> In process of the seasons have I seen,
> Three April perfumes in three hot Junes burned,
> 8 Since first I saw you fresh, which yet are green.
> Ah yet doth beauty, like a dial hand,
> Steal from his figure, and no pace perceived;
> So your sweet hue, which methinks still doth stand,
> 12 Hath motion, and mine eye may be deceived:
> For fear of which, hear this, thou age unbred,
> Ere you were born was beauty's summer dead.

This I think is the most time-centred of all the young man sonnets — no light claim in a sequence where time is so important a character from the very beginning. In the image of the almost perceptible but unceasing movement of the dial's hand time is demetaphorized from the imagining of a bogy-man with sickle in hand to the more chilling experience of actually watching time move on — something to be shared by every modern reader who has a watch with a second hand. [3] Concentration upon the dial, or the watch, is the closest the reader comes to the pure sensation of present time, a sensation which is explicitly presented in Sonnet 104 as an unpoetic, or even anti-poetic, thing. Partly this is reinforced by the representation of time earlier in the sequence. Sonnet 15, for example presented at its begining what would seem to be the ideal description of present time:

> When I consider everything that grows
> Holds in perfection but a little moment,

But that "little moment" is not allowed to remain the second, or even the micro-second we might imagine it to describe. It ceases to be the

quintessential moment of peak perfection, and becomes instead a dilution
which will cover the whole of a man's life. The next two lines begin the
process:

> That this huge stage presenteth nought but shows
> Whereon the stars in secret influence comment.

Already the movement has been extended to two hours' traffic on a stage;
and the second quatrain moves from the tragedy on stage to the tragedy of
life:[4]

> When I perceive that men as plants increase,
> Cheered and checked even by the selfsame sky,
> Vaunt in their youthful sap, at height decrease,
> And wear their brave state out of memory;

This is the key to the poetic representation of time in the body of the
sequence. Like the experience of watching a tragic drama it depends upon a
sense of near timelessness: at the same time as the poet tells us that everyone
and everything is subject to time's devastation he makes the individual
experience seem immeasurably drawn out. In Sonnet 65 the second quatrain
describes the extreme brevity of summer (especially an English summer):

> O how shall summer's honey breath hold out
> Against the wrackful siege of battering days,
> When rocks impregnable are not so stout,
> Nor gates of steel so strong but time decays?

What the reader experiences, however, is the very opposite of brevity, in
surprising contrast with the way the quatrain begins. There could scarcely be
any shorter comparison of summer than to the holding of a breath, but the
image develops, by way of "hold *out*", to encompass first a siege of days, and
eventually to the experience of the aeons it takes for time to break down
impregnable rocks and steel gates.[5] In other words, while the brevity of life is
being asserted, the poetry is taken up with, if only negatively, a description
of near limitless time.

Poetry achieves a similar stretching of present time in Sonnet 73, where the
successive images relating the poet's decay – the yellow leaves on the bough,
the twilight, and the glowing embers – are not so much the vehicles of
finitude the poet declares them to be, as they are for the reader experiences of
long drawn out time.[6] Most importantly, of course, there has always been

the image of one enduring poetic present in the certainty that the poem will survive. In Sonnet 60 time's movement concentrates in the third quatrain in the figure of time the reaper making irresistible progress, but the couplet sets against that image an eternally standing present participle, "praising thy worth":

> Time doth transfix the flourish set on youth,
> And delves the parallels in beauty's brow,
> Feeds on the rarities of nature's truth,
> And nothing stands but for his scythe to mow.
> And yet to times in hope my verse shall stand,
> Praising thy worth, despite his cruel hand.

I wrote, introducing Sonnet 104, that its opening line seems to set it within the same grand poetic tradition of defying time by asserting the poet's sense of his subject's immortality, either because the subject actually is immortal or because the poet can make him so – "To me, fair friend, you never can be old." But the quatrain's development is ominous, with unexpected hesitancies in "as you were" and "seems" in the next two lines:

> For as you were when first your eye I eyed,
> Such seems your beauty still.

Still, the reader is given no immediate answer to his suspicions, and the remainder of the octave moves on to an almost wilfully repetitive description of the change from season to season:

>   Three winters cold
> 4 Have from the forests shook three summers' pride,
>   Three beauteous springs to yellow autumn turned
>   In process of the seasons have I seen,
>   Three April perfumes in three hot Junes burned,
> 8 Since first I saw you fresh, which yet are green.

Although the change from season to season is a common and powerful metaphor for human decay, the sonnet keeps the reader's suspense by preventing him from applying the image to the young man: for all the potential relevance of cold winter shaking away the pride of summer, beautiful spring turning to yellow autumn, and April perfume being scorched away by hot June, the explicit purpose of the lines is merely to register the passing of three years. The reader experiences paradoxical responses. On the one hand, only the passing of three years is being described, so the idea of death and decay implicit in the imagery can hardly apply; on the other, only three years has passed, yet the poet insists upon images of death and decay being applied to the young man. The paradox is sustained in the octave's last line, the reader being forced by the antithesis of "first" and "yet" to make a distinction between the normally indistinguishable epithets "fresh" and "green".

There is, then, in the sonnet's octave, a developed contrast between time as a metaphor and time as an actuality – the cycle of the seasons and the experience of three years. In effect the whole sonnet is aimed at distinguishing between the poet's affection for the young man and his own basic rationality: affection leads him to disbelieve in time – "To me, fair friend, you never can be old" – but reason tells him that even so short a period of time as three years must be called ageing. The sestet makes the distinction explicit:

> Ah yet doth beauty, like a dial hand,
> Steal from his figure, and no pace perceived;
> So your sweet hue, which methinks still doth stand,
> 12   Hath motion, and mine eye may be deceived:
> For fear of which, hear this, thou age unbred,
> Ere you were born was beauty's summer dead.

The distinction is fixed in the contrast between the poet's eye, which, echoing line 2, "when first your eye I eyed", cannot possibly perceive the movement on the dial, and the poet's mind which knows that "your sweet hue . . . hath motion". Present time is trapped in line 12 in the incompatible but simultaneous responses of eye and mind, an incompatibility reflected in the co-existence of the brutal certainty of "hath motion" and the uncertainty of "may be deceived". And the incompatibility of emotional and rational responses to present time governs the couplet: while "For fear of which" maintains the fiction that the eye may, after all, not be deceived, the sonnet closes on the certainty of the death of beauty.

The high formality of Sonnet 104's couplet reinforces the curious detachment of the sonnet. Possibilities of intimacy lie in the first two and a half lines, in its address to "fair friend" and the fond recollection of the poet's first sight of him – but set against these is the disturbing separation, between lines 2 and 3, of the young man from his beauty: the syntax of "For as you were when first your eye I eyed,/Such seems your beauty still" involves an altered perception on the poet's part, replacing intimate concern with more objective observation. Then the ornate phrasing of the rest of the octave, describing the change of seasons, moves the sonnet onto a more consciously poetic level, sustained to the end in the couplet's address to future readers as "thou age unbred" and its description of the young man as "beauty's summer".[7]

Sonnet 104 remains personal in tone, for competing with the rhetoric in each quatrain are simple phrases reminding the reader of the poet's feelings and responses – "To me . . . you never can be", "have I seen", "Since first I saw", "methinks still doth stand", "mine eye may be deceived" – but the reader feels a growing detachment from the young man in the whole sonnet's progression from "fair friend" to "beauty's summer". In one sense the detachment is only a reflection of the sonnet's change of address, from intimate vocative in the opening line to general proclamation in the last, but in this time soaked sonnet the detachment is also the product of a movement from past to future. The first two lines actually make the reverse movement in miniature, from future (although it is a denied future) "you never can be old", to past, "as you were when first your eye I eyed", all aimed at capturing and defining the state of the present, "Such seems your beauty still". But "still" is a word with a range of ominous implications, covering past, present, and future, in the sense of 'so far, at this moment, but with no guaranteed future'.[8] The sonnet then moves from the past through the present to the future. The seasons passage in lines 3–7 is given in a series of past tenses – "have . . . shook", "turned", "have I seen", "burned" – all pointing towards the present state of line 8's "which yet are green". The third quatrain then rests in a grammatical present, although its subject is literally movement from the present into the future:

> Ah yet *doth* beauty, like a dial hand,
> *Steal* from his figure, and no pace perceived;
> So your sweet hue, which methinks still *doth stand*,
> *Hath* motion, and mine eye *may be deceived*.

The future to which time's movement leads is the state of the couplet, although in a typical paradox of grammar its expression has to be in the past tense forms of "were" and "was":

> For fear of which, hear this, thou age unbred,
> Ere you were born was beauty's summer dead.

Both the high tone of Sonnet 104, and its concern with defining and holding on to the present moment govern, to various degrees, the next three sonnets. Sonnet 105 takes up the number three and works a blasphemous conceit of the trinitarian nature of the poet's love and inspiration around the words fair, kind, and true. The unchanging constancy of the poet's love results in unchanging poetry. Then Sonnets 106 and 107 use the grand manner to describe the present state of the poet's and the world's glory in the existence of his love.[9] Sonnet 108 changes the tone, and returns to Sonnet 104's more realistic analysis of time, continuing the contrast of the present with the past – but now it is not beauty's ageing which is analysed, but love's decaying. The three intervening sonnets have all dealt explicitly with the writing of poetry. Now Sonnet 108 seems to start with the same concern, but the degree to which it becomes a further exploration of poetic problems becomes interestingly unclear:

> What's in the brain that ink may character,
> Which hath not figured to thee my true spirit?
> What's new to speak, what now to register,
> 4 That may express my love, or thy dear merit?
> Nothing, sweet boy, but yet, like prayers divine,
> I must each day say o'er the very same;
> Counting no old thing old, thou mine, I thine,
> 8 Even as when first I hallowed thy fair name.
> So that eternal love in love's fresh case
> Weighs not the dust and injury of age,
> Nor gives to necessary wrinkles place,
> 12 But makes antiquity for aye his page,
>   Finding the first conceit of love there bred,
>   Where time and outward form would show it dead.

"Ink" in the opening line, and "conceit" in the couplet, seem pretty clear indications that the poet is examining once more the problems of writing poetry; and the octave is persuasively full of words and phrases which have a recognisable relevance to the craft: as well as "ink", there is "character", "figured", "speak", "register", "express", "say o'er", and "counting" – and "hallowed", in line 8, makes the familiar connection of writing poems to the young man with blessing a saint or deity. But the second quatrain actually does more than merely hint at that connection, it uses the idea of praying – specifically of reciting the Lord's Prayer – to override the sonnet's initial concern with the poet's difficulties in finding original ways of expressing his love for the young man. How far it is overridden is not easy to say – it never completely vanishes, hence the potency of "conceit" in the couplet – but the second quatrain leaves the reader with a vastly different impression from that of a poet struggling for better ways of saying what he feels. What it develops is the sense of repetitiveness which underlies their relationship: "Counting no old thing old" is close to, if not the same as, an admission of hypocrisy, that while time has turned his words and behaviour to things merely habitual, the poet regards them as having still the emotional intensity which they had when they were brand new. Even so extensive a paraphrase hardly manages to register the complexity of the verb "counting", which has partly the sense of valuing, and partly that of reciting by rote, so that "thou mine, I thine" is, simultaneously, a summary of the perfect timeless state when lovers have become so bound together that only so stark an expression of reciprocation can describe them, and a reduction of what was once a true relationship to a mere repetitive form of words.

The sestet does not resolve the paradox. Its introductory phrase, "So that", actually emphasises it all the more, making the assertions about eternal love which follow, both the consequence of the perfect timeless state and the intention of the repetitive exchange of compliments. Thus the reader is forced to experience the true tyranny of time: not the histrionic vision which dominates most of the sequence, of an implacable ravager whose day will surely come, but, more subtle, as the spoiler of the present who makes it impossible for us to know why and what we feel and do even at the very moment we are feeling and doing. What's in the brain is a question only partially answered in the sestet. Whether the vision of eternal love in love's fresh case is the unfulfillable desire which spoils love, or an attainable state which present love points towards is impossible for the reader to resolve. The third quatrain juxtaposes irreconcileables: "eternal love in love's fresh case" has somehow to be set against "the dust and injury of age", and, similarly, "necessary wrinkles" have to go together with making antiquity one's page.[10] And hence comes finally the vagueness of the couplet, which gives the conflicting impressions of a new born love and a sterile relationship.[11]

How to cope with and overcome time's poisoning of human experience is the concern of the final sonnets in the young man sequence, numbers 122–126, and they form the subject of my final chapter. But before considering the kind of resolution which they provide, I shall spend the rest of this chapter on two intermediary sonnets which project, in different ways, further aspects of time's tyranny. They are Sonnets 115 and 116. In 115 the primary conceit lies in the impossibility of our ever knowing when love is at its height:

> Those lines that I before have writ do lie
> Even those that said I could not love you dearer.
> Yet then my judgement knew no reason why

4   My most full flame should afterwards burn clearer.
     But reckoning time, whose millioned accidents
     Creep in 'twixt vows, and change decrees of kings,
     Tan sacred beauty, blunt the sharp'st intents,
8   Divert strong minds to th' course of altering things —
     Alas, why, fearing of time's tyranny,
     Might I not then say, now I love you best,
     When I was certain o'er incertainty,
12 Crowning the present, doubting of the rest?
      Love is a babe: then might I not say so,
      To give full growth to that which still doth grow.

Reduced to its basic argument, this sonnet demonstrates the impossibility of ever being able to say 'now I love you best', and, by extension perhaps, of the impossibility of ever being able to say 'I love you'. The argument is 'proved' by setting the sonnet in the past and showing how and why all the poet's previous statements were false: as with Donne's analysis of the same point in 'Love's Growth' it turns out that love is so dynamic and time-bound an experience that it is impossible to give it the stasis which definition, or even description, requires.

In Donne's poem the argument, for all of its complexity, is aimed towards clarification and enlightenment, showing that love is not the pure abstraction which commentators have described. The twists of syntax hold the reader in suspense, but eventually lead him out of trouble, into comprehension:

     I scarce believe my love to be so pure
       As I had thought it was,
       Because it doth endure
     Vicissitude, and season, as the grass;
5   Methinks I lied all winter when I swore
     My love was infinite, if spring make it more.
     But if this medicine, love, which cures all sorrow
     With more, not only be no quintessence,
     But mixed of all stuffs, paining soul, or sense,
10 And of the sun his working vigour borrow,
     Love's not so pure, and abstract, as they use
     To say, which have no mistress but their muse,
     But as all else, being elemented too,
     Love sometimes would contemplate, sometimes do.

15 And yet no greater, but more eminent,

> Love by the Spring is grown;
>   As, in the firmament,
> Stars by the sun are not enlarged, but shown,
> Gentle love deeds, as blossoms on a bough,
> 20   From love's awakened root do bud out now.
> If, as in water stirred more circles be
> Produced by one, love such additions take,
> Those like so many spheres, but one heaven make,
> For they are all concentric unto thee.
> 25   And though each spring do add to love new heat,
> As princes do in times of action get
> New taxes, and remit them not in peace,
> No winter shall abate the spring's increase.

In comparison with this Shakespeare's sonnet, not least for its conventional sonnet form, is likely to strike the reader as relatively straightforward. It seems to have one of the classic sonnet structures: a first quatrain describes the poet's problem, that he has written lying poetry; a second quatrain, beginning with "But", suggests an opposing view to the first; and a third quatrain, opening with an exclamation, proposes one possible answer, to be overturned finally by a couplet which gives the proper, definitive answer. But it would have to be an excessively casual reader who did not apprehend something seriously wrong at the simple syntactic level between the second quatrain and the third; and for the by now experienced reader of the sequence the peculiar syntactic independence of the second quatrain will confirm his growing suspicions that the sonnet, instead of leading the reader through problems to a solution, in the manner of Donne, is actually taking him in the opposite direction.

The reader's difficulties begin in the first quatrain, but that is where he might expect to find them, and by the end of the quatrain he has not yet begun to lose command of the argument:

> Those lines that I before have writ do lie
> Even those that said I could not love you dearer.
> Yet then my judgement knew no reason why
> My most full flame should afterwards burn clearer.

The sharp contrast in tenses in the opening line, "have writ" and "do lie", alerts the reader to the complexities of time in the sonnet. In other words, they lie *now*: whether they lied *then* is not yet clear. Perhaps the lines were always lies, even at the moment of writing, or perhaps present experience has turned them in retrospect from fact into fiction. The Chinese box nature of the whole sonnet is implicit here, since with the second (and most probable) alternative, the definition of lying has become so flexible that it must, almost inevitably, describe everything written in the past – including the lines of this sonnet when they become, as they are to the reader, part of history. But the reader has a more specific problem: which lines are the lying ones, all the poems which the poet has written, or only some of them? Line 2 provides a typically confusing answer. In fact the modern reader, with his altered emphasis on "even", is likely to be more confused; but even if the Elizabethan reader's understanding of it were restricted to 'namely' – Ingram and Redpath's confident gloss – then the argument will still cause apprehension, in that specifically those sonnets which have made the highest claims have been singled out for description as lies.[12] The third and fourth lines then concentrate on the frame of mind in which those particular sonnets were written. "Then" is an important word in this sonnet: here it emphasises the quatrain's questioning of the poet's thoughts at the time he wrote them. "Then" it was impossible for the poet to know how what had seemed to be the fullest experience could become fuller – but "knew no reason why" is not quite the same as saying 'knew how', for it indicates a questioning of the nature of that experience even at this height, as if some part of the poet's mind had always been weighing cause and effect. This is an important distinction because it organises one of the reader's chief responses to the second quatrain:

> But reckoning time, whose millioned accidents
> Creep in 'twixt vows, and change decrees of kings,
> Tan sacred beauty, blunt the sharp'st intents,
> Divert strong minds to th' course of altering things

The difficulty with the quatrain is that it makes no grammatical sense. It gives every impression of leading to a destination, the reader accepting that for all of the apparent intermediate qualification "reckoning time" will eventually have a verb to itself – probably a predictable one, like lying in wait, or spoiling and destroying. But the third quatrain presents, instead, a new start – "Alas, why, fearing of time's tyranny,/Might I not then say . . ." – so that the reader has to scramble some retrospective sense to lines 5 – 8. They become, and I emphasise that they do so retrospectively, a list of the reasons why the poet's full flame should have burned weaker. In the terms of the first quatrain's concentration upon the poet's thoughts at the time he wrote his sonnets, these lines suddenly have come to demonstrate the complexities of saying "I could not love you dearer", for to say this is also to say that one expects that love soon to diminish. Indeed, the very statement is an indication of the fears and anxieties, not over so vague a matter as time's accidents, but over the effect of time upon even the strongest minds; and the second quatrain is taken up with demonstrating the way such words are the most susceptible to time's millioned accidents. [13] The complexity of the logic is the greater because, as the sonnet's opening line had announced, the poet has said such a thing, and has, therefore, anticipated his love's imminent diminution.

If the reader regains his syntactic equilibrium in the third quatrain by exercising hard revision of what he has just read, his sense of security will soon be betrayed by the quatrain's temporal confusion:

> Alas, why, fearing of time's tyranny,
> Might I not then say, now I love you best,
> When I was certain o'er incertainty,
> Crowning the present, doubting of the rest?

The reader is all at sea with regard to the temporal function of these lines: having negotiated the syntactic hazard of the second quatrain, he takes line 9 as a new direction, the participle "fearing" promising either a statement about the present or a resolution for the future. But lines 10-11 present some confusion with "then" and "When I was". If "then" has the same meaning as in line 3 – i.e. 'at that time' – then the whole quatrain is merely an extension of the second quatrain, underscoring the list of reasons for insecurity in the face of time's accidents with a final defence for having said "now I love you best". But "now I love you best" is a statement which strikes the reader with its present relevance, and he will have already been tilted in that direction by a verb which seems more related to the present than the past, "might I say" rather than 'might I have said'. Its effect is to encourage the reader to interpret "then" as meaning 'therefore', and the whole quatrain gathers a contemporary relevance – even "When I was certain" shedding its historical form and taking on a subjunctive reference, with line 12's participles literally crowning the present moment.

The sonnet is, in the best sense, self-revealing. It is organised around the impossibility of the poet/lover ever being able to say "now" with any certainty, and it forces the reader into a similar confusion about its own "now". The three quatrains have pursued two lines of thought, one a defence for having said "now I love you best" in the past, the other a reasoned argument for saying now, in this sonnet, "I love you best". Their effects upon each other are obvious. If "I love you best" had emerged in the past from a knowledge of time's imminent weakening of the poet's vows and intents, then "I love you best" in this sonnet, at this time, is a fiction. If "I love you best" actually applies now, then "I love you best" in the past was, as the sonnet had begun by admitting, a fiction: the reasoning of the second quatrain is specious, therefore the present statement "now I love you best" will also turn out to be a fiction. The couplet, with its definite opening statement, promises to cut the knot, but like the rest of the sonnet it turns out to be simultaneously an attack on, and a defence of, the poet's right to say, or to have said, "now I love you best":

> Love is a babe: then might I not say so,
> To give full growth to that which still doth grow.

Major confusions come at three separate points, "babe", "then", and "To give full growth". First, to say that love is a babe, in the temporal context of the sonnet, leads the reader two ways: either love is a babe because it never grows out of its infantile state, and so must always be immature, or love is a babe in the most literal sense of infantile, that is not being able to speak so that it cannot define itself ("say so").[14] "Then" presents similar problems to its occurrence in line 10: it is either part of a continuing description of the past — 'at that time [when I wrote those lines]' — or it introduces a resolution for the present and the future — 'therefore [I can not say I love you best]'.[15] In the first possibility, the past, "then" expands the ambiguities of love as a babe in two ways: 'when I said I loved you best I was denying the fact that love must always be immature', or 'because love cannot define itself, when I said I loved you best I was a liar.' If "then" describes the present and future it likewise expands love as a babe in two ways: 'I cannot now say I love you best because I would be denying love's essential immaturity', or 'I cannot say I love you best because the fact that I am in love prevents me from saying such a thing.'[16] Finally, the possible ambiguities of "to" in "to give full growth" leaves the reader in doubt about whether the poet is declaring an intention to destroy or to preserve love: 'if I say I love you best, then I destroy love by turning the babe into an adult', or 'by not saying I love you best I preserve love, my silence allowing love to reach full growth' (which is a kind of "still" growth).

To return from the trees to the wood, the whole of my analysis of the sonnet has so far played down some of the reader's more general problems, in particular the sonnet's tone and the level on which it should be taken. In this respect it is typical of the later sonnets of the young man sequence, demanding that the reader switch from pure facetiousness to earnest conviction, and back again. The second quatrain is as impressively solemn a list of time's effects as any in the sonnets, with its shadowy personification of that enemy as first a mere functionary (reckoning time), then, by way of time's accidents, as a servant (creep in 'twixt vows), an overlord (change decrees of kings), a natural force (tan, blunt), and finally the specific natural force of a river in full flood (Direct strong minds to th' course of altering things). But enclosing this is a beginning and ending of obvious contrivance. The sonnet's opening lines play a joke on the reader by teasing him with the possibility that he is going to witness an outright denial of the poet's love for the young man — "do lie" carrying a powerful implication of deliberate hypocrisy, as opposed to a phrase like 'were wrong'. As it turns out, "lie" is only a retrospective judgment, not a description of the kind of feeling that went into their writing, but the false wit of the opening line hangs over the whole quatrain. False wit, too, governs the couplet: "Love is a babe" seems to be a falling back onto cliché, promising a solution to the problems of time in the hackneyed description of love as the boy Cupid. Reading the sonnet on this level actually reduces the description of time's accidents in the second quatrain to a sustained piece of specious self-excuse — 'if time does this to the strongest minds, how much the more is it bound to do to mine.' Therefore, in tone too Sonnet 115 aims to unsettle the reader. Time is both a destroyer and an excuse, just as time present and time past cancel each other out. Line 11 presents an apt summary of the sonnet's effect by proposing the possibility of being "certain o'er incertainty", which either describes the condition of being uniquely certain in a general state of uncertainty, or of being finally certain that everything is uncertain.

Sonnet 115's confusion spreads from an analytic, and potentially cynical, mind's attempts to use the word "now" — to be certain about the present. In apparently complete contrast Sonnet 116 forgets analysis and cynicism, and irresistibly asserts one way to be certain about the present:

> Let me not to the marriage of true minds
> Admit impediments. Love is not love
> Which alters when it alteration finds,
> 4 Or bends with the remover to remove.
> O no, it is an ever-fixed mark
> That looks on tempests and is never shaken;
> It is the star to every wandering bark,
> 8 Whose worth's unknown, although his height be taken.
> Love's not time's fool, though rosy lips and cheeks
> Within his bending sickle's compass come.
> Love alters not with his brief hours and weeks,
> 12 But bears it out even to the edge of doom.
>   If this be error and upon me proved,
>   I never writ, nor no man ever loved.

It would be an act of critical madness to attempt to analyse this sonnet in the way in which I have just analysed Sonnet 115. Rhetorically the two poems stand in great contrast to each other. In rhythm, syntax, verb tense, and poetic structure, Sonnet 115 encourages the reader to consider and reconsider what is being, and what has been, said. This sonnet does the opposite, its high monotone leading the reader unthinkingly through a series of statements about love: love is not, love is, love's not, love alters not, but love bears it out. The primacy of this idea of defining love can be measured by the reader's reaction to lines 7–8:

> It is the star to every wandering bark,
> Whose worth's unknown . . .

In the process of reading most Shakespearean sonnets the reader might be tempted to take the first half of line 8 as part of the description of the "bark", as in normal English prose syntax; or at the least he would hold in parallel the two possibilities that it refers back either to "bark" or to "star". But here there can be no possible doubt that the proper antecedent is neither "bark" nor "star", but the "it" which begins line 7, love itself.[17]

The contrast with Sonnet 115 is not only formal; in effect 116 provides an answer to the complexities of its predecessor. It proposes a love which exists in an unchanging present, impervious to time's millioned accidents. "Love's not time's fool" is a peculiarly oblique contrast to the image of reckoning time whose accidents "Creep in 'twixt vows, and change decrees of kings", not least because here time is presented as a much more regal figure, despite the overall assertion that his rule can be resisted. This, I think, gives a clue to the ultimate insubstantiality of the sonnet, something which leads so responsive a critic as Stephen Booth to use it as an opportunity to discuss the nature of bombast (whilst denying the label's complete applicability to the sonnet), and which has led other commentators to a general vagueness about its actual subject.[18]

The vagueness is justified because the sonnet's declared subject is non-existent except in the person of the poet himself. "Love is not love which . . ." is the start of a definition which eventually excludes all action, identity, and knowledge. This love fails to respond to human movement in the first quatrain, resists figuratively even the sea's movement in the second, and, ultimately, time's sickle in the third. Its nature is that of the North Star's, the one fixed point in a turning world. But its chief characteristic is its isolation. Unlike, for example, Donne's unique lovers, this love is a solitary figure. The world is both literally and figuratively in contrast with it, in a state of error – " . . . alteration . . . remover . . . tempests . . . wandering

bark . . . time's fool . . . rosy lips and cheeks . . . brief hours and weeks."
That this love is the poet is borne upon the reader by the sonnet's framing,
which is essentially defensive. The couplet, as many commentators have
noted, is pure illogicality, but nonetheless fitting in that it asserts without
possibility of refutation the truth of the poet's description of love; but what
they fail to bring out is that it returns the sonnet to the vulnerability of the
opening lines. "I never writ, nor no man ever loved", in itself a
breathtakingly pompous parallel, is made doubly so in its posing as the
logical consequence to the poet's being in error. What prevents it from being
experienced like that, however, is the reader's sense of the poet's defensiveness from the opening of the sonnet. "Let me not to the marriage of true
minds/Admit impediments" is not quite so trouble-free a request as editors
seem to imply. They feel duty bound to note, although all readers are certain
to pick it up, its echoing of the marriage service, but they largely ignore the
reader's real problem which is to assess whether or not the poet is one of the
'marriage' partners. It is at least possible that the prayer book echo points to
his not being, since the call to admit impediment is made to the other
members of the congregation, not the actual couple. This response obviously
makes "marriage of true minds" an ironic phrase, and it also points clearly
towards the exclusion and exclusivity of the rest of the first quatrain:

> Love is not love
> Which alters when it alteration finds,
> Or bends with the remover to remove.

"Alteration" and "remover" are primarily words to describe infidelity, and
the metaphoric image of the quatrain becomes that of a member of the
congregation at a wedding who could, but out of greater love will not give
cause or just impediment.[19] If, though, the reader is not prepared to treat
"marriage of true minds" ironically, seeing instead the poet as one of the
married pair, then he has to find a way of coping with the marriage in the
context of alteration and removal which the rest of the quatrain insists upon.
The only way is to drive back into the opening lines the sense that the poet
will not be the one to admit impediments, but his partner will: a sense
reinforced by the rest of the sonnet's emphasis on images of uniqueness and
isolation.

"Love's not time's fool" is an unexpected and exciting expansion of the
sonnet's reference, presenting the poet as not only a unique lover, but as a
unique man, whose vision makes his life independent of time's rule. As a
personal vision it seems one way out of the dilemma of a world governed by
time, but it only anticipates the sterile self-dramatisation of Sonnet 121's

" 'Tis better to be vile than vile esteemed''. In the last chapter I discussed the development of the group 117—121 from playful self-defence to total self-elevation. But Sonnet 121 is the logical development of this sonnet too, with "I am that I am" the final way of saying that the poet does not alter or bend.

13 'Hugely Politic': Self-Containment

The final group of sonnets in the young man sequence is 122 – 126, and it is difficult to see these five fitting anywhere else than at its end. It would be possible to make a case for their finality on the grounds that they take up and modify elements from the rest of the sequence, but in a collection so repetitive in imagery and language this would be a weak argument since almost any other five sonnets in the sequence might do the same. A more powerful case for their finality rests on their emotional and intellectual completing of what has gone before. As a whole, and from Sonnet 100 in particular, the sequence has moved from the total dependence of the poet upon the young man towards a realisation of his self-sufficiency. In previous chapters I have discussed the way Sonnets 116 and 121 assert a complete reliance on internal values: but their assertion is just that, bold proclamation that "love is not love which . . ." and "I am that I am". In this final group of sonnets the self assertion is repeated, but now with the depth and conviction of a sustained piece of self definition.

Sonnet 122 depends strongly upon the remembrance of past sonnets, especially the promises of poetic immortality, but the reader is from the start confused about who the poet is and who the subject:

> Thy gift, thy tables, are within my brain
> Full charactered with lasting memory,
> Which shall above that idle rank remain
> 4 Beyond all date even to eternity.
> Or at the least, so long as brain and heart
> Have faculty by nature to subsist,
> Till each to razed oblivion yield his part
> 8 Of thee, thy record never can be missed.
> That poor retention could not so much hold,
> Nor need I tallies thy dear love to score.
> Therefore to give them from me was I bold
> 12 To trust those tables that receive thee more.

To keep an adjunct to remember thee
Were to import forgetfulness in me.[1]

It has been suggested that this sonnet looks back to Sonnet 77, and that it
describes the fate of the vacant leaves which the poet had there given to the
young man.[2] They, it seems, have since been filled and have been given back
to the poet, who, in turn, has given them casually away; and this sonnet is a
defence of that action on the grounds that the poet does not need the young
man's words, having a finer foundation for his love within his own brain.
But, as Stephen Booth points out, one problem with this interpretation is
that line 10 describes a different kind of notebook, one with blank pages
which the poet himself was expected to fill.[3] Ingram and Redpath make a
similar point about the first quatrain, developing from the fuzziness of its
wording three distinct possibilities: '(1) that the tables contained writings by
the Friend; (2) that the writings were by the poet; (3) that the leaves were
blank'. They go on to say that the first two should be ruled out on the
grounds of tact and discretion respectively, and then argue for our seeing
that 'such a book would then have been a more valuable gift than it might
seem now'.[4]

I find both comments too limited, Booth's unusually so. The idea of using
tallies to score love could equally describe reading or writing a numbered
sonnet sequence: "score" is a flexible enough verb to carry a metaphor for
either. More typical, though, is Ingram and Redpath's action of admitting
and then ruling out possibilities, which seems to come from a persistent
desire to make the sonnets a tactful and discreet collection of poems. I shall
argue, instead, for the sonnet's deliberate sowing of confusion. It forces the
reader to hold on to Ingram and Redpath's three possibilities, not only in the
first quatrain but all the way through. "Thy gift" is the poet's to the young
man or the young man's to the poet, either written or blank, and although
the sonnet may veer towards each of these in turn, it allows none to
predominate.[5] Even at the end the couplet's "adjunct to remember thee" is
sufficiently vague to include all possibilities.

If at its most basic narrative level the reader is confused, this is only a sign
of the sonnet's general strategy, which is to undermine the accepted attitudes
of the sequence – and all sonnet sequences – and to replace them with the
total self-sufficiency of the poet. In place of all those sonnets which offer their
poetry as an eternal monument this sonnet offers only the poet, and,
moreover, the poet without his poetry. Consider the lines which close the
first two quatrains, "Beyond all date even to eternity" and "Of thee, thy
record never can be missed." Each, out of its context, belongs to the rhetoric
of the immortalising sonnets; indeed, within the context of the reader's

progress through the sonnet "Beyond all date even to eternity" is initially an immortalising promise of the kind that was made earlier in the sequence. The unexpected qualification which opens the second quatrain, "Or at the least", is a perplexing change of direction, redefining eternity as merely the length of the poet's life; and the reader waiting to see how the tables within the poet's brain could be described as remaining to eternity – and the first quatrain promises some such resolution – finds the answer only by allowing himself to be drawn into the poet's experience of time. For the poet, as for every man, his own life span is eternity, ending as all time will do in rased oblivion. It hardly needs me to note how often the earlier sonnets have accepted the altruistic vision of a poet-less future – times in hope, the eyes of all posterity, after I am gone, when all the breathers of this world are dead — but now the rhetoric of that vision is turned around, and there is no future, for the young man at least, beyond the poet's life.

Reduced to its essentials the second quatrain says that the young man's memory will not die so long as the poet lives. The effect is not so brutal as this summary, though, because the language is the language of eternity, not death. "Brain and heart" is one way of saying 'me', but a way which encourages us illogically to divide the human into separately existing parts, with life spans of their own perhaps extending to the end of time. And although "razed oblivion" does mean, as every editor points out, to oblivion which erases, it also unavoidably suggests, through its misleadingly adjectival structure, the erasing of oblivion. Finally "Till each . . . yield his part" is one way of saying 'till I die', but is so persuasively gentle that the reader can hardly avoid carrying into it the image of a willing reunion of fragments, a shadow of "the judgement that yourself arise".

So "thy record never can be missed" at the end of the quatrain both is and is not a recapitulation of the poet's earlier promises of immortality: is not, because its reference is to only one 'misser', the poet, and not the whole world; is, because the poet is the whole world, with his own eternity which can promise a lasting memory. This is complete self-sufficiency, and it excludes the great image of time as all others – past, present, and future – experience it, namely the written word. That image of permanence is reduced, in contrast to the poet's brain, to images of ephemera: "that idle rank", "that poor retention", "tallies", "an adjunct", "forgetfulness".

After the rhetoric of the octave, the sestet is entirely prosaic – signalled by the five infinitives in the last five times – as the excuse is offered for having given away the book. The reader has, as often, two widely divergent choices facing him. Either this is an extreme example of form imitating content, showing that the written word is actually as bad as the poet claims, or its failure to maintain the poetry of the octave marks down the callousness of the poet's action. Cynicism and sincerity are equally probable sources for the couplet, which casually or idealistically dismisses poetry as a diary entry. But this sestet is the final echo of the excuse mixed with defiance which had informed so many of the preceding twenty sonnets, and here it is conditioned by an octave which forces the reader to accept the universality of the poet's mind. So universal a mind can hardly be capable of forgetfulness, despite the gesture in that direction in the couplet, and as if to demonstrate the point Sonnet 123 takes the implications of 122's octave to their logical extreme, describing an internal mental state not subject to the relativities of time:

> No! Time, thou shalt not boast that I do change.
> Thy pyramids built up with newer might
> To me are nothing novel, nothing strange;
> 4   They are but dressings of a former sight.
> Our dates are brief, and therefore we admire
> What thou dost foist upon us that is old,
> And rather make them born to our desire
> 8   Than think that we before have heard them told.
> Thy registers and thee I both defy,
> Not wondering at the present, nor the past;
> For thy records, and what we see, doth lie,
> 12   Made more or less by thy continual haste.
> This I do vow, and this shall ever be,
> I will be true despite thy scythe and thee.

Line 5 summarises the common human predicament – "Our dates are brief, and therefore . . ." – but the poet transcends common humanity, not being taken in by time's pyramids or time's registers. As the couplet makes clear in opposing "thy scythe" and "thee", it is not merely, as earlier in the sequence, a fear of death and extinction, but the actual nature of time itself and its inevitable distortion of our present experience, which the poet refuses to give way to. It is ironic but typical of the fate of the sonnets that the poem which most forcefully denies the poet's chaining to a particular time should be the one most often used to date the sequence. Whether the pyramids are Pope Sextus's or James I's matters not the slightest. Like all art, this sonnet asserts, they are but a revamping of what has gone before, and in that revamping must be included this sonnet too. The previous sonnet had dismissed writing as something of no account compared with the brain's retention; now writing becomes the prerogative of time – records and registers, the stuff of lives. Between them Sonnets 122 and 123 deny both poetry and history: in their place the poet proposes his own self-sufficiency and, as an extension of that, his truth. "I will be true" is a statement of strange relevance at this stage of the sequence, where it seems no longer a question of being true to anyone, but merely of being whole and complete. It is the language of love poetry used to cap a sonnet whose subject matter is far removed from matters of love.[6]

The next sonnet in the sequence, number 124, develops this image in peculiarly graphic ways, presenting a three sided picture of the poet's love:

> If my dear love were but the child of state,
> It might for fortune's bastard be unfathered,
> As subject to time's love, or to time's hate,
> 4   Weeds among weeds, or flowers with flowers gathered.
> No, it was builded far from accident;
> It suffers not in smiling pomp, nor falls
> Under the blow of thralled discontent,
> 8   Whereto th' inviting time our fashion calls.
> It fears not policy, that heretic
> Which works on leases of short numbered hours,
> But all alone stands hugely politic,
> 12   That it nor grows with heat, nor drowns with showers.
> To this I witness call the fools of time,
> Which die for goodness, who have lived for crime.

This sonnet has been analysed in great detail by both Arthur Mizener and Stephen Booth and shown to be as complex an artefact as any metaphysical poem, but depending upon a crucial vagueness of structure which prevents the reader particularising or confining metaphors to one strain.[7] Rather than retrace their analyses I want to emphasise the sonnet's effect upon the reader, for it claims to be, and its first line palpably belongs to, a love poem. "My dear love" sits uneasily against "child of state", but it is the kind of uneasiness which, as Mizener has shown, stimulates the mind into expectation as to what senses of "child" and "state" will be taken up. Booth, in his commentary, notes the forcefulness of "it" at the beginning of line 2 and, following that, in the sonnet as a whole: 'The key to the poem's power may be in the word "it", which, like all pronouns, is specific, hard, concrete, and yet imprecise and general – able to include anything or nothing.'[8] My sole objection to this is that one thing which "it" cannot include is the addressee of the whole sequence, and for this reason the first occurrence of the word is the most forceful. In a great number of sonnets the reader has become used to finding in a formula like "my dear love" so much unspecificity that it might describe either the poet's lover or the poet's own emotion, or both. Here, quite suddenly, "it" forces out the possibility of "dear love" as a reference to the young man, or to any person for that matter; and the sonnet then develops as a detailed, figurative description of the poet's emotion, aimed at turning something as essentially passionate as love into the same kind of absolute self-sufficiency which led up to the poet's declaration of his truth in Sonnet 123.

The primary metaphors of this "it" are of a statesman, a plant, and a building.[9] "It" has the erectness of these three elements, but does not share in their various vulnerabilities: the sonnet builds up a series of apparently all inclusive doublets, but removes the poet's emotion from any contact with them – neither a child nor unfathered, free from time's love or time's hate, not a weed nor a flower, not affected by heat or by rain, and neither pompous nor discontented. Only one positive statement emerges from the welter of negatives: "But all alone stands hugely politic." The verb provides a moment of possible unity, giving the common denominator of all three metaphors, but the reader can hardly hold them together for the length of the line. "Hugely politic" forces a degree of human reference which destroys the plant and building image, while the figure of the solitary statesman has already been undercut by "it" at the beginning of the quatrain, and it disappears in the botanical imagery of line 12. In effect all that the sonnet allows the reader to add to the poet's presentation of his emotion is that it stands all alone.

So far I have made the sonnet out to be extremely negative, but this is not a completely fair impression, for there is overall a broader picture of the workings of the world and time than its individual parts might imply. It is as if the poet's very exclusion from the order of things, his complete conviction that he stands apart, allows him to see everything much clearer. What I am leading up to is that this sonnet, for the first time in the sequence, presents the process of time as essentially fair. Throughout the sequence time has been vindictive, malicious, hostile to man, the cause of all the evils of the world which, for example, Sonnet 66 catalogues. Time's only act of mercy is, in the terms of that sonnet, "restful death", but in the context of the whole sequence even death is hideous in that it robs the world of the young man. Now, finally, Sonnet 124 sees time in a more detached way. Consider line 4 which sums up the first quatrain epigrammatically, and seems to follow the habit of the sequence by stressing the arbitrariness of time: we are all its victims, whether good or bad –

Weeds among weeds, or flowers with flowers gathered.

But, paradoxically, the image also allows some sense of the fairness of the order of things. Weeds with weeds and flowers with flowers is how things should be, and the reader detects behind the line the shadow of what might have been expected as an epigrammatic summary of unfairness — in, for example, a state where it is better to be vile than vile esteemed — that is, weeds with flowers, or flowers among weeds gathered.

The remainder of the sonnet acts in complete contrast to Sonnet 66, where the catalogue of worldly woe leads to the poet's desire to die; but there the reader sees behind the invitation to accept that everything is inevitably unfair, a developing self-dramatisation as the catalogue becomes more poet centred:

> Tired with all these, for restful death I cry,
> As to behold desert a beggar born,
> And needy nothing trimmed in jollity,
> 4   And purest faith unhappily forsworn,
> And gilded honour shamefully misplaced,
> And maiden virtue rudely strumpeted,
> And right perfection wrongfully disgraced,
> 8   And strength by limping sway disabled,
> And art made tongue-tied by authority,
> And folly, doctor-like, controlling skill,
> And simple truth miscalled simplicity,
> 12   And captive good attending captain ill.
>   Tired with all these, from these would I be gone,
>   Save that to die, I leave my love alone.

Set against this, Sonnet 124 first removes the poet from the poem, with his deepest emotion being given the impersonal pronoun "it", and then it asks us to see the world's woe as matter merely incidental to the huge self-containment which the poet has achieved. The second quatrain raises the poet's love above smiling pomp and thralled discontent: in part these are measures of the poet's internal state, but the impersonal projection of that state directs the reader towards their external application as the two possible conditions of worldly existence according to the fashion of the time; and the couplet reemphasises the point in a sweeping summary of all humanity as the fools of time:

> To this I witness call the fools of time,
> Which die for goodness, who have lived for crime.

It may be that the commentators have had some justification in ignoring

Shakespeare's common description of men as fools, and, instead, relating this couplet, because of its second line, to religious martyrs.[10] I doubt, though, whether such specificity is possible at the end of a sonnet so vague and wide ranging in reference: I am not even sure that an idea as general as death-bed repentence lies behind the last line. If the reader takes, as the phrase and the three quatrains lead him to do, "fools of time" as a description of all men — apart from the poet, that is — then the line becomes a definition of all men, not a specifying qualification. In other words, part of that fairness of the order of things which "weeds among weeds" had summarised, is that while life may be described in the terms of Sonnet 66, death is genuinely providential.

The idea deprived of its poetry is platitudinous, but the reader finds it moving because it so clearly acts as the consolatory emotional and intellectual response which allows him and the poet to close the young man relationship, and the sequence — a successful objective correlative, in fact. These last sonnets move the reader through a developing self-sufficiency which shows the poet transcending all the constraints which had been so important earlier in the sequence. Their effect is rhetorically irresistible, as assertion follows assertion down to the end of this sonnet, where life and death are parts of the greater order.[11] In that context the end of the relationship is both comprehensible and acceptable, not the world ending event which its possibility had been presented as before.

Sonnet 125 is the final sonnet in the group — the final sonnet in the sequence if we describe Sonnet 126 properly as a twelve line couplet poem — and it returns the reader directly to the relationship between the two men, but now using it to affirm an artistic and moral belief:

> Were't aught to me I bore the canopy,
> With my extern the outward honouring,
> Or laid great bases for eternity,
> 4 Which proves more short than waste or ruining?
> Have I not seen dwellers on form and favour
> Lose all and more by paying too much rent
> For compound sweet forgoing simple savour,
> 8 Pitiful thrivers, in their gazing spent?
> No, let me be obsequious in thy heart,
> And take thou my oblation, poor but free,
> Which is not mixed with seconds, knows no art,
> 12 But mutual render, only me for thee.
>   Hence, thou suborned informer! A true soul
>   When most impeached stands least in thy control.

"Simple", "poor but free", "not mixed with seconds", "knows no art", "only me for thee", these are the positive declarations to add to "all alone stands", and to set against the fashionable services of the first quatrain.

In its verbal structure this sonnet puts the reader through three separate experiences, in the first quatrain, the second and third, and then the couplet. The first quatrain presents the Shakespearean sonnet at its most complex. It begins by facing the reader with a worryingly vague opening line: he has to decide whether it relates to something which the poet has done, or to something which he might be capable of doing – 'What does it matter if I have donè this?' or 'What would it matter if I should do this?' By the end of the quatrain that distinction hardly counts, but by then the reader is caught up in the apparent denial of all the poet's work in lines 3 – 4. The language is complex too – "canopy", "extern", "outward", "waste", "ruining", each is a word with ominous but vague suggestion – and the syntax leaves the reader with the problem of deciding whether line 4 describes "great bases" or "eternity". Indeed the whole quatrain is illusory, its *raison d'etre* rapidly disappearing in the non-existence of the rhyme (canopy/ honouring/eternity/ruining). But then, as if in complete contrast,the next two quatrains move the reader into the comfort of predictable rhyming and the formulaic language of conventional love sonnetry, from which I drew the positive statements at the beginning of my discussion of the sonnet.[12] But all is unexpectedly turned around in a couplet unique in the sequence; for, curiously, coming so close to the end as it does, it introduces for the first time the Donne-like impression of our being present at a particular experienced, not imagined, confrontation. At least part of our impression is that the confrontation is with the young man, there being some recall of "thy" and "thou" in the third quatrain, but equally the confrontation reads like one with all mankind, the external world of time's registers in Sonnet 123, the inviting time's fashion in 124, and the dwellers on form and favour of this sonnet. Its effect, too, is to deny completely the possibility of "only me for thee" which the sonnet had seemed to work towards, for such a declaration requires the existence of another capable of mutual render. Again the image is one of standing all alone, with the self-dramatisation of the poet in the dock accused on all sides, and his self-sufficiency borne of freedom from the accusers' control.[13]

The sonnet proposes a nullification of both love and art. To lay great bases for eternity, the principal function of poetry in the sequence, is equated with so superficial an action as bearing the canopy, and the images of the rest of the sonnet have at their back a contempt for the art of comparing which metaphor entails. "Only me for thee" may be morally desirable, but it helps create poetry as bare as "I am that I am". And parallel with this, the act of love as practised between the poet and the young man is doomed by a refusal to pay too much rent or to be outwardly obsequious: "only me for thee" belongs to the world of the phoenix and the turtle, not that of suborned informers and impeachment.

These final three sonnets form an extended and proclaimed self-defence against an accuser who begins in Sonnet 123 as a mere personification, but who ends in 125 as an unmistakeable human figure; and sustained through them is a rhetoric of self-justification:

> No! Time, thou shalt not boast that I do change . . .
> Thy registers and thee I both defy . . .
> This I do vow, and this shall ever be,
> I will be true . . .
> If my dear love were but . . .
> No, it was builded far from accident . . .
> To this I witness call . . .
> Were't aught to me I bore the canopy . . .
> Have I not seen dwellers on form and favour . . .
> No, let me be obsequious in thy heart . . .
> Hence, thou suborned informer . . .

For the reader the effect is puzzling, if not alienating. The sequence has shown enough suffering and certitude to absolve the poet from seeming simply paranoid, but it is evident that this rhetoric only masks the absence of any positive thought – an extended argument for self-containment which rests on little more than the generalisations of Sonnets 116 and 121, and the sense that the world is wrong and that the poet has accusers. Compare it with Sonnet 146 and it seems empty:

> Poor soul, the centre of my sinful earth.
> . . . these rebel powers that thee array,
> Why dost thou pine within and suffer dearth,
> 4   Painting thy outward walls so costly gay?
> Why so large cost, having so short a lease,
> Dost thou upon thy fading mansion spend?
> Shall worms, inheritors of this excess,
> 8   Eat up thy charge? Is this thy body's end?
> Then, soul, live thou upon thy servant's loss,
> And let that pine to aggravate thy store:
> Buy terms divine in selling hours of dross;
> 12   Within be fed, without be rich no more.

> So shalt thou feed on death, that feeds on men,
> And death once dead, there's no more dying then. [14]

Sonnet 146 has a similar plot — persecution, denial of time's influence and death, ultimate self-sufficiency — but its contrast between soul and body gives it the substance of spiritual debate where these sonnets only fall back on the undeveloped image of an accused person in court. In 146 the argument's direction is outwards, moving from the poet's own sense of suffering towards a vision which embraces all mankind. In 123 – 125 the effort is reductive: a succession of images of the world's workings aimed only at revealing the uniqueness of the poet.

As a conclusion to a sequence founded originally upon the uniqueness of the young man, Sonnets 123 – 125 are fittingly limited. Ironically, they present a mirror image of the opening sonnets, with the poet's self-sufficiency and dismissal of the world's demands replacing the young man's. But what pains the reader is the accompanying diminution to the point of dismissal of the poet's art. At the beginning of the sequence this came from the young man, and was acceptable as part of a conventional representation of the sonneteer's beloved. Now, at the end, the poet has himself become art denying, projecting artlessness as one of the necessary elements in his self-containment; and since the sonneteer's convention involves the fiction that his only audience is the beloved, the need to deny his art is bound up with the end of the relationship — but all other readers are caught up in that end, and 125's couplet aims at their rejection as well as the young man's.

Sonnet 125 is a bitter farewell to reader and young man, but the sequence has room for a more nostalgic one. As if in harmony with the newly proclaimed artlessness, the final sonnet in the sequence, number 126, is only a sonnet in the sense that any short poem could be so named. Its couplet, and the appearance of the sonnet on the page — particularly in the Quarto, where brackets are inserted around each of the imaginary thirteenth and fourteenth lines — impress on the reader the poet's ultimate disdain for the sonnet form; the more so in that it is full of echoes of the sequence at its most 'sonnetic':

> O thou, my lovely boy, who in thy power
> Dost hold time's fickle glass, his sickle hour,
> Who hast by waning grown, and therein show'st
> 4 Thy lovers withering, as thy sweet self grow'st —
> If nature, sovereign mistress over wrack,
> As thou goest onwards still will pluck thee back,
> She keeps thee to this purpose, that her skill
> 8 May time disgrace, and wretched minute kill.

Yet fear her, O thou minion of her pleasure;
She may detain but not still keep her treasure.
Her audit, though delayed, answered must be,
12   And her quietus is to render thee.

The obvious envoy-like nature of this poem has often drawn the commentators' notice. Ingram and Redpath, for instance, describe it as seeming to be 'a somewhat deliberate attempt to recapture something of the spirit of the opening sonnets in the teeth of advancing age.'[15] For the reader, as well as the poet, it is almost an exercise in nostalgia, a return to the fond terms of endearment – "my lovely boy" and "thy sweet self" – and the image of the evergreen young man contrasted with decaying lovers, as well as the bogy-man caricature of time with glass and sickle. And the sonnet is packed with actions characteristic of the earlier part of the sequence: holding a mirror, moving forward and plucking back, keeping aside a treasure, and paying a bill. Even the rhymes are familiar, especially the 'couplet's' be/thee which echoes the opening sonnets of the procration group (numbers 1, 3 and 4).

The character of all of this is remembered affection, both for the young man when the poet's love was at its height, and for the sonnet itself as a vehicle for that emotion. But now the point of vision is elevated and all knowing: the apparent fondnesses only prepare the way for a cool final summary of the trap closing. Time will not be disgraced and nature is no more faithful, when bills have to be settled, than evergreen young men are. The reader's experience of this poem is, in miniature, his experience of the sequence. It begins with the young man's power over time and over humanity: in the first four lines he not only holds time's glass up to show other men their ageing, but seems to feed off them, growing – the verb is repeated – by their waning and withering. The rest of the sonnet completes the vicious circle. For all his power over time, the young man is very firmly nature's servant, she holding him back to cheat time; but time, it transpires, is her master, whose final bill she has to pay. The irony of the characterisation of the young man as, first, a figure of power, and, finally, as a coin to pay a bill, will not be lost on the reader who recalls the failure of that same young man either to spend his wealth, in the opening sonnets, or to use his power, as in Sonnet 94. The sequence had opened with a sonnet about prospective, almost imminent, death – and the hope that the poet might salvage a kind of immortality for the young man. It closes with a view of that death as perfectly fitting, a *quietus est* devoid of a sense of loss or remorse, and with as little need for immortality as a poem of six couplets has for a seventh.

Notes

Introduction

1. In *Explorations* (London, 1946) p. 40.
2. W. Empson, *Seven Types of Ambiguity* (New York, 1931); A. Mizener, 'The Structure of Figurative Language in Shakespeare's Sonnets', *Southern Review* v (1940) 730–47; W. Nowottny, 'Formal Elements in Shakespeare's Sonnets: Sonnets I–VI', *Essays in Criticism*, II (1952) 76–84; R. Colie, *Shakespeare's Living Art* (Princeton, 1974) chapters 1 and 2; S. Booth, *An Essay on Shakespeare's Sonnets* (New Haven, 1969) and ed. *Shakespeare's Sonnets* (New Haven, 1977).
3. *Explorations*, p. 59.
4. Two strange alternations in the dark lady sonnets are from the light wit of "black beauty" and playing the spinet in Sonnets 127 and 128 to the vision of lust in action in 129, and from the 'Hathaway' tetrameters in 145 to "Poor soul, the centre of my sinful earth" in 146.
5. Ed. *Shakespeare's Sonnets* (London, 1964) p. 34.
6. It is worth noting, however, that an historically ignorant response to "conceit" might conceivably create a more interesting third quatrain than the Shakespearean one: i.e. that the poet's vision of the young man is generated by a blindly proud belief that his moment will be more constant than that of common humanity.
7. Ingram and Redpath, *Shakespeare's Sonnets*, p. 34; Booth, *Shakespeare's Sonnets*, p. 156.
8. Compare the modern reader's reaction to 104:9–10, 'Ah yet doth beauty like a dial hand/Steal from his figure and no pace perceived'; it is possible for him to make the antiquarian response of imagining a sun-dial, but for the sonnet to be part of his own experience these lines should certainly evoke the experience of looking at the second-hand of a watch.
9. "Influence" had a specific astrological sense, describing the 'Supposed flowing from the stars or heavens of an etherial fluid acting upon the character and destiny of man' (Onions); "comment" is several times used by Shakespeare in senses appreciably stronger than today's, e.g. Hamlet's "the very comment of thy soul" (3.ii.81) and Richard III's "fearful commenting" (= meditation) which is "leaden servitor to dull delay" (4.iii.51–2); "brave", too, had wider range of uses, either as a word of general praise, or, specifically to describe dress; and "waste" Shakespeare in particular used with strong overtones of mortality, as in Sonnet 12's "wastes of time" and Sonnet 100:13, "Give my love fame faster than time wastes life."
10. *Shakespeare's Sonnets*, p. 35.

11. In *The Rhetoric of Renaissance Poetry: From Wyatt to Milton*, ed. Thomas O. Sloan and Raymond B. Waddington, pp. 96–122.
12. Page 97; Waddington describes himself as 'playing Tuve to Booth's Empson', and implies that he is, in part, correcting too laudatory a response to Booth's book, especially the influential review of it by Frank Kermode in *The New York Review of Books*, XV (1970) 33–8.

Chapter 1

1. I refer to the sonnets as a publication, not to any circulation they might have had in manuscript. The 1609 Quarto was not given a second edition, and the next appearance of the sonnets was in Benson's mangled edition of 1640. There are scarcely any allusions to the sonnets in the whole of the seventeenth century.
2. The slight clumsiness of the inversion signals, as often in the sonnets, a possible insincerity on the poet's part: there for the young man to catch if he has the sense.
3. The poet's invention may be 'blunt' because it is dull and clumsy, or because it lacks ceremony, insisting on telling the truth.
4. Booth, *Shakespeare's Sonnets*, p. 332. He notes that in the context of the tone of subservience the word "tend" in line 11 'can colour the line with syntactically irrelevant overtones of servility'.
5. 'Almost gay sarcasm', resulting from a mood of deep depression, is Martin Seymour-Smith's description of it, in his edition of *Shakespeare's Sonnets* (London, 1963) p. 149, and Stephen Booth describes 'the speaker's self-mocking tactics' in this sonnet (*Shakespeare's Sonnets*, p. 257). Earlier commentators were more prepared to read it as innocent in intention: Mark Van Doren called it 'one of the most perfect English poems', in *Shakespeare* (New York, 1939) p. 12.
6. *Shakespeare's Sonnets: Self, Love and Art* (Cambridge, 1972) p. 98.
7. 'The Love Poetry of John Donne – A Reply to Mr C. S. Lewis'; this essay originally appeared in 1938 and is reprinted in the Macmillan Casebook, *Donne: 'Songs and Sonets'*, ed. J. Lovelock (London, 1973) pp. 134–55; and in her book *Five Metaphysical Poets* (Cambridge, 1964) Ms Bennett wrote of 'the cold rage of thwarted lust' which governs the poem (p. 17). Compare Brian Vickers' description of it: 'he imagines himself . . . having been killed by his mistress's scorn, returning to her bed and watching her in the arms of a new (and "worse") lover', in *'Songs and Sonnets* and the Rhetoric of Hyperbole', in *John Donne: Essays in Celebration*, ed. A. J. Smith (London, 1972) p. 135; or, from the same collection of essays, Patricia Thompson's aside on the poem while discussing Donne's *Verse Letters*, that there 'he is not the stock lover, with wreathed arms, pleading for "pitty" from a mistress who shows nought but "disdaine". He is not, that is, in this context, the Donne of "The Apparition"' (p. 321). Clay Hunt observes that the poem's 'brutal sexual realism' is too much for its initial Petrarchanism, but his judgement that 'the convention is entirely out of its element in this poem' reveals his failure to see the poem's joke on the poet; see *Donne's Poetry: Essays in Literary Analysis* (Archon Books, 1969) pp. 8–9.
8. This is to restrict the meaning of the word "by" to its most literal sense. Its range of meanings here is broader than my paraphrase suggests, but the apparent

straightforwardness of the line persuades the reader to perceive "by the grave" as a specific location.

9. 'An excuse for age' is my interpretation of "make my old excuse" in Sonnet 2. Booth's explanation is worth quoting: 'justify, when I am old, the consumption of the beauty expended during my life (taking "old" as an ellipsis for "when I am old"; the context demands that the phrase be understood by synesis, i.e. as meaning what it must mean rather than what its syntax would otherwise indicate ["make my usual excuse"]).' (*Shakespeare's Sonnets*, p. 138.)

10. The "acceptable audit" which the young man should leave to nature reappears in the final sonnet in the sequence, no. 126, where nature's audit payed to time is the young man's death. For "executor" in the sense of 'executioner', cf. *Henry V*, I:ii:202 – 4 (part of the description of the bee-hive): "The sad-eyed justice, with his surly hum,/Delivering o'er to executors pale/The lazy yawning drone."

11. *Shakespeare's Sonnets*, p. 143.

12. 'Formal Elements in Shakespeare's Sonnets: Sonnets I – IV', *Essays in Criticism*, II (1952) 81 – 2.

13. Sonnet 42 in the 1594 edition of *Delia and Rosamond Augmented*.

14. *Shakespeare's Sonnets*, p. 158.

15. The phrase's best known discussion is by William Empson in *Seven Types of Ambiguity* (New York, 1931) p. 71; see also Ingram and Redpath, who list ten possible meanings of the phrase in their edition (p. 38), and Booth's discussion of it in *Shakespeare's Sonnets*, pp. xiii – xiv.

16. *Shakespeare's Sonnets*, p. 160.

17. Compare Henry IV's words of self-criticism: 'My blood hath been too cold and temperate/Unapt to stir at these indignities' (Part I, I:iii:1 – 2).

18. The *NED* cites, from 1592, "So let thy tresses Vntrimmed hang about thy bared necke."

19. The quotation is from Golding's translation of Ovid's *Metamorphoses*, xv, 237.

20. They are not really orders, as becomes obvious in the second quatrain. The reader begins the poem by taking them to be imperatives, but the ordering gradually loses its strength, declining from the first quatrain's "blunt"/ "make . . . devour"/"pluck"/"burn", to "make" and "do"; and the reader retrospectively sees lines 1 – 7 as a series of permissions rather than commands. Something analogous, if opposite, happens in the third quatrain, where the experience of the imperatives in the octave contaminates the pleas "carve not", "nor draw" and "do allow", and turns them into commands.

Chapter 2

1. The word 'mundane' is Booth's; see his account of the sonnet in *An Essay on Shakespeare's Sonnets*, pp. 48 – 9.

2. Cited by Rollins, *New Variorum Edition of Shakespeare: The Sonnets*, I (Philadelphia, 1944) 74.

3. In the Quarto line 12 reads "their sweet respect"; "their" for "thy" is the most common printing error in the Quarto and here, as in most of the other instances, I have followed the generally accepted emendation.

4. In *Shakespeare's Sonnets*, pp. 176 – 8, Booth discusses the sexual innuendo

developed in a series of 'variations on the idea of sharing', and the bawdy overtones of "wit", "conceit", "head", and "all".

5. "This thou perceiv'st, which makes thy love more strong,/To love that well which thou must leave ere long." See my discussion of this couplet in Chapter 5, p. 82.

6. Sonnet 37's connection with 36 is made more obvious by the first quatrain's use of the antithetical rhyme words "delight"/"spite"; the same rhyme appears in 36's second quatrain. See Booth, *An Essay on Shakespeare's Sonnets*, pp. 8—11, for further discussion of the linking of the two sonnets.

7. Booth's comment on "decrepit father" is that 'a metaphor of sexual impotence is dimly apparent throughout quatrain 1' (*Shakespeare's Sonnets*, p. 195).

8. The theme is a common one in the sequence; cf. the third quatrain of Sonnet 113, where the subject is the poet's eye: "For if it see the rud'st or gentlest sight,/The most sweet favour or deformedst creature,/The mountain, or the sea, the day, or night,/The crow, or dove, it shapes them to your feature."

9. *Shakespeare's Sonnets*, p. 225.

10. As in the way Hal uses the word in his opening soliloquy: "I know you all; and will a while uphold/The wayward humour of your idleness" (*Henry IV, part 1*, 1:ii:188—9).

11. The financial metaphor is taken up in "endeared" in the first line of the next sonnet, no. 31, which goes on to repeat the idea of 30.

12. The quatrain's only image is a shadowy financial one, in "lends but weak relief" and "bears . . . the loss". "Loss" in line 12 is usually emended to "cross", a rhyme which occurs in the third quatrain of Sonnet 42, but I prefer to retain any Quarto reading which makes sense.

13. The Quarto reading of line 8 is "Excusing their sins more than their sins are."

14. Compare the interchange between Valentine and Proteus, as they trade literary associations:

> *Val.*   Love is your master, for he masters you;
> And he that is so yoked by a fool,
> Methinks, should not be chronicled for wise.
> *Prot.*   Yet writers say, as in the sweetest bud
> The eating canker dwells, so eating love
> Inhabits in the finest wits of all.
> *Val.*   And writers say, as the most forward bud
> Is eaten by the canker ere it show,
> Even so by love the young and tender wit
> Is turned to folly, blasting in the bud,
> Losing his verdure even in the prime,
> And all the fair effects of future hopes.
>
> (*Two Gent.* 1:i:39—50)

Chapter 3

1. *A Window to Criticism: Shakespeare's Sonnets and Modern Poetics* (Princeton, 1964) p. 82.

2. *Shakespeare's Sonnets*, p. 172.

3. I have kept the Quarto's "steeld" in line 1 in preference to the common emendation (adopted by Booth) of "stelled". Ingram and Redpath give a detailed discussion of the cases for and against the two readings (*Shakespeare's Sonnets*, pp. 60–2). Their preference is for the Quarto reading.

4. 'Ingenuity of interpretation is only needed if "it" be misread as appositional to "perspective". Shakespeare is not saying that such clever projections are the highest form of pictorial art, but that his heart's image of the Friend is a perfect portrait, though to realize this we must see it through the poet's eye.' (*Shakespeare's Sonnets*, p. 63.)

5. One conceit which underlies line 14 is that the young man becomes an artist too: his heart, which the poet does not know, is (on the analogy of line 2) his painting of the poet – but because the young man is *not* a poet revealing himself to his subject that painting will remain an unknown image.

6. See chapter 2, pp. 31–3.

7. *Shakespeare's Sonnets*, p. 141.

8. *Shakespeare's Sonnets: Self, Love and Art*, pp. 71–3.

9. The Quarto punctuates lines 6–7 thus:

> Th' imprisoned absence of your liberty,
> And patience tame, to sufferance bide each check,

10. *Shakespeare's Sonnets*, p. 141.

11. In his 1918 edition Pooler suggested that 57 should follow 58.

12. As, for example, in 39:10; 57:7; 94:13.

13. As in 54:5; 70:7; 95:2; 99:13.

14. Note that both 36 and 39 offer excuses for separation.

15. The Quarto reads "this self deceivest" in line 7.

16. In the sonnets "spite" usually describes the actions of fortune, as in 107:11.

17. For example (from Tilley): 'Where beauty is there needs no other plea'; 'Youth will have its course'; 'More favour lusty youth than crooked age'.

18. Malone suggested in 1780 that line 8 misprints "she" for "he"—it should be "till she have prevailed". This suggestion has been followed by most editors, which shows, as Dover Wilson wrily commented, how little they knew human nature.

19. But some commentators have been prepared to take the sentiment at face value. In the New Variorum edition Rollins cites Gregor (*Shakespeare*, 1935) to the effect that 'such superhuman forgiveness . . . must bring forth the deepest loneliness of a spiritual art' (p. 119); and Seymour-Smith argues strongly for the sonnet's seriousness of intent: 'Critics have found the "superhuman forgiveness" evinced in it hard to accept. The metaphor of the Friend who possesses all Shakespeare's love is, however, meant to be just as difficult to accept as Shakespeare found it.' (*Shakespeare's Sonnets*, p. 132.)

20. Compare the couplet of Sonnet 61, where "for" conveys a similar ambiguity: "For thee watch I, whilst thou dost wake elsewhere,/From me far off, with others all too near."

21. More than in most cases an editor's punctuation of this sonnet will be governed by his interpretation of its meaning. The key lines are the closing ones of the three quatrains, 4, 8, and 12. The Quarto punctuates 4 with a comma after "respects", 8 with a full-stop after "gravity", and 12 with a comma after "part".

Booth puts a dash after all three; Ingram and Redpath have colon, colon, full-stop.

22. The suggestion was first made by Gerald Willen and Victor B. Reed in *A Casebook on Shakespeare's Sonnets* (New York, 1964).

Chapter 4

1. In his 1924 edition Tucker wrote that 'the only real reason . . . for suspecting that the piece may not be by Shakespeare is to be found in the rather pointless repetition of "heaven's air," '; but the repetition is not pointless – the pun on "heir" mimics the praising ideal of sonnets such as 18. .

2. In line 2 the Quarto spelling, "poor'st", hints at a punning connection with "want subject" in line 1.

3. "Dumb" does not have the modern sense of 'stupid', but means 'of poor expression, insensitive'.

4. *Shakespeare's Sonnets*, p. 197.

5. I have kept the Quarto's "dost" in line 12, rather than follow the common emendation to "doth" (which Booth accepts).

6. *Shakespeare's Sonnets*, p. 198.

7. Also the characteristics of the canker blooms in Sonnet 54 recall the characteristics of the young man in the procreation group; "live unwooed and unrespected fade", cf. 2:4; 5:1 – 4; 7:8 – 12; 11:6; 12:9 – 12; 13:9 – 12;15:5 – 8; "die to themselves", cf. 1:6, 14; 3:7 – 8; 6:4; 7:14; 9:14; and "distills", which recalls the whole of Sonnet 5.

8. Note in the first quatrain of this sonnet the contrived clumsiness of the expletives (a not uncommon trick in the sequence, cf. 94:1 – 2):"O how much more *doth* beauty beauteous seem,/By that sweet ornament which truth *doth* give./The rose looks fair, but fairer we it deem/For that sweet odour which *doth* in it live."

9. The Quarto ends the opening line with "monument".

10. *Shakespeare's Sonnets: Self, Love and Art*, p. 158.

11. *The World's Body* (New York, 1938) pp. 287 – 88.

12. There is a possible contrast in the sonnet's first quatrain between, in line 1, "marble" and "monuments", and, in line 4, "unswept stone", rather than "unswept stone" being merely a summary of the first two – line 1 setting out the graves of princes, line 4 the uncared-for grave of the young man.

13. This is the Quarto punctuation. Booth removes the parentheses, using a dash after "lie" and a semi-colon after "eyes".

14. *Shakespeare's Sonnets: Self, Love and Art*, p. 106.

15. Rather than the modernised form "travelled" I have kept the Quarto's spelling "travailed" in line 5 in order to help the reader see the pun.

16. Not only Ovid's *Metamorphoses* again, but also Horace's "aere perennium" = "brass eternal"; notice the wrenching effect of "brass eternal" next to "slave", which forces the reader to consider its classical status rather than what would be its normal English syntactic sense (i.e. brass as eternal slave).

Chapter 5

1. The distinction had not only been made in the immortalising sonnets, but also in a sonnet like 61, where a series of rhetorical questions in the octave builds up a picture of the young man's concern for the poet. But line 9 reveals this to be mere wish-fulfilment – that his motives might be the same as the poet's.

2. Something analogous happens in Sonnet 61 (see previous note) in the poet's picturing of himself lying awake at night.

3. In the Quarto line 4 begins "Bare rn'wd quiers".

4. Cited by Rollins in the New Variorum edition, p. 189. Other comments include 'a superb sonnet' (Beeching, 1904) and 'a sonnet of ever-living loveliness' (Clemen, 1936).

5. See in particular Booth's discussion of this sonnet in *An Essay on Shakespeare's Sonnets*, pp. 118–30.

6. It is impossible to make any absolute groupings in the sequence. In terms of subject matter Sonnets 71–74 seem to form a self-sufficient group, but 75, which takes up a different subject (the poet's sporadic meetings with the young man) nonetheless continues 74's financial metaphor.

7. *Shakespeare's Sonnets*, p. 170.

8. I can best describe it as a 'blocking metaphor', one which prevents the reader from making the necessary equalization of images – so that what fixes in the mind is only the image of his being marched off to gaol, not his actual dying. Contrast it with the dying images of 73 where the bare trees, the sunset, and the dying embers all encourage the equalization.

9. *Shakespeare's Sonnets*, p. 172.

10. Note the way "contains" echoes the opening phrase of the sonnet, "But be contented".

11. I have followed Booth in two emendations of the Quarto text: line 1, the Quarto reads "how thy beauties were" ('were' is a common Elizabethan spelling for 'wear'); line 10, the Quarto has "these waste blacks" (one assumes the loss of a nunnation mark).

12. I have ignored the common emendation of "the vacant leaves" to "these vacant leaves" in line 3. Any sense of the young man as a writer rather than a reader is cancelled by line 4 which seems to refer specifically to this book of poems – giving a retrospectively ironic meaning to "vacant" in line 3 (i.e. vacant to the young man because he is unable to comprehend them).

13. Notice the regular patterning of the three quatrains: the first gives one line to the glass, one to the dial, and two to the book; then in the second and third quatrains these amounts are doubled, two lines to the glass, two to the dial, and four to the book.

14. *Shakespeare's Sonnets*, pp. 156–7.

15. Note also the grammatical ambiguity of these verbs, where the reader is never quite certain as to whether they are imperatives or introductions to hypotheses.

16. The sonnets which have one syntactic break are 13, 74, 117, and 140 (and, possibly, 123).

17. "Willing to die" = I am prepared to if I have to; "lucky to die" = I want to die.

Chapter 6

1. Most commentators leave 81 out of the group; see my discussion of it *infra*.
2. The Quarto has "fel my name" in line 7.
3. For the sexual overtones of "argument", cf. *Rom. & Jul.*, 2:iv:93 – 6, "I would have made it short, for I was come to the whole depths of my tale, and meant, indeed, to occupy the argument no longer."
4. This is to limit "love" in line 14 to 'affection'. Even if we admit the word's other meaning, i.e. 'my *beloved* caused my decay', the beloved's power is still lessened by the nearly dismissive introductory phrase, "The worst was this . . "
5. *Seven Types of Ambiguity*, p. 69.
6. *Shakespeare's Sonnets*, p. 288.
7. These words describe the poetry as well as the poet, but the identity of the two is unavoidable.
8. The common metaphor is of inspiration: first with the wind in his sails, and then through the "spirits" and affable ghosts.

Chapter 7

1. For "travail" in line 2, rather than the modernisation 'travel', see note 15 to chapter 4.
2. The common emendation of "guil'st" in line 12 is to "gild'st"; but the Quarto may easily be understood as a shortened form of 'beguilest', a more attractive reading than the emendation.
3. Compare also the deliberateness of lines like 27:8, "Looking on darkness which the blind do see", and 27:12, "Makes black night beauteous, and her old face new". Both seem rather too obvious products of poetic toil.
4. I do not mean to claim that the situation is real in any historical sense, but that the impression is of reality taking over from poetic fantasy.
5. Again, in some ways the choice of these four sonnets as a group is highly subjective. A good case could be made for including Sonnet 66; and a reader might not be happy at my tying together two third-person sonnets, 67 and 68, with two second person sonnets, 69 and 70.
6. Also, as Booth points out in stating his preference for the Quarto's "seeing" over its suggested emendation to "seeming", the phrase "dead seeing" carries 'morbid overtones of "a viewing of the body"' (*Shakespeare's Sonnets*, p. 250).
7. This is to make the metaphoric connection between hair and grass which the second quatrain encourages. Line 11 has the more general sense of not exploiting others' youth to keep oneself young.
8. Martin, *Shakespeare's Sonnets: Self, Love and Art*, p. 79.
9. E.K. feels the need to gloss "yore" in *The Shepheardes Calender* as "long agoe" ('July', 116). Booth notes in "holy antique hours" a pun on 'wholly (or holey) antic whores' (*Shakespeare's Sonnets*, p. 252).
10. The Quarto prints "end" as the rhyme word for line 3; "done" was first suggested by Gildon in 1714, and has been generally accepted. Two other Quarto readings need comment: "their outward thus" in line 5 is normally emended to "thy outward thus" on the analogy of the other occurrences of this

error, but here it would be possible to make a case for the Quarto. And in line 14 "solye" is generally accepted to be a misprint for "soyle", but editors have suggested, amongst other possibilities, "toil", "solve", "foil", and "sole". Ingram and Redpath give the suggestions careful consideration, choosing "soil" as the most reasonable (*Shakespeare's Sonnets*, pp. 160–1).

11. "Confound" is one of the characteristic items of the sequence's vocabulary: its effect is quite shocking here because of its normal associations with time, as in 5:6; 60:8; 63:10;64:10.

12. There is a further irony if the reader takes "this" in the couplet in its common sense in the sequence, as 'this poem'; i.e. 'it is my poetry which reveals your vice'.

13. Line 3, which describes "suspect" as beauty's "ornament", does not seem to be about conflict, but the next line's image of the crow directs the reader towards an ironic interpretation of "ornament"; i.e. it is as much an ornament to beauty as a crow is to a clear sky. There are further ironies here since it is impossible for the reader to avoid the implication that beauty itself chooses the ornament. There is even the possibility that the line may be read as if "ornament of beauty" were merely a periphrasis for "beauty", which makes the crow in line 4 the referent for "beauty" not "suspect".

14. "And" is a significantly vague link-word to introduce this line, allowing the reader to see it as a simple connection with the preceding line, or to go so far as to connect "thou present'st" with the canker.

15. Note the pun in "charged": attacked in battle and accused in a court of law.

16. *Shakespeare's Sonnets*, p. 149.

17. "Lascivious" is superficially a criticism of the comments, but the reader automatically refers it to the sport which is being commented on.

18. For the proverb, Booth compares (from Tilley) 'Everything is the worse for wearing' and 'Iron with often handling is worn to nothing' (*Shakespeare's Sonnets*, p. 311).

19. Compare Sonnet 15 where the poet is an engrafter.

20. Marvell creates a similar ambiguity in 'An Horatian Ode', 36–40: "Though Justice against Fate complain,/And plead the ancient rights in vain:/But those do hold or break/As men are strong or weak", where it is not clear whether the ancient rights hold because men are strong or because they are weak, or whether they break because of men's strength or weakness.

21. Note, too, the way that "that to thee resort" echoes the deception of 95:10, "chose thee out".

22. "Translated" means, as in Bottom's 'translation', transformed; but may also have its modern sense of having been turned from one language into another. This sense goes back at least to the fourteenth century; cf. *Henry IV, part 1*, 4:i:47–8, where the two senses unite: "Wherefore do you so ill translate yourself/Out of the speech of peace, that bears such grace,/Into the harsh and boist'rous tongue of war."

Chapter 8

1. The most affecting element is the intimacy of the elision, "y'have".

2. The last line imitates, in its mechanical weariness of expression, the view of life which the quatrain proposes.

3. Compare Booth's comment on line 10: 'the involved syntax of lines 9– 10 and the two ambiguous appearances of "for" make this line demonstrate a reality in the fanciful fusion of identities that the poem discusses: within the line, to safeguard either is actually to safeguard the other.' (*Shakespeare's Sonnets*, p. 171.)

4. The Quarto prints "right" as the rhyme word for line 6; it is, of course, a common Elizabethan spelling for 'rite'. Unlike "travail"/"travel" (see notes 15 on chapter 4 and 1 on chapter 7) the reader is more likely to see the pun if the modernised form is printed.

5. 'Pouring the compliments out' may seem an insensitive paraphrase to apply to a sonnet which deals with true love. I use it for two reasons: the sonnet is principally about unappreciated love – the implication being that the young man needs more than simple sincerity – and the word-play in "love's rite" carries some sense of a patterned exchange of compliments.

6. In line 9 I choose to read, with the Quarto, "books" rather than the common emendation "looks".

7. The Quarto punctuates the end of line 13 with a comma. Booth's decision to employ a full-stop marks the rarity of this couplet's structure: the only other two which he punctuates in this way are 92, where line 13 is a question and 14 its answer, and 37, where the connection between the two lines is closer than here: "Look what is best, that best I wish in thee./This wish I have, then ten times happy me."

8. *Interpretations in Shakespeare's Sonnets* (Berkeley, 1963) p. 45.

9. The point which Landry glosses over is that the sonnet develops "appetite" as a metaphorical comparison, not an alternative: between the first and second quatrains the reader's expectations are changed from the belief that "love" should be more constant than "appetite" to the plea that it should have the same constancy.

10. There is an ambiguity here. Some critics take "sad interim" as the trough described in the octave, when love has diminished. Others take it to refer to a period of absence or estrangement. Landry goes so far as to include it in 'the sonnets clearly written in absence' (*Interpretations in Shakespeare's Sonnets*, p. 27).

11. I retain the Quarto text of the couplet, not the common emendation of "as" to "or".

12. Compare Booth's comment: 'in these lines it becomes practically impossible to remember whether one is thinking about harvest in terms of childbirth or childbirth in terms of agricultural harvest' (*Shakespeare's Sonnets*, p. 316).

13. "Or" indicates the same kind of conscious metaphorising which I described in Sonnet 56.

14. *Shakespeare's Sonnets*, p. 161.

15. *Shakespeare's Sonnets*, p. 324.

16. Compare Seymour-Smith's comment on Sonnet 100: 'Here opens a new and entirely different series of sonnets (100– 115), addressed to the young man. From the abrupt change in tone and from internal evidence it is clear that some time has elapsed since the series ending with 96 had been written' (*Shakespeare's Sonnets*, p. 161).

17. Sonnet 17 in the 1529 text of *Diana*.

18. Commentators have differed in their judgements as to what quality of the buds of marjoram it is which is being related to the young man's hair. Suggestions

include their colour (auburn, brown, or golden), perfume, shape, and inclination to curl into knots.

19. Booth explains the action of "annexed" like this: 'added to his robbery — to his booty, to what he had already stolen ("annexed" also suggests "appropriated", and thus, despite the syntactic limitation of the "annexed to" construction, "annexed thy breath" meaning "stole thy breath" may also impinge on a reader's consciousness to enrich the line by presenting a syntactically unharnessed extra description of the same theft)' (*Shakespeare's Sonnets*, pp. 323–4).

20. Booth has a long, interesting note on these lines, see *Shakespeare's Sonnets*, pp. 322–3. While the violet is called a "thief", line 5 describes it as dying the veins of the young man. The logical conclusion — although it is actually nonsense — is that the violet gets its fragrance from the young man, and he gets the colouring of his veins from it.

21. In Milton's description of the Fall, the first casualties are the roses; see *Paradise Lost*, IX, 892–3.

Chapter 9

1. The basic difference is that putting the lines into direct speech attributes the sententiousness to the Muse, while seeing them as a summary makes the sententiousness the poet's, in his description of what the Muse says. A further complication is that it is all in the poet's mind anyway.

2. The denigration of artifice covers both painting and poetry. The metaphor is essentially related to painting — "colour" and "pencil" lead to "lay" in the sense of putting on canvas; but "lay" also picks up an echo from 100:7, "Sing to the ear that doth thy lays esteem", and looks forward to 102:6, "When I was wont to greet it with my lays".

3. Booth notes that "Philomel" means simply the nightingale, adding that it is used here 'simply as a poetic name for the species, with no active reference to the myth of Philomela' (*Shakespeare's Sonnets*, p. 330). I am not so certain since the sonnet's couplet puts a calculated emphasis on the poet holding his tongue. As a metaphor for the silencing of a poet, but his triumph over that silencing, the Philomela myth has interesting implications for this sonnet.

4. Or "his pipe" if one keeps to the Quarto's gender.

5. In line 12 "sweets grown common", although it refers literally to the nightingale's song and figuratively to the poet's verse, also acts contra-logically to remind the reader of the young man's decay — "sweet" being one of the stock epithets applied to him throughout the sequence. And in line 14 "dull you" has, as well as its primary meaning of 'bore you', the innuendo that the poet's verse, in contrast with the poetastry of the other flatterers, would make the young man seem less shining (by being more truthful about him).

6. The degree of autobiographical emphasis of modern commentators varies. To Stephen Booth it has a little importance; his headnote to Sonnet 111 begins: 'Like Sonnet 110, this sonnet derives extra precision from its reader's knowledge that William Shakespeare, actor, provided for himself by public means' (*Shakespeare's Sonnets*, p. 359). In contrast, Edward Hubler sees the matter as

central to the sonnets' presentation of the poet as 'The Natural Fool of Fortune'; after several pages' analysis he judges that these sonnets demonstrate Shakespeare's awareness of 'an indecency inherent in the practice of literature. He felt that it involved a certain violation of privacy. . . . One may find exaggeration without denying the residuum of truth in Shakespeare's repeated statements that the self-revelation of his poems was embarrassing' — *The Sense of 'Shakespeare's Sonnets'* (Princeton, 1952) pp. 120—1. Of course, this is a matter contingent upon the expectations which the reader brings to the sequence. To see the Sonnets as poems addressed to a real lover, describing actual moods and deeds, removes from them the order and planning of a work of art, and substitutes for it the haphazardness of life.

7. See Booth's analysis of the word play of this quatrain, *Shakespeare's Sonnets*, pp. 351—2.

8. The second line, too, may bear a future subjunctive reading.

9. But see my comments on Sonnet 125 in chapter 13, p. 222.

10. The interlocutor seems to bind 110 and 111 together, too: 110's couplet asks for welcome to the beloved's breast and 111 opens by responding to the beloved's complaint against fortune, "O for my sake do you with fortune chide."

11. There is a further, accidental irony in the probable misprint in line 1 in the Quarto text, ". . . doe you *wish* Fortune chide." Seymour-Smith finds the Quarto reading defensible — see *Shakespeare's Sonnets*, p. 165.

12. This applies whether one interprets it as "means" breeding "manners" or *vice versa*.

13. "Gored", for example, has a specific meaning which relates it to the jester's motley, but with the object "thoughts" it is impossible for the reader to ignore the word's wider associations, particularly 'pierced' and 'made filthy'; see Booth, *Shakespeare's Sonnets*, pp. 354—5.

14. Compare Hubler's comments: 'The idea in the couplet is of course pertinent to what goes before if only because an assurance of friendship is always proper to a series of poems addressed to a friend; but in this case the assurance comes with such a diminution of force that one wonders why it was allowed to stand. . . . The artistic failure of the couplet is so accentuated by the double rime that one wonders if at the time of composition the ingenuity of the rime seemed to justify the couplet' (*The Sense of 'Shakespeare's Sonnets'*, pp. 24—5).

15. It is worth adding that the comparison only pretends to be a simile: not 'I shall be like a willing penitent who drinks vinegar', but 'as if I were a willing penitent I shall drink vinegar'.

16. Suggestions have included:

besides me, thinks I'm	besides methinks they're
besides me thinks I'm	besides methinks y'are
besides, me thinks, are	besides methinks are
besides you thinks are	besides me thinks you're
besides me-thinks, is	besides methinks are
besides methinks they are	

Chapter 10

1. I retain Quarto's "still" in line 12 in preference to the generally accepted

emendation "skill". Ingram and Redpath discuss the matter in detail, ending with a preference for "skill" (*Shakespeare's Sonnets*, pp. 240–2).

2. *Shakespeare's Sonnets*, p. 139. Compare Seymour-Smith's comment that line 14 'can be read as a compliment, by understatement; but is almost certainly meant literally' (*Shakespeare's Sonnets*, p. 143); and Booth's on the same line: 'The figure – litotes, understatement – is usually hyperbolic in its effect; here it also undercuts the speaker's position by echoing idioms by which a speaker praises by comparison with something even less praiseworthy' (*Shakespeare's Sonnets*, p. 239).

3. Ingram and Redpath say that "wight" is not an archaism. Booth argues otherwise: 'the word should have carried the tone of self-consciously affected archaism that made it a favourite with Spenser. . . . Shakespeare uses the word eight other times: once in the context of witchcraft, once in a mock-proverb by Iago, once in Iago's ballad of King Stephen, once by Gower, once to describe Armado, and three times in the mouth of Pistol' (*Shakespeare's Sonnets*, p. 340).

4. "Chronicle of wasted time" includes: (i) consumed time; (ii) time spent idly; (iii) time's catalogue of destruction. Note also the effect of the singular: 'chronicles' would merely have referred to the poems, but "chronicle" indicates the whole of recorded history within which the poems are placed.

5. The line might easily have read 'In praise of ladies fair and lovely knights'; the difference of effect is obvious.

6. That is to take 'prophetic' in its primary sense of reading the present correctly (and therefore the future).

7. But note the way that the typological metaphor becomes poetic fact: from old poetry as praise of the young man's beauty the sestet moves to a vision of past time as a prophecy of his godhead. "Praise" is a powerful word on which to end the sonnet. Its meaning develops through the sonnet: in line 4 it stands for conventional poetic praise, in line 9 it signifies prophecy, and in line 14 the Psalmic praise of the godhead.

8. *Shakespeare's Sonnets*, p. 336.

9. *Shakespeare's Sonnets*, p. 163.

10. *Shakespeare's Sonnets*, p. 336.

11. *Shakespeare's Sonnets*, p. 340.

12. Ingram and Redpath give "yet" detailed discussion, seeing four possibilities in it: '(1) temporal = "as yet" . . . or (2) = "after all", or (3) a meaningless expletive, or (4) a word intended to emphasise the magnitude of the fears and anxieties – almost equivalent to an "even" placed after the "not" in line 1. We prefer (4) and (2) in that order' (*Shakespeare's Sonnets*, p. 245). See also Booth's long discussion, in *Shakespeare's Sonnets*, pp. 343–44.

13. See Hotson's discussions of the sonnet in *Shakespeare's Sonnets Dated and Other Essays* (London, 1949) pp. 4–21, and *Mr. W. H.* (London, 1964), pp. 73–84.

14. *Shakespeare's Sonnets*, p. 347.

15. Even the editorial gloss makes the young man the probable referent if we recall the opening of Sonnet 58: "That god forbid, that made me first your slave/I should in thought control your times of pleasure."

Chapter 11

1. Martin, in *Shakespeare's Sonnets: Self, Love and Art*, only cites Sonnets 117–120 in passing; Hubler gives them less than half a page's discussion in *The Sense of*

'*Shakespeare's Sonnets*'; and J. B. Leishman, in *Themes and Variations in Shakespeare's Sonnets* (London, 1961), devotes only half a page to Sonnet 117 and nothing to the others. For G. Wilson Knight's discussion of Sonnet 121, see *The Mutual Flame* (London, 1955) pp. 49 – 52.

2. *Shakespeare's Sonnets*, p. 392.
3. For example, Richard II on the death of kings, Lear and Hamlet on suffering humanity; hence Eliot's 'objective correlative' which might equally apply to Sonnet 116 – Booth's discussion of the near bombast of the sonnet picks up this point too.
4. The qualification in my 'almost' is because of the possible implications of "bonds" in line 4 and "dear purchased" in line 6. Either or both might convey some sense of the poet's unwilling attachment to the young man.
5. In *The Language Poets Use* (London, 1965), Winifred Nowottny compares the sonnet unfavourably with the one which follows it. In 118 she describes Shakespeare as reducing a 'complex experience into a forced correspondence with something already known, and understood as "rational", the result being a 'repetitive and heavily argumentative sonnet' (pp. 63 – 4).
6. Booth glosses "eager compounds" as 'pungent concoctions'. Chaucer put the same idea into *Troilus and Criseyde*: "O, sooth is seyd, that heled for to be/As of a fevre, or other gret sikenesse,/Men moste drynke, as men may ofte se,/Ful bittre drynke; and for to han gladnesse,/Men drinken ofte peyene and gret distresse" (III, 1212 – 16).
7. "Appetites" has obvious sexual connotations in the way that the singular 'appetite' would not have.
8. For example, Pooler (1918) 'undesirable people'; Tucker (1924) 'inferior people'; Ingram and Redpath 'inferior company'; Seymour-Smith 'people . . . whom he knew to be inferior'.
9. Booth's note on "ne'er cloying" as an equivalent for the Quarto's "nere cloying" points up my simplification here: 'This is one instance in which unavoidable modernization demonstrably diminishes a poem. Both "ne'er cloying" (i.e. "never-cloying") and "near cloying" make sense here, and their paradoxical amalgamation in a single self-negating expression constitutes an emblem of the whole poem; a seventeenth century reader would not have known which of the two opposing ideas was meant or which of two lines of argument . . . "nere cloying" served' (*Shakespeare's Sonnets*, p. 395).
10. But Booth gives plenty of other possible meanings – see *Shakespeare's Sonnets*, pp. 397 – 8. If "rank" does mean 'gorged with', then it gives life to a never quite stated image of eating until one makes oneself sick – gluttony being its own emetic.
11. The main point of the limbeck image is to begin the subdued alchemical metaphor which runs through the sonnet.
12. *Shakespeare's Sonnets*, p. 171.
13. *Shakespeare's Sonnets*, p. 400.
14. Dr Johnson's 'fatal Cleopatra'; by which I think he was probably referring to the dying Cleopatra's pun on the cause of her death and its result – "That I might hear thee call great Caesar ass/Unpolicied" (*Ant. & Cleo.*, 5:ii:305 – 6).
15. There are further problems in the couplet: "So I return rebuked to my content/And gain by ills thrice more than I have spent." Do we read the final line as the confidence trickster's give-away (as Booth does), or treat its

mercenary overtones as figuratively neutral, as in Sonnet 146, for instance, which is packed with financial imagery, but where no-one would seriously argue for a mercenary attitude on the speaker's part? Also, "rebuked to my content" raises enough of the spectre of the poet responding to the young man's censure to threaten to return the whole sonnet to the mood of 117's "Accuse me thus . . ."

16. 'Complex', to distinguish it from grosser narratives like the triangle group of 40–42, where the development lies more in the action than in the mind.

17. The reader may well have been struck by the gradual fading out of the addressee. Sonnet 117 is, as I have shown, a poem at least as much about the young man as it is about the poet. In 118 his position is relegated to being merely a sounding-board for the wit. In 119 the poet is entirely self-absorbed, "you" having completely disappeared – a disappearance emphasised by the third quatrain's use of "true" as its first rhyme word: instead of its response being "you", as in 118's couplet, we get " . . . when it is built anew" (a possible pun on 'on you').

18. *Shakespeare's Sonnets*, pp. 407–8.

19. Its action is analogous to a verb like 'bewhored'.

20. The reader does not, though, lose the 'exchange' possibility. This is the kind of syntactic ambiguity which editors' paraphrases almost always do damage to. Ingram and Redpath paraphrase this whole sonnet, and the way they deal with its first two lines demonstrates one way of simplifying the complexities of Shakespeare's poetry: 'The fact that you were once unkind to me serves me a friendly turn; for otherwise, when I recall the anguish that I then felt . . .' (*Shakespeare's Sonnets*, p. 276).

21. In fact the instinctive paradox comes primarily from the sonnet's apparent definition of a tyrant as one who does *not* take something.

22. Suggestions include: 'some one occasion of great sorrow' (Wyndham, 1898); 'the dark days when both were unhappy' (Pooler, 1918); 'the period of our estrangement' (Young, 1937); 'a direct reference to the action of the Friend which produced Sonnets 34–35' (Seymour-Smith).

23. There is a potential irony in the contrast of the salve's literal superficiality and the poet's "deepest sense".

24. Early commentators saw the sonnet as a defence against Puritan attacks on the stage; then Pooler, in 1918, thought the subject some particular slander of Shakespeare or the young man. The problem lies in judging the context of the sonnet – the stage? homosexuality? some unnamed crime? – and then in following its meaning from line to line (e.g. in the first quatrain what kind of connection does "and" in line 3 make between lines 1–2 and lines 3–4; and, in the same line, does "so" refer backwards to "pleasure", "just pleasure", or "vile"?) There are also difficulties in understanding individual words: the most notorious is "salutation" in line 6, where the normal sense of 'greeting' hardly fits the meaning of the line. (Is it possible that, on analogy with 'salutary', the word might mean 'warning'?)

25. *Interpretations in Shakespeare's Sonnets*, pp. 88–9.

26. *Shakespeare's Sonnets*, p. 410.

27. Self-justifying questions and assertions: "Why should others' false adulterate eyes . . .?"; "Or on my frailties why are . . .?"; "I am that I am"; "they that level/At my abuses reckon up their own"; "I may be straight"; "my deeds must not be shown".

Real or imagined persecutions: "receives reproach"; "deemed/Not by our . . . but by others' . . ."; "why should others' . . .?"; "why are frailer spies,/Which in their wills count bad what I think good"; "they that level/At my abuses"; "they themselves be bevel"; "By their rank thoughts"; "this general evil they maintain".

28. The procreation sonnets harp on this condition unremittingly, but Sonnet 94 has the most clear description of it: ". . . and will be none/That do not do . . . moving others are themselves as stone /Unmoved . . .".

29. Similar self-identifications are used by other Shakespearean negative forces, especially at their moments of crisis: Richard III, "Richard loves Richard, that is, I am I" (5:iii:183); Iago, "'Tis in ourselves that we are thus or thus" (*Othello*, 1:iii:321); Parolles, "Simply the thing I am/Shall make me live" (*All's Well*. 4:iii:310 – 11).

Chapter 12

1. The whole sonnet becomes a set of Chinese boxes. The vile ones do the esteeming, so whoever they esteem to be vile is likely not to be, and *vice versa*. If the poet is esteemed vile by them, then he clearly is not vile, so "'Tis better to be vile" is only a separate wish, not the prediction of an actual choice. (When the reader begins the sonnet he gets an impression of the perverseness of such a society in his unsureness about the opening line. By the end of the quatrain it has become clear that "vile esteemed" means 'thought to be vile', but at first it may well be taken to mean 'vilely esteemed' – in which case the line means something like 'It is better to be vile than not to be given due respect': a sentiment which mocks the society of the vile esteemers.)

2. "Prevent" has the primary sense of 'come before, anticipate'. The sub-text of the couplet is one of frenetic movement, with the muse working hectically to keep one step ahead of time.

3. The sonnet's image is of a sun-dial, where the movement of the shadow is impossible to perceive second by second. Thus the reader who observes the second-hand of his watch moving has a more realisable experience of time's movement, but, for that reason, perhaps a less acute sense of its insidiousness.

4. My analysis of these lines is not entirely fair to the sonnet: although the "that" which introduces line 3 makes it, and line 4, an amplification of lines 1 – 2, it does not prevent the reader from seeing the "little moment" as, in fact, opposed to the descriptions of extended time which follow. This does not affect my basic point, however, that the sonnet seems to promise the reader, at its beginning, an examination of the specific moment of greatness of an individual life, but it turns out to be a meditation on the extensiveness of life.

5. The slide from holding a breath to holding out in a siege is only one part of a complex movement of images in the quatrain. The reader never loses sight of summer as the main point of reference, but he perceives, simultaneously, a whole series of variously related images of time's ruin. The development goes like this (although I do not pretend to include everything): "Summer's honey" is the conventional sweetness of the season, but then "summer's honey breath" personifies the season to the image of a sweet human being (both eventually

decay). "Hold" suggests that the human holds his breath; but "hold out" introduces the idea of his (and the season's) being besieged, an image clarified in "wrackful siege" and "battering days". The image of breath as a wall being battered gives way to "rocks impregnable" being battered, but rocks impregnable are themselves an image of destruction at sea, following "wrackful" ('wreck') and "battering" (waves). "Stout" and "strong" may relate equally to the human being or the implied ship; and the violence of "wrackful siege of battering days" is replaced at the end by the slowness and imperceptibility of "decays", which is, ultimately, the breath of decay infecting summer's honey breath (i.e. an inner destruction, not one from outside).

6. Consider the order of "When yellow leaves, or none, or few, do hang/Upon those boughs", rather than the apparently more logical '. . . or few, or none . . .' It is not the process of decay which is being described, but the period of time which seems so drawn out when one expects the process to be over but is never sure that it is.

7. For the formality of the octave, compare Leontes' opening words to Polixenes: "Nine changes of the watery star hath been /The shepherd's note since we have left our throne/Without a burden. Time as long again Would be fill'd up, my brother, with our thanks . . ." (*W. Tale* 1:ii:1 – 4).

8. The sonnet plays on three similar words to make similar effects: "still" (lines 3 and 11); "first" (2 and 8); "yet" (8 and 9).

9. I use "love" since the sonnets are purposefully unclear about whether the person or the emotion is being described.

10. The verbs "weighs not" and "gives . . . place" are both calculated to maintain these ambiguities. "Weighs not" = (i) ignores what is there (ii) refuses to be swayed by; "gives place" = (i) gives way to (ii) allows to appear.

11. Compare Booth's summary of line 13 in *Shakespeare's Sonnets*, p. 350, which ends: 'the line allows for simultaneous assertion of miraculous youthfulness and for the attribution of the sentimental value of a relic, a reminder of its former self.'

12. Booth calls his reader's attention to "even" in 59:5 – 6, where it seems to be used in the modern sense; "O that record with a backward look,/Even of five hundred courses of the sun."

13. "Tan sacred beauty" becomes almost the case in point – i.e. the way the poet's strength of love will be weakened by the merest ageing of the young man.

14. Note the implications of both of these possibilities. Love as always immature is a cynical definition: love, to stay love, must always have the prospect of growth before it, so that it must be impossible for a lover to say 'I love you best'. Love as non-speaking makes all love poetry, by definition, hypocrisy.

15. The three occurrences of "then" have become progressively more difficult to give a past meaning to; but assuming that the reader carried a strong sense of the past into "might I not then say" in line 10, then "then might I not say" is so obvious an echo here that he is tempted to read the line as an answer to line 10's question.

16. The problem is, of course, that the sonnet says 'I love you best' all the while, a fact which the reader grasps from the conventional melodrama of the opening line.

17. The one trick which the sonnet does play on the reader comes in the next two lines: "Love's not time's fool, though rosy lips and cheeks/Within his bending

sickle's compass come." So strong is the influence of "love" on the sonnet that momentarily the reader expects "his" in line 10 to have "love" as its subject, not "time".

18. Booth gives the sonnet detailed general discussion in *Shakespeare's Sonnets*, pp. 387–92. Seymour-Smith notes that 116 'begins a new group of sonnets (116–126), not altogether coherent as a group, and among the most enigmatic of the whole sequence' (*Shakespeare's Sonnets*, p. 168). Ingram and Redpath describe it as 'neither a plea to the Friend to be faithful, nor an apologia for the poet's own conduct, nor a defence against suspicions of his infidelity, but a meditative attempt to define perfect love' (*Shakespeare's Sonnets*, p. 268).

19. "Alteration" has also the sense of time's alteration, i.e. ageing, but "remove" admits no compromise.

Chapter 13

1. I have kept the Quarto punctuation of lines 4–6. Booth has a dash after lines 4 and 6.

2. The two sonnets were compared by Lee in 1907. In his 1918 edition Pooler first made the specific suggestion that this sonnet harked back to 77.

3. *Shakespeare's Sonnets*, pp. 412–13.

4. *Shakespeare's Sonnets*, p. 280.

5. The doubt as to whether the book is empty or written in is teasingly maintained through the tables within the poet's brain. They are either "full charactered" in the sense of 'fully remembered' — so treasured that they have been got by heart, word perfectly — or they are "full charactered" in contrast to the pristine state of the young man's gift. "Idle rank" works in a similar way: either an empty file of pages, or lines of writing which remain unread.

6. The only reminder of love in the opening lines is "that I do change": but that becomes more a matter of personal immortality than a claim that the poet will remain faithful.

7. Arthur Mizener, 'The Structure of Figurative Language in Shakespeare's Sonnets', in *A Casebook on Shakespeare's Sonnets*, ed. G. Willen and V. B. Reed (New York, 1964) pp. 219–35; this is a revised form of the essay which appeared in *Southern Review* in 1940. Booth, *Shakespeare's Sonnets*, pp. 419–26.

8. *Shakespeare's Sonnets*, p. 419.

9. Man: "Child of state . . . bastard . . . unfathered . . . subject to . . . suffers . . . smiling . . . falls . . . inviting time . . . fashion . . . fears not . . . but all alone stands."
Plant: "weeds . . . flowers . . . all alone stands . . . nor grows . . . nor drowns."
Building: "it was builded . . . nor falls . . . leases . . . all alone stands." ·

10. For 'fools' as a simple equivalent to 'men', cf. "Well, thus we play the fools with the time" (*Henry IV, part 2*, 2:ii:154); "merely thou art death's fool" (*Meas. for Meas.* 3:i:11); "this great stage of fools" (*K. Lear* 4:vi:187); "we fools of nature" (*Hamlet* 1:v:54).
In his Variorum edition Rollins lists a variety of suggestions as to the line's specific reference, starting with Steevens (1780), 'perhaps this is a stroke at some

of *Fox's Martyrs*'; Palgrave (1865), 'plotters and political martyrs of the age'; Tyler (1890), the Earl of Essex and his companions; Wyndham (1898), death-bed repenters; Lee (1907), 'penitent traitors, who expiated their crimes with piety on the scaffold', Alden (1913), 'all those whose love is what the foregoing lines have said that the poet's love is not'; Serrazin (1914), Catholic priests executed in 1594–5; and so on.

11. Note, for example, the rhetorical "no" used in 116, 121, 123, and 124.
12. Add to these "form and favour", "all and more", "compound sweet", and "simple savour".
13. The couplet echoes the situation of 124's couplet, calling a witness in court.
14. The Quarto repeats "My sinful earth" at the beginning of line 2, the most famous crux in the sonnets; there is an apparently limitless number of suggested emendations.
15. *Shakespeare's Sonnets*, p. 288.

Index

The index falls into two parts: 1, references to the sonnets and 2, references to other works by Shakespeare and to works by other writers. An italicised entry indicates detailed commentary on a poem.

1 The Sonnets

2 Other Works